Antonio SANDU

BETWEEN PUNISHMENT AND REHABILITATION: HOW PROBATION OFFICERS BUILD THEIR PROFESSIONAL IDENTITY

A Comparative Study of Restorative Justice, Community Supervision, and Penal Culture in Post-Communist Europe

2026

EDITURA LUMEN
în elita editurilor românești

Antonio SANDU: BETWEEN PUNISHMENT AND REHABILITATION: HOW PROBATION OFFICERS BUILD THEIR PROFESSIONAL IDENTITY. A Comparative Study of Restorative Justice, Community Supervision, and Penal Culture in Post-Communist Europe

Lumen Publishing House is accredited by CNCS and CNATDCU
redactia@edituralumen.net
www.edituralumen.ro

Descrierea CIP a Bibliotecii Naţionale a României
SANDU, ANTONIO
Between punishment and rehabilitation : how probation officers build their professional identity : a comparative study of restorative justice, community supervision, and penal culture in post-communist Europe / Antonio Sandu. - Iaşi : Lumen, 2026
Conţine bibliografie
ISBN 978-973-166-662-4

316
343

Contents

1. Theoretical Perspective on the Social Construction of the Probation Counselor Profession

The scholarly literature[1] [161] concerning the social construction of probation practice — with particular reference to the British system and its potential for generalization — argues for the necessity of analyzing historical perspective when implementing new standards in probation practice, given that probation systems are path-dependent on the historical contexts in which they have developed and continue to evolve. A comparison between the American and British systems reveals that the two have evolved differently according to the meaning attributed to the term *offender*[2]. The historical as well as theoretical origins of various probation services have had a significant impact on practice — which aspires to be evidence-based and scientific — on professional ideology, and on the standardization of probation service delivery. The constructionist perspective leads to the proposition that systemic change imposed through administrative mandate undermines the social practice of probation services, and that demands for the uniformization — globalization — of social work practice within probation services should therefore be resisted [161, pp. 5–18]. The most recent research indicates that the supervision of offenders by specially trained probation officers[3] yields significantly more favorable outcomes compared to situations in which supervising officers lack relevant professional qualifications [139].

[1] Substantial portions of this chapter have been previously published in Sandu, A. (2016). Cadre normativ-instituționale ale construcției sociale a profesiei de consilier de probațiune în zona de N-E a României și în Republica Moldova [Institutional regulatory frameworks of the social construction of the probation counselor profession in North-Eastern Romania and the Republic of Moldova]. In: *Sociologie Românească*, vol. XIV, no. 1/2016. ISSN 1220–5389.

[2] In the original English-language sources, the term employed is *offender*. We have preferred the Romanian equivalent *făptuitor* (literally: *perpetrator* or *doer of the act*) over *infractor* (literally: *criminal* or *lawbreaker*), as we consider the former to be more consonant with the specific character of the restorative justice paradigm, which we regard — at least in part — as one of the foundational frameworks of modern probation systems.

[3] In the original English-language sources, the term *supervision officer* is used instead of *probation officer*.

In our view, these studies provide theoretical confirmation of our position that the institutional perspective and the professional socialization of probation officers exert a formative influence on the construction of their professional identity and, consequently, on the quality of practice, directly affecting the outcomes of probation work. A further observation arising from the terminological shift from *probation counselor* to *supervision officer* — borrowed from the terminology specific to American probation services — clearly highlights the differentiation in the function of probation, which in the American conception is centered on surveillance, whereas in the European tradition it is oriented toward counseling and rehabilitative practice. The translation of the term *officer* as *ofițer* in Romanian-language probation literature also strikes us as imprecise, as a more semantically accurate rendering of the American expression would be *public official within probation services*.

One of the constitutive instances of professional identity is represented by the institutional perspective, encompassing both the social and socio-legal institutions involved and the organizations delivering probation services [95]. The institutional perspective constitutes the framework within which probation activity unfolds, and as such, the specifically institutional values [214] permeate social work practice [193]. The interpretive paradigm applied to the meaning of social work practices [42] in the sphere of offender rehabilitation and social reintegration, and of social alternatives to incarceration, transforms the discourse on practice in ways that are difficult for professionals to consciously perceive, given that they are already infused with the constitutive values of practice derived from the respective theoretical paradigm. For instance, values such as equity understood as retribution — being tributary to the retributive justice paradigm — will generate a discourse on practice oriented toward the correctness of punishment, the necessity of punishment, and the labeling of probation service subjects as offenders, regardless of whether they have been formally convicted. The purpose of probation services organized from the perspective of the retributive justice paradigm consists in supervising the execution of non-custodial sanctions. Conversely, a probation practice infused with ethical values derived from the restorative justice paradigm — namely, social responsibility and solidarity — will have as its objective the restoration of the social equilibrium disrupted by the act deemed antisocial; more precisely, the equilibrium within the victim–offender–community triad. The person who has committed a criminal act is more appropriately referred to as an *offender* in the sense of *perpetrator* (*făptuitor*) rather than a *criminal* (*infractor*) — particularly when restorative justice-based probation practices are applied during the trial or probationary period (*perioadă de probă/încercare*) — hence the term *probation* — insofar as the sentence has not yet been pronounced and the person has not yet been convicted, and therefore remains under the presumption of innocence. The discourse on practice will focus primarily on the construction of the autonomy and responsibility of the person who has committed criminal acts, while simultaneously pursuing the restoration of the victim's prior condition [128] and the redress of the inequities suffered as a result of the offender's actions.

Normative changes at the legislative level alter the frameworks of practice and, along with them, the discourse on practice. A legislative framework that mandates probation primarily as a service for supervising the execution of non-custodial sanctions will generate a discourse on practice centered on surveillance and behavioral control of persons under supervision. A legislative framework that proposes as the objective of probation practice the restoration of the social equilibrium disrupted by acts of potential antisocial character will generate a discourse on mediation, engagement, autonomy — self-determination [61] — and responsibility. The dependence of professional discourse on its normative context is consistent with the theory proposed by David Cooperrider and Suresh Srivastva [204], which underpins appreciative inquiry, according to which a social system and/or organization evolves in the direction in which its development is questioned. Dependence on context — normative, theoretical, and otherwise — constitutes the framework within which the constructive process takes place and acquires meaning. This framework has a limiting and, to some extent, transcendent character relative to the constructive process itself, although it is itself evidently the product of a prior process of social construction. The evolution of the normative–institutional framework leaves its imprint on the social construction of the probation officer's professional identity precisely through the redefinition of the operational definitions with which the professional works and around which the discourse on practice is organized. The operational definitions of terms such as *punishment*, *sanction*, and *reintegration* undergo interpretive drift in the very process of modifying the interpretive and ideological — theoretical — context that underpins professional practice. This interpretive drift can be traced through an examination of the normative and ideological frameworks that demarcate practice, and of the interpretive consensus that emerges around them within the professional community in which practitioners operate. In our view, the first stage in understanding a process of social construction may consist in identifying the limiting frameworks — situated at a different discursive level, as products of a prior and/or parallel constructive process — which function within the system under investigation as boundaries to the discursive freedom of the subjects of communicative action.

1.1. Theoretical Paradigms and Ideological Models of Probation Practice

From the perspective of the role of sanctioning action, the scholarly literature [30, pp. 16–28] identifies four theoretical models:

Retributive Justice [93] constitutes the classical paradigm for understanding punishment, originating in the *lex talionis* and grounded in the principle of reciprocity, with the purpose of punishment being the retribution of the offender for the act committed [125]. This position is supported empirically by research examining public perceptions of the purposes of punishment [137, 141, 155, 156]. Retributive justice is concerned with the distribution of justice [172]. The individualization of punishment takes into account the social cost of the offense, the (socially constructed) [49, p. 196] gravity of the act, and the circumstances of its commission [81, 129]. The theory of retributive justice is grounded in distributive ethics [52, p. 92], and particularly in the work of John Rawls [88]. Justice as fairness is transposed, in this context, as proportionate punishment for the act committed [49, p. 197]. In our view, the assessment of social danger cannot constitute a justification for sanctions within a purely distributive theory, as such an analysis would be consequentialist rather than intentionalist in character. The principles of distributive justice sanction primarily the enacted intention, or foreseeable negligence [51], with the consequences of the act being relevant rather to the individualization of punishment. The exclusive retribution of intention would deprive the sanction of its deterrent capacity. In judicial practice, factors such as the social danger of the act, the risk of recidivism, and the recovery of damages are likewise taken into account in the individualization of punishment [49, p. 197]. The retributive function of punishment is oriented predominantly toward the past — focused on the harm itself produced by the criminal behavior — and on proportionality between the offense and the sanction [196, pp. 455–482].

We consider the retributive paradigm to be tributary to universalist and deontological ethics, according to which one may speak of a transcendent character of justice and the administration of justice [49, p. 198]. The exclusive focus of the retributive justice model on sanction has been criticized [30, p. 176] for its failure to emphasize the educative and social therapeutic function of punishment.

Utilitarian Justice holds that the purpose of applying a sanction is the prevention of future criminal acts, the utilitarian theory of punishment being grounded in deterrence, rehabilitation, and the incapacitation of the individual from committing further offenses [49, p. 199]. In contrast to retributive justice, which is oriented toward the past, the utilitarian–consequentialist justice paradigm is oriented toward the future [74]. International practice in probation based on utilitarian justice as of 2015 places emphasis on cooperation between probation services and community opinion leaders[4] in order to reduce the illegitimate opportunities — the chances of committing new offenses — available to persons under supervision in the community [157]. Studies have demonstrated that the probation officer's preference[5] for methods based on strict surveillance versus communicative strategies [179] influences the quality of practice [159] through the choice of intervention techniques incorporated in case management [163]. The same study indicates that in cases of continuous or repeated non-compliance by the subject of probation services, the majority of officers, regardless of their theoretical orientation, are willing to employ punitive strategies. Regrettably, neither the Romanian nor the Moldavian context is characterized by transparency with respect to case management, although Romanian legislation — beginning with the New Penal Code — has generalized the concept of probation service involvement in community supervision of persons convicted with suspended sentences. Romanian penal legislation has, however, taken a retrograde step by excluding from the New Code of Criminal Procedure any reference to the functions of punishment. The most significant functional component of the utilitarian approach is that of rehabilitation, understood as the reduction of the potential risk of the offender [102] committing further criminal acts; in this sense, the former Penal Code stipulated that "the purpose of punishment is the prevention of new criminal offenses," constituting both a coercive measure and a means of re-educating the convicted person

[4] The original English-language term is *community handlers*.
[5] Grounded in the institutional paradigm from which it derives [*authors' note*].

(Art. 52, para. 1) [49, p. 199]. The utilitarian justice paradigm identifies [30, pp. 16–28] three principles: the deterrence of future criminal acts — both by the offender in question and by other individuals; exemplary severity — whereby the severity of the sanction contributes to the rational decision of whether or not to resort to illegitimate means of need satisfaction; and the principle of proportionality (gradation) — which proceeds from the presumption of the offender's rationality and their capacity to weigh the subjective advantages procured through the commission of the offense against the disutility of the punishment [49, p. 200; 57, pp. 117–124].

Human Rights-Oriented Justice proceeds from the premise that society — represented by the state — bears co-responsibility for the disruption of social relations through the criminal act [63, 64, 65, pp. 65–75, 172]. Human rights-oriented justice [30, pp. 16–28] proposes a synthesis between the retributive principle of proportionality and the utilitarian principle of offender rehabilitation, supplemented by considerations pertaining to the personality of the offender. The state is obligated to contribute to the rehabilitation of the offender, its prerogative being not merely the right to punish, but also the assumption of obligations regarding the character of the punishment and the limits of its execution [49, p. 204]. The state has the power to withdraw certain rights from the convicted person, correlated with an obligation to protect that person against inhuman and degrading treatment [30, pp. 16–28]. The protection of the victim, alongside that of society, constitutes the justification for the application of a sanction, which consequently may not exceed the risk to which society — including the victim — would be exposed in the absence of any sanction whatsoever [25, 30, pp. 16–28, 49, p. 205, 81].

Restorative Justice is grounded in the premise that the role of punishment is to facilitate social rehabilitation and reintegration [175], with theorists holding the state co-responsible for both processes. The operational definition of rehabilitation, which will be employed throughout this work, is as follows: rehabilitation is the outcome of a complex process combining corrective actions targeting the offender's conduct, the offender's personal development under the condition of promoting social responsibility and values. Within the rehabilitation process, social responsibility, social justice, active participation, the process of empowerment, and the development of skills for independent and prosocial living are promoted [234]. The term *reintegration* refers to the actions involved in the offender's return to society and the process of social reintegration — resocialization. A number of authors, including Munting [234], avoid the use of the term *rehabilitation*, employing *reintegration* as a synonym. The difficulty with using the term *rehabilitation* arises from its lengthy history within the medical and psychological model of probation, which has been superseded by social models through a shift in the discourse on practice — that is, in its constitutive elements. Whereas the notion of *rehabilitation* connotes the restoration of a social norm, that of *reintegration* refers more broadly to the reestablishment of functional equilibrium, rendering it more suited to models grounded in restorative justice. The critique of the concept of reintegration is that it is too closely linked to that of exclusion, such that practice grounded in reintegration presupposes the social exclusion of the offender. Nevertheless, practices based on reintegration — on the social dimension of probation — are considered to offer greater prospects for reducing the risk of recidivism compared to those based on rehabilitation — on the strictly psychological or psycho-legal dimension [234].

Whereas the reparation proposed by the retributive model is unilateral — through the incarceration of the offender — restorative justice is premised on the reaffirmation of shared community values through a process that is at least bilateral — offender–victim — if not trilateral — offender–victim–community [178]. Whereas retributive justice raises questions concerning the relationship between the act of power and the transgression represented by the antisocial act, the second penal philosophy raises questions about the essence of shared values and the ways in which the social identities of both victim and offender are constructed and can be reconstructed through the identification of values shared between the parties. The purpose of punishment within this penal philosophy is oriented both toward the offender and, in particular, toward the restoration of the victim's rights through the offender–victim mediation process [53, pp. 65–75, 172]. At the center of the restorative justice paradigm lies the mediation of the offender–victim relationship [73]. Restorative justice places the victim's position at its core, along with strategies for compensating the damages suffered as a result of the criminal act [49, p. 206], as well as the offender's understanding of the harm caused and their acceptance of responsibility for repairing the damage [126]. Probation service practice integrates the restorative justice model through the organization of active reparatory programs and programs aimed at raising the offender's awareness of the impact of the offense on the victim [30, pp. 16–28]. The objective of restorative justice is the decriminalization of the sanction [82]. Restorative justice emerged from a questioning of the sufficiency and even the necessity of punishment — as instituted in modern penal systems — for the reestablishment of justice following the commission of a socially harmful act. Alternatives to punishment grounded in retributive theories have gradually coalesced into a new ideological and instrumental paradigm known as restorative justice [67, 68, 132, 133, 134, 135, 201, 202, 203]. The implementation of restorative justice accentuates the social dimension of criminal responsibility [83, 205]. In order to demonstrate its efficacy as a form of social therapeutics, the response to crime must involve the triad of victim–offender–community. The victim–offender relationship is considered essential to the success of probation programs grounded in restorative justice theory. The study conducted by Saulnier Alana and Sivasubramaniam Diane [174], examining the importance of the offender's apology to the victim in the process of social recovery, demonstrates that the actual presence of the victim at the stage of the offender's expression of regret has a heightened impact on the subjective perception of the apology and its relevance. The presence of the real victim, rather than a symbolic or surrogate one, facilitates a greater ease in expressing regret, acknowledging and accepting guilt — elements with significant implications for the subjective economy of the offender's social recovery [174]. This finding is of considerable importance for the development of faith-based restorative justice programs, which include confession before a priest invested with the symbolic authority to grant forgiveness in the name of Jesus Christ. We are convinced of the cathartic power of the confession of sins before a representative of the divine and of its exceptional importance in the social recovery of persons who have committed criminal acts. Another category of social therapeutic programs involves the acknowledgment of the act and of the status of offender within therapeutic and support groups, and the general expression of regret before a surrogate victim.

The restorative justice paradigm is — in its theoretical form — situated at the antipode of retributive justice, which it comes to replace [194]. In practice, elements of restorative justice coexist with those of retributive justice, as well as with those of human rights-centered and transactional (contractualist) justice. The models that have informed the formation of the restorative paradigm are heterogeneous, but all are grounded in the restoration of justice to the hands of those directly concerned: the victim, the offender, and the community [178]. Injured parties must be active participants in the criminal process — not only with respect to civil damages, but also in determining the strategies for the offender's social recovery, which replace punishment proper [158]. The model is premised on a thorough understanding of the context in which the act occurred and of its consequences for the injured party. The narrative perspective brings the parties into contact not from an adversarial position, but from one in which each comprehends the other's story, what each brings to the social mediation interaction, how each party relates to the act committed, and how each has internalized the experience. This approach leads to the realization of the ideal of giving voice to the victim [78]. The theory of communicative action [31] demonstrates that in the process of achieving consensus — and more broadly, reflective social equilibrium — some parties manifest their capacity as moral agents, while others assume or are assigned the role of moral patients, individuals incapable of making their voice — their perspective, aspirations, and needs — heard. Restorative justice theories emphasize the social construction of the offender's autonomy and responsibility in the process of interaction with the victim, or even with other individuals who have assumed or been assigned a victimized position in their personal narratives. The offender may be required to provide direct compensation to the victim, or even to perform a series of services in their favor, leading to real redress for the dissatisfaction suffered as a result of the criminal act. In this way, social justice — understood as equal opportunities in accessing the resources necessary for the pursuit of one's own well-being, and as compensation for the advantages obtained through illegitimate access to resources — is restored [132]. The deliberative process is what generates social therapeutics, both in the case of the victim and in that of the offender [67, 201]. Theorists of the paradigm invoke dialogical morality in understanding the communitarian perspective on restorative justice [67]. Reference is made to the postmodern experience of deconstructing universalist claims to justice [210], with justice being understood rather as a social construction, and social morality as the outcome of ongoing negotiation. Doina Balahur [5] considers restorative justice as a conceptual framework paradigm for non-custodial sanctions. The author identifies two senses of the term *probation*: that of strategies limiting the offender's contact with the formal criminal justice system, and that of an alternative to custodial sanctions. Through probation practice based on restorative strategies, the aims pursued are both the decriminalization of the sanction and the reconstruction of the networks of organized reciprocity and "civic solidarity" [180].

1.1.1. Punishment as a Discourse of Power

In order to understand the social construction of the probation officer profession, it is necessary to outline certain theories of punishment as a discursive strategy. Such a general theory of punishment, from a discursive–postmodern perspective, is developed by Foucault, who traces the distinction between "words and things" in the context of the discourse of power and the power generated by discourse, as well as the relations of power that it produces [15, 49, p. 188]. Power, as Foucault [22] argues in *Discipline and Punish: The Birth of the Prison*, requires a discourse to legitimize it [54]; history and social space are nothing other than pretexts for the exercise of discursivity upon reality, radically modifying the interpretation conferred upon a social fact — and the context of interpretation — thereby altering "reality" itself. In Foucault's view [206], as well as in constructionist sociologies, the substitution between reality and its representation is affirmed [51]. Power is internal and constitutive of discourse [54]. In the construction of probation, the idea of establishing relations of power as a determining factor in the functioning of probation is supplemented by that of reducing the risk associated with criminal conduct [149]. Anglo-Saxon practice, in particular, regards probation as a form of exercising power — which we would characterize as a form of *soft power* [85, 86, 87] — coupled with a strategy for limiting the associated community risk arising, on the one hand, from criminality and, on the other, from the effects of incarceration. Foucault's vision positions probation as an intermediary space, situated at the intersection between carceral punishment and liberty [153]. Foucault [22] presents the birth of the prison as a transformation in the technologies of power. Punishment is viewed as a form of codifying power, with the prison as its external manifestation [182]. Non-custodial sanctions can be interpreted in a Foucauldian sense as a major transformation in the codification of power — from coercive and restrictive power to cooperative power grounded in influence and co-participation, replacing force-based power. Cooperative power, of which probation practice is one expression, is a product of the social deconstruction of the totalitarian valences of the state [160] and of its pretension to impose the social contract. According to Foucault [22], punitive power organizes three dispositifs, each with its own discourse [49, p. 189].

The first conception of power is that of the external regulation of individuals. This type of discourse produces the statization of juridical power, giving rise to the function of the prosecutor as representative of the state [54]. The uniqueness of the Sovereign was a consequence of the essentialist vision of the world, upon which it is grounded and which it propagates. The uniqueness and order of the world presupposes the existence of a single truth, giving rise to the inquest (*enquête*) as a form of knowledge thereof. The inquest initially replaced the probatory procedure of medieval canon law, which presupposed a form of judicial duel — a direct and often lethal confrontation between the accused and the accuser. Contemporary forms of probation grounded in restorative justice theory return to the primacy of the offender–victim relationship, not from the perspective of confrontation, but of cooperation in restoring the social equilibrium disrupted by the act committed. In this context, the literature speaks of a hyper-racial dimension to systems of incarceration and, by extension, of racial segregation [153]. An over-representation of Black inmates in American prisons has been observed. A similar situation may be found in both Romanian and Moldavian prisons, where the Roma ethnicity exhibits a significantly elevated rate of incarceration. From a Foucauldian perspective, the predominance of a minority group in the carceral spectrum can be interpreted as a rejection of alterity and a legitimization of power constructed upon the guilt of being different.

With the emergence of contractualist theories, a reform of punishment took place through the limitation of arbitrariness [54, pp. 203–210]. The violation of the law no longer represents an offense against the Sovereign, but against society as a whole, with crime being redefined from the perspective of social danger. The contractualist technologies of power remove corporeality from the spectrum of sanctions. In practice, any sanction involving bodily harm to the person is deemed illegal and denounced under the European Convention for the Prevention of Torture and Inhuman or Degrading Treatment or Punishment. Regrettably, both Romania and the Republic of Moldova have received convictions from the European Court of Human Rights for ill-treatment of detainees and for inhuman and degrading treatment — both in penitentiaries and in pre-trial detention, and in institutions providing involuntary psychiatric internment [236]. Punishment acquires an active role in defending the interests of society and public order, losing its retributive character as an act of vengeance for the offense against the Sovereign. Symbolic punishment and the representation of punishment are gradually replaced by corporal punishment. "Sanction proceeds only from an investigation carried out in the manner of scientific inquiry. This penal philosophy is grounded in realistic humanism" [54, pp. 203–210].

The third penal philosophy is situated by Foucault around the institution of the prison, its objective being "control over acts, but above all over the possibility and virtuality of the act" [51, pp. 117–124]. Foucault regards contemporary society as one of generalized surveillance, with the coercive system producing delinquency. For Foucault, the prison produces rather than discovers delinquents, who are an institutional product of incarceration. Incarceration generates social stigmatization, for both the prisoner and their family. The carceral environment constitutes a context of alternative — deviant — socialization, with the risk of recidivism being significantly elevated for former detainees [153]. From a probation perspective, the Anglo-Saxon model of suspended sentencing enables the accused to remain outside the carceral space — not only physically, as in Romanian and Moldavian law, but also symbolically. Since guilt has not been declared and the presumption of innocence remains operative, the offender does not acquire the status of a convicted person, thereby avoiding the associated stigmas of the prisoner/convict status. The person whose sentence has been suspended nonetheless retains the status of a convicted individual, and the symbolic incarceration limits their trajectory of social reintegration. The technology of power is different in the first case: the refusal to pronounce a conviction represents a refusal of explicit power and a genuine co-participation of the state in maintaining the offender–victim–society equilibrium. In the second case, the symbolic exercise of power through the act of conviction has a repressive character, with society as represented by the state failing to assume its share of responsibility toward either the offender or the victim. In Foucault's view, with the processes of modernization and secularization of society, a transformation of the styles of power codified in juridical norms takes place. The maximization of efficiency and good governance are collateral effects of the process of "reinventing society" in its totality on the model of the prison [22, 49, p. 191]. As a result of the emergence of the penal system as a central element of the modern state, the prison gradually replaced traditional forms of punishment — capital punishment, deportation, corporal punishment, and so forth [4]. Imprisonment became the predominant sanction in modern society, through which both retribution — still considered necessary — and prevention could be achieved [49, p. 192]. The paradigm of punishment in modern societies is prisonocentric. Doina Balahur [4] considers incarceration the essential reference point of conventional penal systems.

1.1.2. Some Considerations on the Prisonocentric Paradigm and Possible Social Alternatives

Imprisonment is regarded by both the general public and specialists in penology as the sanction carrying the highest level of punitive severity. It is considered the most rigorous and yet the most appropriate response of the community to crime and criminals [185]. The prison represents a total institution, following the model described by Goffman [28] for the asylum. Carceral culture is imposed upon the individual, redefining their way of life and transforming them into a career criminal. The necessity of gradating punishment, and the need for a less severe societal response commensurate with a reduced estimated level of social danger assessed at the community level and implemented by the courts, has led to the emergence of various forms of non-custodial sanctions. These are viewed as alternatives to imprisonment in terms of punitive intensity [4].

Probation grounded in the alternative-to-imprisonment model remains tributary to the prisonocentric paradigm; even in its humanized form, imprisonment remains present in the discourse on punishment and on the social recovery of the offender [185]. Symbolic incarceration definitively ties the offender to a carceral past, even though the absence of the actively criminogenic environment of the prison significantly reduces the risk of recidivism. The prisonocentric paradigm remains dominant even in states where non-custodial sanctions account for over 70% of all convictions pronounced, as is the case in Japan, Germany, Slovenia, Finland, Austria, and Egypt [4]. In our view, the prisonocentric paradigm is fundamentally retributive in nature, with the sanction remaining the societal response to crime [49, p. 194]. The non-custodial sanctions mentioned above remain within the retributive logic, not constituting, in effect, a genuine decriminalization of the sanction.

The dominant currents supporting social alternatives to imprisonment indicate that society has come to recognize the disadvantages of incarceration in the social recovery of offenders. In our view, among the most significant causes — and consequences — of incarceration in its etiology is poverty [119], both material and symbolic. Through a systematic analysis of 23 of the more than 300 studies in the literature examining the impact of incarceration versus alternative solutions on reducing the risk of recidivism, Martin Killias and Patrice Villetaz [150] find that the results appear, on balance, to favor non-custodial sanctions. In 11 of the 27 cases compared, recidivism is more frequent among subjects who underwent incarceration than among those who benefited from alternative sanctions. However, the meta-analysis conducted by these authors with regard to the gravity of the acts for which the subjects were convicted indicates that the risk of recidivism is nearly equal in cases of serious offenses sanctioned by imprisonment versus alternative solutions. The apparent reduction in the risk of recidivism for those who served non-custodial sanctions, the authors argue, may also be attributable to the minor nature of the antisocial act committed, its low degree of social danger, and the exclusion or limitation of any intent to commit a genuinely serious offense. This may be correlated with the fact that alternative solutions to incarceration are directed at offenders with a low degree of social danger and, consequently, of recidivism risk, and it cannot therefore be asserted that the alternative solution is what produces the reduction in recidivism [150]. In our view, this observation is correct and consistent with the incapacitation function attributed to punishment. Punishment as social prophylaxis maintains the offender who has committed particularly serious acts outside the capacity to commit further acts, keeping society at minimal risk from antisocial behavior. A criminal career is, in our view, facilitated by the carceral environment and the habituation of the detainee to it. In some cases, incarceration becomes a career in itself, with the penitentiary environment being perceived as a survival resource — particularly in the case of those who have undergone long-term detention and whose social support networks have been subsequently disrupted. Such individuals no longer find the resources for adaptation to a non-carceral environment, which leads them to commit criminal acts with the express intention of returning to prison. Once the carceral experience becomes habitual, it loses its function as an inhibitory factor on antisocial behavior. Research conducted in Moldova indicates that on 1 April 2005, a total of 1,950 persons were serving prison sentences for the second time, 1,332 for the third time, and 930 for the fourth time or more — compared to 2,458 detainees who were serving their first sentence, representing only 36.9% of the total prison population in Moldova at the time of the study [185].

A genuine alternative to the prisonocentric paradigm would be one derived from restorative justice, eliminating the notion of sanction and not merely that of punishment, transforming it — at least at the discursive level — into educational measures of social reintegration. The fact that Romanian legislation associates educational measures with sanctioning measures contributes to the perpetuation of a retributively grounded penal philosophy, even though a step forward is represented by the conceptual separation of *sanction* from *punishment*. This separation is, however, only partially productive, insofar as neither the general public nor the great majority of practitioners perceive or operationalize the distinction in probation practice. The operational definitions of *sanction* and *punishment* nonetheless constitute a separate object of empirical inquiry that falls outside the scope of the present research.

1.2. Theoretical Perspectives Underpinning the Practice of Probation Services in Romania and the Republic of Moldova

We have sought to identify the penal ideologies that underlie the institutional construction of probation at the global level, with particular reference to Romania and the Republic of Moldova. The scholarly literature contains a number of theories according to which the concept of sanction may be extended to include rewards as positive sanctions [6], consolidating the distinction between positive deviance — as a manifestation of the need for social change that merits recognition — and negative deviance and delinquency proper, which merit punishment [49, p. 185]. From a sociological perspective, punishment may be understood as a societal response to the deviant behavior of its members. Punishment may encompass both formal and informal sanctions, presupposing the existence of a direct relationship between the nature and gravity of the deviance, the norms violated, and the severity of the sanction [49, p. 186]. In essence, the sanction represents society's reactive response to undesirable behavioral patterns. Beyond its retributive character, the sanction also acquires a number of educative and restorative functions [196]. From the perspective of the constitution of probation as a practice of community-based control of deviance and delinquency, the sanction becomes autonomous in relation to punishment [123]. In general, the specialist legal literature places emphasis on the retributive factor, regarding punishment as "the sole criminal sanction designed to ensure the restoration of the legal order disrupted by the commission of a criminal offense" [41]. This view reflects the powerful retributive current present in both Romanian and Moldavian society — one that is deeply favorable to custodial measures and strongly marked by discrimination against persons who have committed criminal acts, including after their release from the carceral environment. We consider that the profound distrust of institutions and the attitude of intolerance toward various forms of social deviance — including minor forms of delinquency — is characteristic of post-totalitarian societies, whereas established democracies tend rather toward tolerance and the maintenance of social equilibrium. This view is supported by a United Nations survey demonstrating a high degree of acceptance of non-custodial sanctions in developed states and a markedly lower acceptance in less developed states [57]. At the level of the Republic of Moldova, a survey conducted in the municipality of Chişinău indicates that although Moldavian citizens express willingness to participate in the social reintegration of persons subject to probation, only 27% indicate that they would be willing to offer concrete, practical assistance [57, p. 190, 223–229]. The situation revealed by the survey may differ at present from the year in which it was conducted — prior to 2009, the year of the book's publication — precisely because the Probation System has since evolved and become more firmly established in public awareness. Respondents in the cited survey considered that responsibility for probation practice — with particular reference to the prevention of recidivism — should rest with the state, while also suggesting the need for the establishment of non-governmental organizations to deliver services in this field. Another survey conducted in the Republic of Moldova [3] indicates that 26.23% of respondents would refuse outright to assist a former detainee seeking help with food, shelter, protection, and social understanding; only 14.75% would agree without reservation, while 56.56% would deliberate on the advisability of assisting a former prisoner. The same survey provides data on the social stereotypes held by Moldavian citizens toward former detainees: caution and fear — 67%; hostility — 2%; no particular feeling — 20%; other — 11% [3, 94]. With regard to the visibility of the probation service in the Republic of Moldova, a study published in 2011 indicates that few community members (approximately 21%) are well or very well acquainted with the activities of the probation service. The majority — 52% — have little or no knowledge of these activities. Most respondents identified their sources of information about the probation service as acquaintances, colleagues, friends, family, and the mass media. The same study revealed a limited degree of public knowledge about the probation service, a finding confirmed by results obtained among legal practitioners (prosecutors and judges). While 62% of prosecutors and 53% of judges reported being well or very well acquainted with the activities of the probation service, this implies that 38% of these practitioners have only a limited knowledge of the matter. It is a cause for concern that one in five judges and one in ten prosecutors have very little or no information about the activities of the probation service [17]. Surveys conducted in Romania reveal a similar situation, with probation services being poorly known among the general public, including among legal practitioners — 14% of the lawyers surveyed were unable to provide an explanation of the term *probation* [108].

The functions of punishment are addressed in both the sociological and legal literature: retribution, deterrence, incapacitation, and rehabilitation [196]. It is not entirely clear whether, in the view of both the Romanian and Moldavian legislators, the same functions can be associated with non-custodial measures. In our view, non-custodial measures are oriented rather toward social prophylaxis and the rehabilitation of persons — in particular minors — who have committed criminal acts. It should be noted that the New Penal Code and the New Code of Criminal Procedure [37, 38][6] in Romania avoid defining the functions of punishment, abandoning any legislative positioning with respect to the utility of punishment [177]. The former Penal Code was dominated by the educative and rehabilitative function of punishment, which situated the Romanian penal system within a human rights-centered justice paradigm and, partially, within that of restorative justice. The retributive function of punishment, although implicitly present in the form of the notion of a sanction owed by the offender as a consequence of the violation of the law, was not discursively present at the level of the legislative text. Romanian penal doctrine appears to insist on the retributive character of punishment, this being considered the dominant function by many authors [186]. Although this doctrine originates — as is evident — from the beginning of the last century, it remains, regrettably, present in judicial practice and in public opinion, which holds that the purpose of the sanction is to punish the guilty person [99]; the label of guilt being affixed in most cases from the moment of the criminal investigation, through the gratuitous and irrational violation of

[6] In the context of the present work, NCP (*Noul Cod Penal* — New Penal Code) and NCPP (*Noul Cod de Procedură Penală* — New Code of Criminal Procedure) refer to the legislative codes specific to the Romanian state, whereas CP (*Cod Penal* — Penal Code) and CPP (*Cod de Procedură Penală* — Code of Criminal Procedure) refer to the corresponding legislation of the Republic of Moldova. The Romanian codes cited throughout this work have been sourced from: Lupașcu, D. (2014a). *Noul Cod Penal: legislație consolidată* [New Penal Code: Consolidated Legislation], 10 February 2014. Bucharest, Romania: Editura Universul Juridic; and Lupașcu, D. (2014b). *Noul Cod de Procedură Penală: legislație consolidată* [New Code of Criminal Procedure: Consolidated Legislation], 10 February 2014. Bucharest, Romania: Editura Universul Juridic.

the presumption of innocence. The legislation of the Republic of Moldova [96, 97, 98, 100, 103, 104, 105, 106] is equally non-transparent in defining the functions of punishment, and the penal doctrine consulted by us makes reference to "the fulfillment of the functions of punishment" without explicitly specifying what these are [101].

From a discursive perspective, the lack of concern with the functions of punishment in doctrine — specialist legal literature — leads us to conclude that the retributive paradigm is dominant at the level of public discourse, such that scholars in the field neglect to interrogate these functions, treating them as a matter of common knowledge — even though the legislative changes that have occurred derive from "legal imports" from legal systems that have adhered to a different penal philosophy and, by extension, to a different operational definition of the functions of punishment. The process of social construction of punishment — and, by extension, of probation as an institution involved in the management of the execution or non-execution of punishment — undergoes a deconstruction arising from the aforementioned semantic shift, a process of which society — and indeed many practitioners — are not adequately informed. Transparadigmatic practice generates an incoherent discourse that attempts to justify, in the terms of one paradigm — the restorative — elements of social practice that originate in the retributive paradigm. The institutions of the retributive paradigm do not lose their relevance; rather, they gradually undergo an interpretive drift as the restorative paradigm takes root among practitioners. An interpretive cleavage is undergone by the concept of punishment, and correspondingly by that of probation as a social and professional practice. Probation services are designed to supervise the execution of non-custodial sanctions at the intersection between institutions with a primarily social work mandate — namely the probation service, oriented toward reintegration and rehabilitation — and legal institutions, focused on the idea of retributive justice, as well as institutions within the Prison Directorate system, oriented toward a carceral paradigm. This intersection of professional values creates an inequality of discourse and, at the level of power normalization strategies, among the respective institutional representatives and public opinion. The normalization of power relations and the achievement of an institutional status quo may place the prestige of social work services — including probation services — in either a position of strength or, conversely, one of marginality. Professional prestige enables the probation officer, as an institutional actor, to participate more or less extensively in the perpetual social negotiation of the very meaning of criminal justice and punishment, as well as their respective functions. The social pressure to which social institutions are subjected is likewise variable, depending on public expectations regarding social justice [215]. These expectations may be situated along a continuum ranging from the value of solidarity — which leads to restorative practices — to the value of collective retribution — which leads to practices of a retributive nature.

1.2.1. Responsibilities of Probation Systems in Romania and the Republic of Moldova

The tasks entrusted by the legislature to probation services in accordance with Romanian and Moldavian legislation [215, p. 21] are as follows:

Table 1. Professional Activities and Responsibilities of the Probation Officer in Romania and the Republic of Moldova [215, p. 21]

Activity / Responsibility	RO	MD
Supervision/organization of community service / corrective labor[7]	✓	✓
Preparation of social inquiry reports / pre-sentencing reports	✓	✓
Supervision of the execution of sanctions / probation conditions	✓	✓
Supervision of persons serving a suspended / conditional sentence	✓	✓
Supervision of court-mandated drug/alcohol treatment and other therapeutic programs	✓	✓
Supervision of educational and vocational training programs, and of the execution of educational measures	✓	✓
Supervision of persons released on parole / on license / serving an interrupted sentence	✓	✓

[7] The term *corrective labor* is understood here to encompass unpaid community service work, labor activities carried out by detainees within penitentiary settings, and the now-defunct practice of sentence execution at the offender's place of employment.

Activity / Responsibility	RO	MD
Provision of criminal mediation services / victim support		
Primary and secondary prevention		✓
Assistance and support for incarcerated persons; preparation for release; sentence management		✓
Supervision of the execution of special measures for addiction treatment		
Participation in the assessment of incarcerated persons for the purposes of conditional release	✓	
Counseling and assistance for defendants subject to house arrest or electronic surveillance (suspension of pre-trial detention)		
Supervision of offenders not criminally liable due to mental illness / supervision of involuntary psychiatric commitment		
Supervision of offenders whose sentencing has been conditionally deferred		
Supervision of electronic monitoring		
Supervision of the execution of open-regime imprisonment (semi-liberty)		
Supervision of the execution of semi-open regime imprisonment (semi-detention)	✓	
Support services for amnestied persons	✓	
Post-release aftercare		
Day centers for persons on conditional release		
Mandatory registration of domicile	✓	
Monitoring of compliance with court-imposed prohibitions (e.g., prohibition from holding a specific office or position)	✓	
Supervision of the execution of restraining orders in cases of suspended sentence, including situations involving sexual abuse and abuse risk		✓
Provision of supervision and assistance services for persons in pre-trial detention		

Activity / Responsibility	RO	MD
Support services for the families of incarcerated persons		
Supervisory authority over conditionally released persons		
Supervision of the non-coercive enforcement of court-imposed measures	✓	
Coordination of voluntary services within prisons		
Assistance (conducting interviews/examinations) in hearings involving minors		
Preparation of offenders for sentence interruption and supervision of interrupted sentence execution		

Anton M. van Kalmthout and Ioan Durnescu [215, p. 21] indicate that among the most significant responsibilities of national probation systems should be the following: providing judicial authorities and courts with social inquiry reports and assessment documents containing relevant information about the offender's personal circumstances and social situation; implementing (non-custodial) sanctions and supervising offenders; developing organizational and community-based services for the implementation of community measures; offering financial, psychological, and social work assistance and support at any stage of the offender's engagement with the criminal justice system — pre-sentencing, post-sentencing, custodial, non-custodial, and post-penal. Alongside these functions, the provision of support to crime victims and victim–offender mediation are regarded as being of comparable importance, albeit with a lower degree of international prevalence. With regard to the responsibilities assigned to the probation service of the Republic of Moldova, we note the absence of any mandate to conduct social inquiries into the offender's circumstances and to prepare pre-sentencing reports that would assist the court in individualizing the sentence [17, 18]. Another significant gap in the responsibilities of the Moldavian probation service concerns primary and secondary prevention [2, 8, 9, 10, 12]. Romanian legislation fails to assign to the probation service any responsibilities relating to victim–offender mediation, given that criminal mediation remains limited in scope, leads to the dismissal of criminal liability only in a small number of cases, and is left to private services and firms specializing in mediation [29, 32]. Another significant responsibility absent from the activities of probation officers in Romania is the supervision of conditionally released or paroled persons, as this form of release does not exist in Romanian penal enforcement law [1]. These institutional differences across national probation services shape the specific character of the social construction of the probation officer within each national context. A mandate that is absent from the repertoire of a National Probation Service is necessarily reflected in the discursive practice relating to professional activity and professional identity [62]. The absence of prevention-related responsibilities may generate, at the discursive level, an excessive preoccupation with control and surveillance, which may derive from the internalization of the role of supervisor of the supervised person's behavior rather than that of a provider of social services aimed at populations at elevated risk of criminal behavior. The absence of victim–offender mediation responsibilities may translate, at the discursive level, into a disregard for victim-related issues [46, 47, 48, 58, 59, 60] and for victims' needs, thereby rendering the implementation of a restorative justice-based probation paradigm in Romanian legislation particularly challenging.

Ioan Durnescu [144] develops a classification of contemporary probation systems according to their constitutive values [138] and the purposes assigned to them in relation to the national criminal justice system [191]. The first model, operative in Turkey and Estonia, is premised on the promotion of community measures and sanctions. In our view, the ethical values informing this model are connected to the social responsibility of the community and to the value of the individual within the community, beyond their condition of self-induced vulnerability [39] arising from the social disequilibrium created by the commission of an antisocial act. The second model, in which Ioan Durnescu [144, p. 274] includes the Romanian system, has as its primary purpose the support of the judiciary in reaching the most appropriate sentencing decisions. Given this stated objective, the professional discourse of probation officers will tend to incorporate references to judicial practice, and the construction of their professional identity will be associated more closely with the legal professions than with social work — the field from which probation practice historically derives [7]. The rehabilitation model and the protection of the population against criminogenic risks have been developed in countries such as France, Austria, the Czech Republic, Denmark, Germany, and Bulgaria [131, 188]. We situate the Moldavian probation system within this model, on the basis of the responsibilities identified above. The final model discussed by Ioan Durnescu [188, p. 19] is the British model, grounded in punishment and its implementation [112].

1.2.2. The Establishment of the Romanian and Moldavian Probation Systems

Elements of restorative justice practice can be identified as far back as Greco-Roman antiquity. The origins of restorative practices may be traced to Aristotelian ethics, where the principle of restoring an equitable situation appears alongside those of justice, community, and punishment [76]. Modern probation systems are grounded in the gradual development of alternatives to incarceration and the practice of conditional release [66]. The earliest practices of this kind were *recognizance* and *surety*. Release on recognizance was granted upon the offender's promise not to commit further criminal acts, while release on surety required the existence of a third party who would stand as guarantor for the offender. The origins of the term *probation* are linked to the British criminal justice tradition, where it denoted the temporary suspension of a sentence pending a royal pardon, or the conditional release of petty offenders [188, p. 8]. One of the earliest practitioners of probation was John Augustus (1784–1859), who served as guarantor for pre-selected offenders in the city of Boston, pledging that they would refrain from further criminal conduct and appear at their scheduled hearings. Offenders for whom Augustus had vouched, and who succeeded in reforming their conduct and abstaining from further criminal activity, benefited from the discontinuation of criminal proceedings, with the court treating the offense as though it had not occurred [49, p. 214]. This practice forms the contemporary basis for the institutions of deferred or suspended sentencing, which are prevalent in jurisdictions across the United States and Europe [190].

In Romania, the New Penal Code (NPC) introduced several new legal instruments, including: *waiver of the application of punishment* (Arts. 80–82), whereby the person in respect of whom this measure has been ordered is not subject to any forfeiture, prohibition, or incapacity arising from the offense committed [Art. 82, para. (1) NPC]; *deferral of the application of punishment* (Arts. 83–90), whereby the person in respect of whom deferral has been ordered is obligated to receive visits from the probation officer [Art. 85, para. (1), letter b, NPC], with the court having the additional power to impose a range of obligations such as: attendance at a course, performance of unpaid community service, participation in a social reintegration program, submission to medical treatment or care, and so forth [Art. 85, para. (2), letters a–d, NPC]. Where the person in respect of whom deferral of punishment has been ordered has not committed any further offense prior to the expiry of the supervision period, and where revocation or annulment of the deferral measure has not been ordered, the punishment shall no longer be applied and that person shall not be subject to any forfeiture, prohibition, or incapacity; *suspension of the execution of punishment under supervision* (Arts. 91–98) is ordered by the court where the sentence imposed does not exceed three years' imprisonment and the defendant has not previously been convicted of a sentence exceeding one year, or where rehabilitation has intervened. The defendant is required to perform unpaid community service [Art. 91, para. (1), letter c, NPC] and is supervised by the probation services; *conditional release* may be ordered after the execution of at least two-thirds of the custodial sentence [Art. 100, para. (1), letter a, NPC], or after at least twenty years in the case of a life sentence [Art. 99, para. (1), letter a, NPC]. Supervision measures administered by the probation service are mandatory [Art. 101, para. (1), letter a, NPC] [49, p. 216].

The probation model initiated by John Augustus in Boston, as adapted to the characteristics of modern penal systems, has since expanded internationally, with probation being regarded as an alternative sentencing solution that prevents mass incarceration — particularly of juveniles and young offenders — thereby reducing the adverse consequences of the custodial environment and constituting a significant component of the social rehabilitation of offenders. The Romanian model, as embodied in the NPC, introduces probation as a public service directly involved in the supervision, rehabilitation, and social reintegration of offenders [49, p. 217]. The first probation legislation was enacted in the United Kingdom in 1887 under the title *Probation of First Offenders Act*, developed on the basis of the American probation model — following the Augustus model — with the aim of maintaining first-time minor offenders at liberty under supervision and support [190]. The institution of suspended sentencing emerged as a response to criticisms directed at the Augustus model of maintaining offenders at liberty, whereby those who refrained from further criminal conduct over a given period were entirely exonerated. Critics of this model argued that the absence of a sanction predisposed offenders to recidivism. The conditional release model, contingent on the offender's abstention from further criminal conduct, reduces the potential inequity arising from the absence of a conviction [33]. A conviction is pronounced, but its application is suspended for a probationary period; once that period has elapsed without incident, the sentence is extinguished, and rehabilitation may ensue. The declaration of guilt in the act of conviction clearly signals the position of the court — and, by extension, of society — with regard to the act committed. Suspended execution of sentence differs from the Anglo-Saxon probation model, in which the court does not pronounce a sentence, thereby preserving the presumption of innocence in favor of the defendant [49, p. 218]. As noted above, acquittal following probation under the Anglo-Saxon model precludes the existence of a criminal record, given that no conviction has been handed down. In certain jurisdictions — including Romania prior to the introduction of the NPC — there was no statutory requirement for the supervision, within the community or by probation officers, of persons convicted with suspended sentences. The NPC introduced the novel element of probation service oversight of convicted persons not serving custodial sentences [49, p. 219].

In Romania, the earliest manifestations of practices relating to conditional release appear in the *Law on the Prison Regime* of 1874, which is considered among the most progressive penal legislation of its era [188, p. 10]. Prior to this first formal codification of conditional release, the Romanian principalities had known a range of practices whereby the defendant could be made a bondsman of the victim, who retained the power to release them, or could appeal directly to the clemency of the ruling Prince. Medieval practice included such forms of conditional release — for instance, when a person condemned to death was chosen as a husband by a young noblewoman, with marriage bringing with it a pardon for the condemned. In Romania, "non-custodial legal provisions" and elements of probation practice existed as early as the pre-war period. The institution of *supervised liberty* was defined by Article 146 of the 1936 Penal Code as the placement of the minor, for a period of onc year, under close supervision — either in the care of a legal guardian, a state institution such as a children's home, or a trusted individual who assumed the corresponding responsibility [49, p. 220]. The court would defer the pronouncement of its judgment until the expiry of the probationary period. The person or institution entrusted with the supervision of the minor was obligated to exercise that supervision on a continuous basis and was required, upon expiry of the probationary period, to report to the court on the minor's conduct [188, p. 11]. Where the minor under supervision had not committed any further criminal acts during the probationary period, no sentence of conviction was pronounced, and the defendant was accordingly not convicted. Subsequent legislation replaced this measure with suspension of the execution of sentence or, under the NPC, deferral of the execution of sentence under supervision — which entails a conviction and a formal declaration of guilt on the part of the defendant. Even under the current legislative framework, forms of this practice of non-pronouncement of guilt may be found in the institution of *removal from criminal investigation*. Removal from criminal investigation is ordered by the prosecuting magistrate who, on the basis of an assessment of the degree of social danger and the risk of future criminal conduct, proposes the removal of the defendant from criminal investigation. This practice is not, however, connected to probation, as it does not entail a probationary period or supervision by a specialized service. The communist period also gave rise to various alternatives to custodial punishment, the most significant of which was *sanctioning and rehabilitation through labor*, instituted by Decree No. 218/1977 [188, p. 12]. Labor was considered a method of social rehabilitation and served as a substitute for sentences of up to five years' imprisonment. The penal policy of the communist regime pursued the de-institutionalization of criminal punishment for minors, leading to a reduction in the incarceration rate in Romania from 66% in 1976 to 29.4% in 1979 [188, p. 12]. The model applied may be considered analogous to unpaid community service, a sanction available in the criminal legislation of the United States and numerous other states. At present, unpaid community service does not exist in either Romanian or Moldavian legislation as a sanction *per se*; it may be imposed by courts only in the form of the conversion of a criminal fine into days of unpaid labor. A criticism that may be leveled at the system of sanctioning and rehabilitation through labor is that supervision was left entirely to the collective of fellow workers and to the militia and security organs, without any recognition of the need for professionals in the fields of psychology, sociology, and social work to supervise the community supervision [91] of persons who had committed criminal offenses. Another practice prevalent during the communist period was the frequent recourse to amnesties — including general amnesties under which detainees were released and amnestied on condition that they refrain from committing further criminal acts [49, p. 221].

Following 1989, Romanian legislation introduced the following measures: *suspension of the execution of sentence under supervision* (Law No. 104/1992); and *execution of sentence at the place of employment* (Law No. 140/1996). The establishment of probation services in both Romania and the Republic of Moldova was aimed at developing alternative sanctioning measures that would allow for the reduction of the financial and social costs of incarceration [187]. Relevant statistical data from the Republic of Moldova indicate that the penitentiary system is severely overcrowded; surveyed detainees reported that 38.7% considered conditions in Moldavian penitentiaries to be very harsh or even inhumane, a further 18.5% described them as harsh, only 21.1% as good and normal, and 20.7% as tolerable [185]. The institution of probation has assumed an increasingly significant role in the administration of the execution of sentences and educational measures — both custodial and non-custodial — as well as supervision measures in cases where the implementation of a conviction has been deferred, suspended, and so forth. The first pilot project aimed at the experimental introduction of probation services in Romania was conducted at the Arad Penitentiary, followed in 1998 by the extension of the project to nine further cities across the country. From 2000 onwards, a specialized Directorate has operated within the Ministry of Justice, overseeing 41 local probation services at county level throughout the country, which were subject to dual subordination to both the Ministry of Justice and the local Tribunal [112, 188, p. 20]. In the Republic of Moldova, probation was introduced relatively recently, after 2001, alongside other alternative measures to detention, including criminal mediation and unpaid community service [183]. We note that these three components — probation, criminal mediation, and unpaid community service — which together constitute the paradigm of restorative justice, are treated separately as alternatives to incarceration, rather than as a unified system of social intervention in the sphere of the protection and social reintegration of persons who have committed criminal acts and of victims, through the mobilization of existing community resources. Probation is conceived as operating across two phases of the criminal process: the pre-sentencing phase and the sentencing phase. The pre-sentencing phase concerns the provision of social and psychological assistance to persons charged with the commission of criminal acts. During the pre-sentencing phase, the probation officer prepares the psychosocial assessment report on the offender [61] — particularly in the case of juvenile offenders — which constitutes a significant element in the individualization of the sentence. The sentencing phase concerns the application of rehabilitative and reintegrative measures under supervision of the offender within the community [195]. Sentencing-phase probation encompasses sentence management, the establishment of the sentence execution regime in the case of custodial sentences, and so forth. We observe an overlap between the activities of the probation officer and those of the social worker within the penitentiary. Through the exercise of rehabilitative activities, sentence management, and preparation for release, the work of the probation officer acquires a predominantly social work character, which takes precedence over the dimension of controlling the execution of (non-custodial) sentences. The probation officer is a social work specialist whose client is the person who has committed criminal acts. Participation in the administration of justice confers upon both the Romanian and Moldavian probation systems a particular institutional character — namely, that of functioning with the objective of the social rehabilitation of offenders, the reduction of the risk of further criminal conduct, and the enhancement of community safety [49, p. 245]. The paradigm within which such a probation system is situated is a communitarian one: the functioning of probation is oriented toward community interests — the social rehabilitation of persons who have committed criminal acts on the one hand, and the enhancement of community safety on the other. A further major objective of the probation system is the reduction of the costs of executing criminal sanctions, including the social costs entailed by the dysfunctions that the prisonocentric paradigm may generate [49, p. 246].

1.2.3. The Institutional Context of the Establishment and Operation of Probation Services in Romania and the Republic of Moldova

The analysis of the institutional context governing the operation of probation services has been the subject of a study [112] conducted within the Probation Service attached to the Bucharest Tribunal (PSB), which operated under the legislative and institutional framework in force in Romania in 2007. The institutional relationships of collaboration and subordination developed with other institutions — including the Ministry of Justice, the National Prison Administration, tribunals and courts of first instance, penitentiaries, and other regional probation directorates — were examined. The resulting diagram highlights the relationships of collaboration and subordination within which the probation service is embedded.

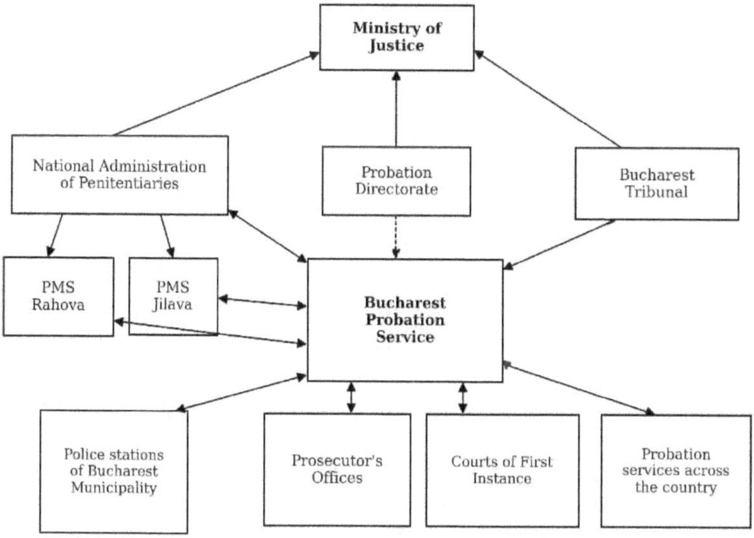

Fig. 1. The Bucharest Probation Service — Institutional Relationships of Subordination and Collaboration [112, p. 306]

Although the diagram represents the institutional relationships in which the Bucharest Probation Directorate was embedded in 2007, under the provisions of the former Probation Act, the institutional relationships established by probation services may be considered broadly similar — at least with regard to cooperation with the courts, criminal investigation bodies, penitentiaries, and so forth. The generalizability of this model renders it applicable to probation services in both Romania and the Republic of Moldova, and it may serve as a point of departure for the analysis of the institutional relationships in which the probation services of both countries are involved. In the process of constructing the probation officer profession, the institutional relationships of the organization to which the practitioner belongs lead to the identification of formal and informal social networks — both latent and manifest — that constitute the interactional context within which the practitioner constructs their professional identity. The Probation Directorate investigated in the aforementioned study (which operated under the auspices of the Bucharest Tribunal) was, at the time of the research, confronted with a chronic shortage of personnel, accompanied by a more than tenfold increase in workload, which placed considerable pressure on probation officers. The solutions identified included the introduction of professional supervision of practice, the computerization of the service and the establishment of a database encompassing the full range of the institution's activities, as well as the conduct of advocacy activities that led to legislative amendments, thereby enabling a reduction in the institutional pressure to which probation officers were subjected [112].

Worthy of particular note is the significant role played by community justice centers in the development of services for convicted persons and former detainees. These centers aim to represent the community's interest in assuming an active role in crime prevention and in the social reintegration of former offenders, promoting active restorative justice measures. In the Republic of Moldova, the first such center was established in 2005 at the initiative of the Penal Reform Institute, in the city of Ungheni. The center's stated purpose is to assist public institutions in promoting penal reform, with a view to implementing alternatives to detention and supporting the social reintegration of persons released from penitentiary institutions [3]. The cited source indicates that by 2009, fifteen community justice centers were operational in the Republic of Moldova. In Romania likewise, non-governmental organizations have developed restorative justice programs based on community justice centers [120], including those implemented by the *Asociația Alternative Sociale* (Alternative Social Association) in Iași[8], and the *Centrul de Mediere și Securitate Comunitară* (Center for Mediation and Community Security)[9], also based in Iași. We observe that community justice centers have played an active role in promoting restorative justice and in establishing the necessity of probation services in both countries. In Romania, pilot juvenile justice programs — such as those implemented by the *Asociația Alternative Sociale* — provided the foundational basis for the policy development of probation services, effectively conducting extensive exploratory research on the adaptation of probation techniques and methods to the Romanian socio-cultural context. In the Republic of Moldova, by contrast, the establishment of Community Justice Centers did not precede the adoption of probation as an alternative measure; rather, both developed in parallel, with the centers functioning as support services for the public institutions

[8] For the programs of the Association, see: http://www.aoc.ro

[9] For the programs of the Center for Mediation and Community Security (CMCS), see: http://www.cmsc.ro

implementing penal reform — including probation as a social practice. This relationship between probation and community security across the two countries helps explain why the legislation — although broadly favorable to elements of restorative justice in both states — does not place particular emphasis on restorative justice in the organization of probation services, with community involvement being left to the private sphere of non-governmental organizations pursuing community justice and security programs.

The formal establishment of probation services in Moldova was initiated through pilot programs supported by the Resource Center of the Penal Reform Institute. The practical implementation of the probation service commenced on 1 January 2004, through the piloting by the Penal Reform Institute (PRI) of pre-sentencing probation in relation to juvenile offenders, in the Central District of the Municipality of Chişinău. The pilot activities, incorporated within the project *"Alternatives to Detention and Legal Assistance for Children in the Criminal Justice System"*, implemented by the Penal Reform Institute (PRI) in partnership with the UNICEF Moldova Representation, encompassed the following:

- the establishment of a pilot pre-sentencing probation service for juvenile offenders within the Penal Reform Institute;
- the preparation of the conditions necessary for the conduct of probation activities;
- the methodological development of probation assessment reports;
- the extension of probation activities to additional pilot districts;
- the evaluation of pre-sentencing probation activities;
- the identification of possibilities for the nationwide generalization of pre-sentencing probation activities [65].

The same pilot-based approach formed the foundation of the Romanian Probation System, drawing on pilot programs in the field of restorative justice for juveniles conducted between 1998 and 2001.

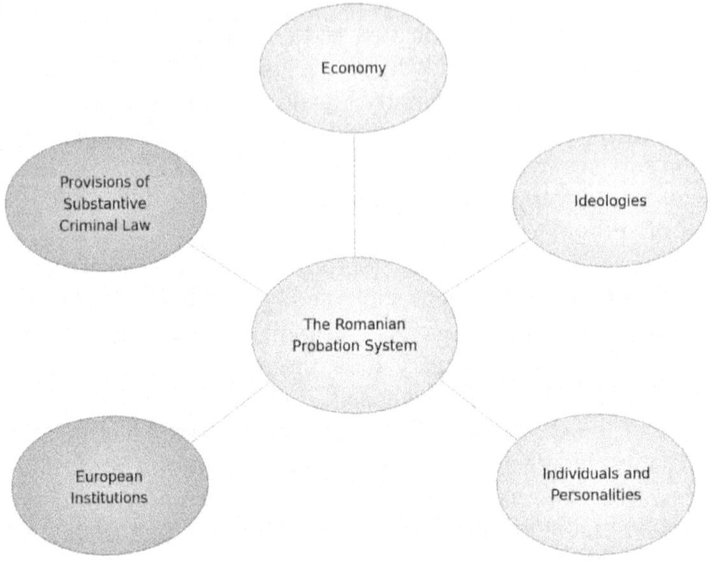

Fig. 2. The Paradigm of the Establishment of the Probation System [188, p. 13]

The paradigm proposed by Ioan Durnescu [188, p. 14] for the Romanian probation system — which, in our view, is equally applicable to the situation of the Republic of Moldova — identifies a range of causes and contributing factors that have led to the emergence and development of probation services. Non-custodial measures are consistent with socio-democratic corporatist or conservative corporatist social policies, characterized by pronounced income inequality and moderate, conditional social rights [130], and are consonant with the humanistic vision that informs public policy in Romania. The replacement of custodial sanctions with non-custodial alternatives leads to a reduction in costs within the national penitentiary system [49, p. 251]. A particularly significant contribution to the development of the probation system has been made by Romania's and the Republic of Moldova's accession to the European Conventions — including the European Convention on Human Rights and the European Convention for the Prevention of Torture and Inhuman or Degrading Treatment or Punishment [188, p. 16]. The modernization of the penal legislation of both countries has necessitated the establishment and development of the probation system and, concomitantly, the emergence of the probation officer profession.

1.3. Methodology

1.3.1. The Ontological and Epistemic Framework of the Social Construction of the Probation Officer Profession

The theoretical models and epistemic strategies underpinning the research are drawn from the sphere of sociology, with the analysis being conducted from the perspective of the theory of communicative action. Habermas [31, 80] regards communicative action as the preferred model for the exercise of power in contemporary society [49, p. 21]. The ontological and epistemic framework of the research is grounded in the vision of social constructionism [77, 148], concerned with explicating the processes through which people come to describe, explain, and account for the world in which they live and of which they are part [15, 49, p. 15]. Constructionism — as a paradigm of social thought — refers to the manner in which the individual operates with constructs, understood as operational definitions applied to segments of reality. A social construct represents an interpretive-behavioral model, resulting from a process of social negotiation of the interpretation that members of a community assign to a given thing or phenomenon. Whereas constructivism situates the formation of constructs at the level of the individual, constructionism locates them at the level of interactions within the social environment, with the individual internalizing and subsequently projecting them back onto the social environment [50, 146]. The vision underpinning our research is of a transmodern constructionist character [55], postulating the existence of a society embedded within a network of interdependencies, which presupposes a transformation in the structure of social action — namely, its reconstitution as the co-construction of social reality by members of interpretive communities situated at communicational nodes [162]. Our aim has been to identify the socio-legal perspectives on the social construction of the probation officer profession in the context of its institutional redefinition in Romania and the Republic of Moldova.

From a socio-economic standpoint, the North-Eastern region of Romania — comprising the counties of Iași, Suceava, Botoșani, Neamț, and Bacău — is among the most economically deprived regions in Romania and in the European Union. As a center of poverty, the region presents an elevated criminogenic profile, with many of the offenses for which individuals are registered with probation services being directly linked to a low standard of living. The Republic of Moldova formed part of the USSR until 1991, when it proclaimed its independence. The majority population is Romanian-speaking, with pronounced regional characteristics that were clearly discernible in the interviews conducted. The country's multi-ethnic character is attributable primarily to the effects of the Soviet occupation. The Republic of Moldova comprises 32 administrative districts and 2 autonomous regions. The standard of living is relatively low compared to other European states, with a substantial proportion of the population having emigrated to the European Union or to Russia. A high degree of corruption is frequently cited by the population as a cause of the low standard of living. Post-Soviet mentalities of an anti-democratic or even totalitarian character are also invoked — mentalities oriented toward social relations grounded in personal authority rather than the rule of law. These mentalities persist in the post-Soviet era despite legal provisions enshrining democracy and the rule of law. The Republic of Moldova is currently engaged in a process of modernization and development, both economically and socially.

Our research is based on a mixed methodological approach, encompassing both qualitative and quantitative dimensions, each of which constitutes an independent study in its own right. The qualitative dimension is represented by the study entitled *Axes of the Social Construction of the Probation Officer Profession: A Qualitative Study in the North-Eastern Region of Romania and in the Republic of Moldova*, conducted through the Grounded Theory method, drawing on data collected through interviews and focus groups, followed by a partial validation by means of an online questionnaire administered to probation officers in Romania and the Republic of Moldova. The quantitative dimension is represented by the survey-based study entitled *Retributivity and Public Perception of Non-Custodial Sanctions: A Study in the North-Eastern Region of Romania and in the Republic of Moldova.* The two studies are complementary: the first focuses on the perspectives of probation stakeholders — heads of probation services and offices, service users, and other categories of persons involved in the social reintegration of offenders — while the second examines public perceptions of non-custodial sanctions and of the activities of probation services. The two perspectives allow for methodological triangulation, designed to enhance the validity of the research.

1.3.2. The Study Axes of the Social Construction of the Probation Officer Profession: A Qualitative Study in the North-Eastern Region of Romania and in the Republic of Moldova

The purpose of the study is to identify the specific characteristics of the social construction of the probation officer profession. The research context concerns the specific features of communicative action as the preferred mode of action in the implementation of probation services in the North-Eastern region of Romania and in the Republic of Moldova.

1.3.3. Research Objectives

O1. To develop a study aimed at diagnosing the institutional context of the operation of probation services in Romania and the Republic of Moldova, from the perspective of justice reform. We seek to identify the meanings that professionals assign to their own activities. We are equally concerned with the meanings that offenders on probation attribute to the probation service, and with their understanding of their relationship with professionals within the system.

O2. To develop a theoretical framework concerning the role of the probation officer in the social construction of autonomy and responsibility among persons on probation — particularly juveniles — as well as the contexts and processes of resocialization for juvenile delinquents. On the basis of a diagnosis of probation practice, we will develop a theoretical model describing communicative practices and communicative action itself, which serves as an instance of the social (re)construction of the autonomy and responsibility of (juvenile) delinquents. The methodological literature on Grounded Theory — the methodological approach adopted for this research — regards it as essential that the researcher refrain from employing hypotheses derived from the specialist literature, and even from conducting a literature review that might foreground theoretical perspectives susceptible to being transformed into hypotheses. Such a prior review of the literature, conducted before the construction of one's own theoretical core, is considered counterproductive for research intended to be carried out through Grounded Theory [121].

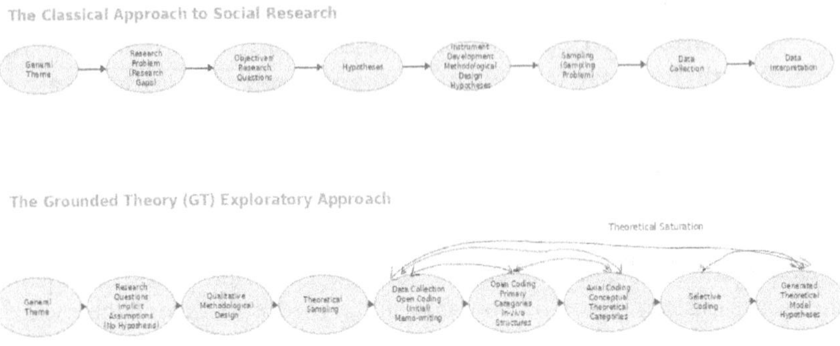

Grounded Theory is premised on the progressive identification of the significance of data and the generation of semantic categories derived from the direct analysis of data and their aggregation into a theory. The aim of Grounded Theory is to generate a theory concerning a studied social phenomenon, rather than to verify an existing theory. Grounded Theory proposes an inverted perspective on the relationship between theory and data: research proceeds from direct field data, operationalized successively, in order to generate a theoretical model, rather than departing from such a model to be verified in the field. The process of theoretical generation is inductive rather than deductive. Inductions are successive, continuing until the construction of a theoretical model of the highest possible degree of generality. GT aims to anchor social theory in perceived reality, remaining sensitive to the social context. Theory derives from experiential data rather than from prior theories. GT is influenced by phenomenological sociologies and symbolic interactionism. GT may be employed either as a comprehensive research method — encompassing the data collection stages, which are conducted through GT-specific strategies involving theoretical sampling, theoretical model saturation, and so forth — or as a method for the qualitative analysis of previously collected data (GT in its abbreviated form): document analysis. In the present work, we have chosen to employ GT in its integral form, applied to the data collection process.

The distinguishing feature of GT is that it does not rely on hypotheses, which constitute only a final product generated in the course of analysis rather than derived from the specialist literature. Research objectives and questions guide the inquiry, grounded in implicit presuppositions, without the formulation of hypotheses. There is no clearly defined research problem (Research Gap) in the classical sense, departing from a review of the domain literature. Analysis begins with the proposal of a series of constitutive axes (directions) of the theme to be explored, which will guide the exploratory endeavor and which may be modified at any point during the research in accordance with the directions identified in the category generation process. The initial thematic axes serve to guide the research and do not coincide with the conceptual thematic axes generated through axial coding. Research objectives and directions are reconstructed as data are collected and analyzed. The methodology encompasses a series of inductive processes, termed coding processes, through which the relationships between data are analyzed.

Open coding involves the continuous comparison of one's own data with results presented in the literature and with the respondent's discourse. In this process, initial categories are established through the identification of primary relationships between the key concepts identified in respondents' discourse.

Axial coding constitutes the second inductive process. At this stage, conceptual theoretical categories are generated at a higher degree of generalization, distinct from those resulting from the open coding process. Within this coding process, the connections between categories are made explicit, and a first analytical model is formulated.

Selective coding involves the identification of the central category and the relationships between categories, through the constant comparison of categories and the identification of possible discursive patterns.

Memos. Their introduction enables researchers to record ideas concerning the evolution of thc theoretical generation process across all stages of open, axial, and selective coding [71, p. 67]. Memos constitute theoretical notes pertaining to a particular set of data (their association with multiple categories, convergence/divergence with results from the literature, correlations between categories).

1.3.4. Data Collection

Data collection was carried out through 24 individual interviews with probation officers and heads of probation services — 12 from the North-Eastern Region of Romania (the counties of Botoșani, Suceava, Iași, Neamț, and Bacău) and 15 from the Republic of Moldova (the districts of Bălți and Ungheni, and 4 services from the districts of the Municipality of Chișinău, as well as the Central — National Office based in Chișinău). In the data analysis, references to interviews are designated

IRO for those conducted with respondents from Romania, and *IMD* for those conducted in Moldova. Additionally, 7 interviews were conducted with persons under the supervision of probation services in Romania and 8 in the Republic of Moldova. These were supplemented by a focus group conducted in Romania, in which, alongside representatives of the Probation System, 8 further professionals involved in the implementation of probation were also included (social workers, psychologists, and forensic medical practitioners). As an additional component, 3 interviews were conducted with a forensic medical practitioner, a lawyer, and a social worker, respectively, each of whom collaborates in various capacities with the probation service. The respondents who were probation officers were predominantly female — 10 of the 12 probation officers interviewed in Romania, and 10 of the 15 probation officers in the Republic of Moldova — a gender distribution consistent with that of employees within the probation services of Romania and the Republic of Moldova. With regard to the respondents who were supervised persons, 14 were male and 1 was female. Probation officers with between 2 and 17 years of professional experience were selected for participation in the interviews; two of the Romanian respondents and three of those from the Republic of Moldova had been in the system since the period of the experimental projects conducted through NGOs in the years 1997–2001 in Romania and 2003–2004 in the Republic of Moldova, respectively. Telephone and electronic correspondence was conducted with representatives of the National Probation Directorates and probation services, with the timing and duration of the interviews being established in consultation with service heads. Within each service, the selection of respondents was based on the snowball sampling method. The interviews were semi-structured, organized around a series of thematic axes including the description of professional practice and its specific characteristics, institutional cooperation, and models of probation practice.

1.3.5. Qualitative Sampling

Theoretical sampling was employed, whereby the inclusion of each new respondent in the sample was determined following the analysis of previous respondents, with new sample members being selected until theoretical model saturation was achieved. In order to ensure data saturation for the purposes of theoretical model construction, a saturation grid was used in accordance with the methodology set out by Brod and collaborators [136], Rubin and Rubin [89], Onwuegbuzie and collaborators [122], and Fusch and Ness [116]. The saturation grid takes the form of a table in which the inductively obtained categories are listed vertically and the interview or focus group respondents are listed horizontally. In order to confirm sample saturation, it is important to demonstrate that the contribution of the final respondents to the category table does not exceed the categories already obtained for the *n-2* respondents.

Table 1. Sample Saturation Grid for Probation Officer Respondents (RO)

	IRO01	IRO02	IRO03	IRO04	IRO05	IRO06	IRO07	IRO08	IRO09	IRO10	IRO11	IRO12	FG
C1	X						X	X			X		
C2	X	X	X	X	X	X	X	X			X		X
C3			X	X			X	X	X		X		
C4	X	X	X	X		X	X	X	X	X	X	X	
C5	X	X	X	X	X	X	X	X		X	X	X	X
C6	X	X	X	X	X	X	X	X	X	X	X	X	X
C7	X			X	X	X	X	X	X		X	X	X
C8	X	X	X	X	X	X		X					
C9				X	X	X	X	X	X	X	X		
C10	X				X	X	X	X	X	X			
C11		X					X						
C12											X		
C13	X		X	X		X				X	X		
C14				X				X					
C15	X			X					X		X		
C16	X					X		X	X	X	X		
C17	X			X				X	X		X		
C18	X	X		X	X	X	X	X		X	X		
C19						X		X			X		
C20	X								X				

Table 2. Sample Saturation Grid for Probation Officer Respondents (MD)

	IMD01	IMD02	IMD03	IMD04	IMD05	IMD06	IMD07	IMD08	IMD09	IMD10	IMD11	IMD12	IMD13	IMD14	IMD15
C1	X	X	X	X	X	X		X							
C2		X	X	X		X		X			X	X			
C3		X			X	X		X							
C4	X	X	X	X	X	X		X			X				
C5	X	X		X	X	X	X	X			X	X			
C6	X	X	X	X	X	X	X					X			
C7												X			
C8															
C9															
C10															
C11															
C12															
C13															
C14															
C15					X										
C16															
C17			X												
C18															
C19															
C20															

Table 3. Sample Saturation Grid for Service User Respondents (RO)

	IBRO01	IBRO02	IBRO03	IBRO04	IBRO05	IBRO06	IBRO07
C1							
C2							
C3							
C4							
C5							
C6							
C7							
C8							
C9							
C10							
C11							
C12							
C13							
C14							X
C15							
C16	X						
C17							
C18	X		X		X	X	
C19							
C20							

Table 4. Sample Saturation Grid for Service User Respondents (MD)

	IBM01	IBM02	IBM03	IBM04	IBM05	IBM06	IBM07	IBM08
C1								
C2								
C3								
C4								
C5								
C6								

	IBM01	IBM02	IBM03	IBM04	IBM05	IBM06	IBM07	IBM08
C7								
C8					x			
C9								
C10								
C11								
C12								
C13								
C14		x					x	
C15								
C16								
C17	x	x						
C18	x	x	x	x	x	x	x	
C19								
C20								

LEGEND:

I. Categories

C1. Normative framework of operation | C2. Institutional framework of operation | C3. Evolution of probation practice in Romania and Moldova | C4. Responsibilities of the probation officer in relation to service user typologies | C5. Professional socialization | C6. Professional identity of probation officers | C7. Professional dilemmas and challenges in probation practice | C8. Specific characteristics of the probation officer–supervised person relationship | C9. Case management between supervision and counseling | C10. The probation officer–supervised person relationship as a therapeutic relationship | C11. Narratives of practice | C12. Power-balancing strategies | C13. Working instruments and tools | C14. Attitudinal change toward society and normativity | C15. Constitutive values | C16. Operational values of practice | C17. The moral dimension of probation practice | C18. The rationale for the punishment of offenders | C19. Victim–offender mediation as a constitutive element of the restorative justice paradigm | C20. The functional paradigm of the profession: restorative justice, human rights-centered justice, and retributive justice.

II. Interview Codes

IRO — Interview with a probation officer from Romania | **IMD** — Interview with a probation officer from the Republic of Moldova | **IBRO** — Interview with a service user from Romania | **IBM** — Interview with a service user from the Republic of Moldova | **FG** — Focus group respondent.

1.3.6. Discussion

From this perspective, it is to be expected that discourse on probation will make reference to ostensibly objective benchmarks such as the normative framework, but above all to the effective functioning of institutions — that is, to the models of communication that operate within them. Consistent with social constructionism, social reality is understood as a process of reconstructing the interpretations of various social events and of the manner in which subjects represent their social world, with no distinct pursuit of an objective description thereof. The social constructionist perspective calls into question the notion of the absolute objectivity of social reality, which is instead regarded as the outcome of an interpretive process applied to the values, norms, institutions, and instruments that demarcate social action [77, 90]. From the constructionist epistemological perspective, we speak of the *credibility* of data rather than necessarily of their *validity*. The credibility of data interpretation was ensured through constant reference to respondents' own expressions, marked in quotation marks. The acceptance of interpretations by the interpretive community to which respondents belong was achieved through the partial presentation of the results of data analysis from the focus group conducted, and through the confrontation of the focus group respondents' views with those of the probation officers interviewed. Upon completion of the qualitative data analysis, the results were made available to senior personnel within the National Probation System of both countries, as well as to coordinators from the regional probation directorates and to the persons interviewed. The preliminary report was made available for consultation on the website of the LUMEN Center for Socio-Human Research, with interested parties — and in particular research participants — invited to formulate critical responses to the research conclusions, which were taken into account in the drafting of the final report. Model saturation was verified for each generated category, with the selection of new respondents being discontinued when new interviews ceased to yield significant new data in any of the research's thematic axes. Researcher triangulation and data source triangulation were pursued with a view to minimizing as far as possible the sources of subjectivity in data interpretation, with the researchers acknowledging the subjective nature and exploratory character of the research. The interviews were conducted in Romanian, the language in which the data coding process was also carried out.

Ethical considerations were examined by the research team. Data confidentiality is ensured through the anonymization of responses and the destruction of recordings upon completion of the research. The nature of the questions does not produce a heightened degree of discomfort for respondents beyond that of their routine professional activities, and participation in the research does not constitute an additional source of stress. Respondents were informed that they could withdraw from the research at any point during the interview, and that they could likewise choose not to respond to some or all of the questions. The selection of the two regions was grounded in a series of geographical, economic, cultural, and ethnic similarities. Linguistic, historical, and cultural particularities led us to conduct a comparative analysis of the two regions in order to understand the effects of diverse historical contexts and the potential frameworks for the construction of the probation officer profession (the historical, social, political, economic, cultural, and attitudinal framework).

1.3.7. Specificities of Data Analysis

For the interpretation of data, Grounded Theory (GT) was employed [13, 24, 71, 79], involving a process of systematic generation of concepts and conceptual categories of progressively increasing levels of generality that account for the researched theme. We consulted with particular interest studies conducted through GT methodology on the subject of probation and alternatives to custodial punishment, seeking methodological consistency with this body of research [109]. The approach was inductive, with successive stages of work proceeding from the information provided by the research subjects, thereby aiming at the generation of a new theoretical corpus rather than the validation of a set of prior hypotheses [13, 165]. Thus obtained, the results — synthesized in the form of a model — may constitute working hypotheses for future research aimed at clarifying the resulting model and establishing the extent of its validity. Data coding was carried out in multiple phases: *initial coding* and *selective/focused coding* [111], with the aim of identifying significant themes or categories; this was followed by *focused coding*, through which a categorization of data closer to theory was achieved by means of subdivision into categories and subcategories, and the consolidation of semantically adjacent initial categories. In the first stage, *open coding* was employed. A second stage in the data analysis process was *axial coding* [13], through which the thematic axes yielded a series of theoretical constructs with an explanatory role in the development of the instrumental model for understanding the social construction of probation in the North-Eastern region of Romania and the Republic of Moldova, following the penal reform that took place in both countries.

1.3.8. Results

The results are presented in the form of the thematic axes of categories and subcategories, as generated during the process of *open coding* and subsequently transformed through *axial coding*.

1.3.9. Model Confirmation

The results obtained through qualitative methods were subjected to partial validation through the administration of an online questionnaire distributed to all probation services in both countries. The questionnaire addressed a series of questions concerning the importance of initial professional training in probation practice, the types of activities carried out, the relationships between probation officers and other professionals, the relationship with civil society, the specific characteristics of institutional communication within probation services, the constitutive ethical values of the profession, and the degree of adherence to the retributive or restorative model of probation service operation [222]. The questions were generated on the basis of the inductively constructed categories, with a view to examining the extent to which the model — generated through the qualitative analysis of interviews with probation officers — may be considered partially generalizable across Romania and the Republic of Moldova, and not solely with respect to the persons interviewed. From Romania, 24 respondents replied, of whom 14 were female and 10 male; from the Republic of Moldova, 34 responded, of whom 25 were female and 9 male. The small number of respondents means that the data obtained are not statistically representative; however, the convergence between the qualitatively obtained data and the respondents' questionnaire replies may contribute to the credibility of the model in the sense of its acceptability within the professional community of probation officers. The low response rate is attributable, in our view, to the limited size of the professional community of probation officers in the two countries — in Romania, for example, the number of officers at the time the interviews were conducted was 350. A further cause of the low response rate is the professional overload experienced by probation officers.

The absence of statistical representativeness does not call into question the generated model, although it equally does not permit its absolute statistical certification. The exploratory nature of the research nonetheless allows for an enhanced relevance of the model, with premises for generalization to the entire professional community in both countries, enabling us to assert that the generated model possesses a high degree of plausibility.

1.3.10. The Study Retributivity and Public Perception of Non-Custodial Sanctions

This study was conducted on the basis of the sociological survey technique using a questionnaire, and aimed at highlighting public perceptions regarding non-custodial sanctions and their implementation through probation services.

Hypotheses:

1. In both Romania and the Republic of Moldova, a strong retributive current predominates, with a low degree of social tolerance toward persons who commit criminal offenses. The formulation of this hypothesis originates in the presupposition that general living conditions influence the degree of social tolerance.
2. Non-custodial alternatives constitute socially acceptable sanctions, particularly for the punishment of offenders whose acts do not present a very high degree of social danger.
3. In both Romania and the Republic of Moldova, the activity of probation services is relatively little known, a fact which may lead to lower acceptance of non-custodial sanctions.

The sample comprised over 1,056 respondents from the North-Eastern region of Romania and 432 from the Republic of Moldova. Participants in the questionnaire-based study [40] from the North-Eastern region of Romania numbered 1,056 (484 male and 572 female), while from the Republic of Moldova 432 respondents replied (202 male and 230 female). The age distribution of Romanian respondents was as follows: 49% under 35 years of age, 31% between 35 and 45 years of age, and 20% over 45 years of age. The age distribution of Moldavian respondents was: 63% under 35 years of age, 18% between 35 and 45 years of age, and 19% over 65 years of age. The educational level of Romanian respondents was: 4% with no formal education, 44% with secondary education, 47% with university-level education, and 5% with postgraduate education. The educational level of Moldavian respondents was: 5% with no formal education, 32% with secondary education, 53% with university-level education, and 10% with postgraduate education. The income level of Romanian respondents was: 32% earning up to 1,000 Romanian lei, 34% between 1,000 and 2,000 lei, 11% between 2,000 and 3,000 lei, 5% over 3,000 lei, and 18% non-responses. The income level of Moldavian respondents was: 23% earning up to 1,000 Moldavian lei, 38% between 1,000 and 2,000 lei, 24% between 2,000 and 3,000 lei, 17% over 3,000 lei, and 8% non-responses. The specific results of this secondary study will be detailed in Chapter 3 of the present work.

Conclusions

The evolution of probation in Romania and the Republic of Moldova, viewed from an institutional perspective, follows an ascending trajectory, with both countries appearing to recognize — at least at the level of public policy — the need for alternatives to custodial punishment. Penal reform has incorporated probation as a central social institution within the system for the rehabilitation of persons who have committed criminal offenses. Regrettably, its character as a novel institution persists even after 10 and 15 years, respectively, since the first programs aimed at implementing restorative justice. The public remains somewhat reticent, being deeply indebted to the retributive paradigm, while the socio-economic context of both countries and the influence of the mass media lend the retributive emphasis a distinctly vindictive character. The foundational basis of probation in both the Romanian and Moldavian models is retributive in nature; however, recourse to the international standards required by the conventions to which both countries are party ensures the incorporation of a number of restorative elements.

The restorative perspectives identified find it difficult to gain purchase within the current normative framework, in which the function of punishment remains retributive and sanctionary. The fact that Romanian legislation no longer formally defines the functions of punishment — leaving this definition to the discretion of practice and legal doctrine — is regarded by us as a step backward relative to prior legislation, which ensured that the role of punishment was rehabilitative rather than strictly coercive. On the other hand, a step forward is represented by the exclusion of juvenile offenders from the possibility of criminal punishment. Sanctionary educational measures are not classified as punishments and, accordingly, the juvenile offender acquires no criminal record upon their completion. This would constitute, in our view, a model of good practice for which probation officers in the Republic of Moldova should engage in active advocacy.

2. Axes of the Social Construction of the Probation Officer Profession. Qualitative Research in the North-Eastern Region of Romania and in the Republic of Moldova

2.1. Thematic Axis I. The Instrumental and Institutional Framework

2.1.1. The Normative Framework of Operation

The analysis of the normative framework governing probation services focused on how it directly influences the functioning of probation services. Being a constructionist analysis, the normative framework was understood as an instance of the *social construction* of the probation officer profession, constituting the benchmarks within which their practice evolves. The normative framework directly shapes the meaning that professionals assign to their own activity, its role, and in general any discourse about practice.

Deficiencies of the Normative Framework | Referring to the specific operating framework of Probation in Romania, the respondents consider it ambiguous, being in the opinion of some respondents a step backward compared to the previous legislation, in terms of its clarity and applicability. The lack of methodological clarifications regarding the effective implementation of the new codes requires probation officers to make an additional effort to identify good practices in compliance with the legislation in force.

> *The current legislation is much more ambiguous, and the New Criminal Code and the New Code of Criminal Procedure do not clarify all aspects; where they are not clarified, we try to find what is most correct (IRO08).*

The legislation in force (post-2014), especially the Criminal Code, is considered kaleidoscopic, based on normative frameworks adopted from different legal systems, without taking into account during their elaboration the Romanian specificity of the executionary system and of probation.

> *Indeed, the New Criminal Code borrows several elements from different legislations. It is an amalgam, a hotchpotch; things that were truly necessary were not properly pieced together. My opinion is that the Codes should be elaborated and Probation [should be based] on Romanian specificity (IRO08).*

Another difficulty highlighted by the respondent concerns the relatively large number of normative acts regulating probation practice: primary legislation regarding the New Criminal Code and the New Code of Criminal Procedure, specific legislation regarding the execution of non-custodial sentences, and the law on the organisation of the probation system. In addition, there is secondary legislation, consisting of regulations and other normative acts designed to implement the criminal reform. Moreover, due to the relatively recent change in criminal legislation, some cases were tried by courts and sentenced based on the provisions of the old Criminal Code, and others based on those of the New Code – depending on the time of the offence and the most favourable criminal legislation for the defendant. This normative plurality is liable to generate confusion in the supervision of the execution of non-custodial measures.

> *We work under 2 laws, Law 252 regarding the probation system and Law 253 regarding non-custodial measures, and we work under the Criminal Code. Most of the sentences we receive now are under the New Code, but we also have the old Code [under which] sentences are still being issued. We work on the basis of what constitutes the internal regulations and all the normative acts that have come since the change of the code (IRO11).*

Regarding the Moldavian normative framework, we were able to obtain few opinions, which generally referred to the strict observance of the law by probation officers. We detect in the respondents a heightened degree of obedience towards the normative system in force. The obligation to respect the law should not lead to an axiological reflection on it. The question solicits an opinion regarding the reason why offenders are punished, aiming to clarify the respondent's personal adherence to the retributive or restorative paradigm of probation; the respondent affirms his profound adherence to the law.

We consider that the law proceeds correctly (IMD04).

In our opinion, the attitude of refusing to comment on a criminal policy on the grounds that court decisions are executed and it is not the role of probation officers to comment on them constitutes an abuse of obedience and at the same time an abuse of rights. Not contesting court decisions is not the same as not discussing public policies in the sphere of justice, not expressing one's position regarding adherence to a restorative or restitutive model of organising the practice of criminal sentence execution and, implicitly, the organisation of probation. Moreover, the execution as such of court decisions, a fundamental principle of the act of law, should not be conceived in the absence of the right to appeal those decisions. The probation service should be in a position to consider itself a party and even to formulate opinions, at least before the execution courts, including the ability to appeal non-custodial sentences when, for example, the body of the decision contains measures that become impossible to execute due to objective conditions in the community.

> *I am not entitled to discuss the sentences issued by the Court. A sentence is not discussed, but executed. And if I were a judge, I might answer your question, but as it is, what we have is what we do (IMD05).*

The Specificity of the Normative Framework Governing Probation Services | The particularities of Romanian normativity regarding non-custodial measures are viewed by the respondent in the broader context of the particularities of the Romanian judicial system, from criminal prosecution to the phase of conducting the criminal trial and executing the sentence. The limits of the sentence are considered reasonable by the respondent, both in terms of their limited extent, by comparison with sentences in force in other legislations that may extend over decades or even hundreds of years. The individualisation of sentences is also appreciated by the respondent (IRO07). The respondent shows that in the 15 years of probation's existence in Romania, the system has become personalised, adapting to the general frameworks of the Romanian legal system. Referring to his own reflections on the national specificity of probation, based on the exchange of experience with professionals from other countries, the respondent indicates that the main differences between probation systems concern the implementation of legal obligations, the orientation towards the letter of the law in the case of probation systems in Nordic countries, and towards the spirit of the law, interpersonal communication with the offender, and the counselling emphasis in Romania. In turn, Moldavian respondents emphasise the predominance of the assistential dimension of probation practice (IMD08), the social assistance of the supervised person constituting a framework for professional success, defined as the completion of supervision without recidivism. Respondents discuss a series of normative particularities of probation practice within the Romanian criminal executionary system, which differentiate it from the British system – on the basis of which the probation system partially operated during the experimental period and respectively during the period before the 2014 criminal reform. The mentioned differences refer to the existence of strict supervision deadlines, the existence of sanctioning measures that must be enforced by the probation officer, and accessory obligations incumbent upon the convicted person (IRO11). Presenting the Romanian specificity of probation services, the respondents indicate that a large part of the working methodology is borrowed from the model of other probation systems, even though the legislation expressly requires the adaptation of all practices to the national framework. However, the majority of respondents indicate that the borrowings from other legislations have been adapted to this Romanian specificity, which is, however, a largely hypothetical one, insofar as we were unable to identify elements of originality in practice highlighted as such by respondents. Rather, what is original is the methodological synthesis itself of European probation models – British, Norwegian, etc. – adapted to the specificity of Romanian society.

> *The practice of probation services has borrowed, let us say, elements from several countries and has adapted them to the Romanian specificity. Our legislation provides that the supervision of convicts, their assistance, and the running of programmes with inmates shall be conducted according to the specific legislation (IRO01).*

The Moldavian respondents, who showed reluctance to discuss the normative dimension, affirm a post-Soviet perspective on the normative and *institutional* framework governing the functioning of probation. The respondents express their optimism regarding the institutional modernisation of probation services in Moldova.

Many practices have remained from the Soviet Union, but over time, slowly, slowly, things are changing and we are adopting other practices from other European countries on the basis of trainings, round tables, and workshops (IMD01).

Moldavian respondents indicate a diversification of service duties, which extend from supervision and control to reintegration, resocialisation, and re-education. The retributive model based on excessive supervision is being replaced by an assistential one, with the probation officer effectively providing a range of social services aimed at the social integration of the offender, assistance in finding employment, housing, obtaining occasional social benefits, etc. (IMD02). The methodological dimension of practice has evolved in step with the changes occurring in Moldavian society. Progress achieved in the de-penalisation of sanctions is highlighted, as well as in the reduction of the number and duration of custodial sentences (IMD04; IMD03). The working methodology was especially the result of the work of Moldavian officers (IMD02; IMD08), with special mention being made of colleagues at the Central Office, and the support of Romanian colleagues being appreciated (IMD08). No methodological imports from other European services were mentioned, but such methodological cross-pollination is inevitable. The most frequent references to the normative specificity of practice concern the unconditional adherence of probation officers to the law (IMD01; IMD02; IMD06). Respondents also indicated the existence of a large number of normative frameworks that must be observed, but unlike their Romanian colleagues, they did not make observations regarding possible ambiguities, overlaps, or discrepancies between normative acts. On the contrary, the legislative abundance is considered beneficial for the activity of officers, who are thus helped to carry out their work as smoothly as possible.

We operate under the Criminal Code and the instructions regarding probation, the Execution Code, the Code of Criminal Procedure, and certain articles that are useful to us and help us (IMD06).

2.1.2. The Institutional Framework of Operation

The institutional framework extends the normative one in delineating the intrinsic (defined as quasi-transcendental) [166] limits of the social construction of the probation officer profession. While normative frameworks establish the limits of a social practice, the institutional framework determines the concrete manner in which that practice functions in society. Consistent with the constructionist perspective adopted, we shall privilege the analysis of institutional discourse, of the interpretive consensus regarding probation, referring only in passing to a series of structural and functional elements of the institutions. Respondents complain about a chronic lack of resources in probation services in both countries. Romanian respondents highlight the absence of a vehicle fleet, as well as the poor condition of existing vehicles, the lack of human resources – not only those occupying probation officer positions, but also other categories of personnel, such as drivers, needed for probation officers' fieldwork. A degree of bureaucracy is also mentioned, as well as unrealistic demands placed on staff compared with existing resources, etc.

> *The lack of resources. That is clearly a Romanian specificity. They loaded us in the Criminal Code with duties for three other institutions, without making any hires. They did not provide any resources. We have 2 cars, a single driver; the cars are very old – with one of them we had a flat tyre twice in one day and had to pay out of our own pockets to have it repaired because we were in the middle of nowhere, and of course, a request was then made to Bucharest. It is not normal to pay out of your own pocket. We had the car repaired in a village at a so-called service centre, but the man there did not give us any receipt, and our famous Directorate says: 'Well, we'll help you, but get a receipt.' Well, I would like to see them going to villages like those and completing all the formalities that they later require. In other words, the demands exist, but the resources do not. This is typically Romanian (IRO02).*

Moldavian respondents emphasise the lack of resources in the system, insisting on the demotivating potential of this situation (IMD12). Another particularity of the probation system in the two countries is the "omni-specialisation" of officers, who all carry out all specific activities: assessment, supervision, work with persons released on parole, etc. This state of affairs contrasts with that existing in other European countries, with the hope of resolving this situation: *[...] when the context will be favourable* (IRO03; IMD08). Probation services are not yet organised into distinct departments, each dealing with one of the specific activities: pre-sentence reports, supervision, social reintegration programmes, etc. The need for such a distribution is felt by the research participants, whose discourse shows that the large volume of cases under their management overwhelms them and creates burnout problems.

> *We all have the same duties. That is, no one handles programmes, another pre-sentence reports, and another supervision. This should be done, but there are too few of us. And from my point of view, given the number of cases I currently have, I am already experiencing mental gridlock (IRO04).*

Possible directions for the development of probation, as envisaged by the respondent, concern specialisation into offices (departments) that would deal with each of the areas of professional duties: assessment, supervision, counselling, etc.

> *I repeat, we have become accustomed to making soup; not everyone can make soup – some should make stew and some should make soup. But we hope that in the end, especially since this is also the future context of the probation service, where there are large services of more than 15 people, a division of activities will be made, so that there are officers specialised in assessment, supervision, and counselling activities (IRO11).*

In the opinion of those interviewed, a specific feature of probation practice is the exceptional dedication of those working in the field, who demonstrate conscientiousness, professional competence, and perseverance, and can rightfully be considered *people of quality* (IRO05). A major difference between Romanian probation and that in other states, but which exists even between the specificity of probation in different regions of the country, is the specificity of criminality. Since crime differs from country to country and from region to region within the same country, probation services must adapt to these situations. Beyond the particularities of probation deriving from the dominant penal philosophy at the level of a country, the type of crime and the etiology of criminality at the local level require a methodological particularisation of probation services.

> *There is a single element: criminality. There is a distinct criminality. I am referring to the model of practice in probation, not to the level of legislation, [...] so I cannot say that there is something 100% specifically Romanian. [...] Because, for example, in the Moldavia region (the North-Eastern region of Romania) we have property offences, thefts, robberies, violence against the background of excessive poverty; in Transylvania, this type of offence does not predominate. It must be adapted to our specificity (IRO08).*

Borrowing from other legislations is insufficient without a genuine adaptation to local specificity, since a series of methods and techniques that may be efficient, for example, when working with 20–30 cases, as is the case in Great Britain or Norway, function entirely differently when the caseload of Romanian and Moldavian officers is approximately 150–300 cases per officer.

> *They initially tried to take from the English what could be taken, under conditions where, for example, in England a probation officer works with 20–30 cases and has time for intervention, or in Norway, where the intervention is not measured in years, but in hours (IRO08).*

Respondents identify the need for changes in the Moldavian probation system. Referring to the protests of probation officers in Romania that took place between July 2015 and April 2016, the respondent indicates that, although he considers such manifestations necessary in the Republic of Moldova as well, probation officers are afraid of unpleasant consequences, including the possibility of losing their jobs. This response can be correlated with the reluctance to answer questions soliciting a personal value judgement regarding the penal philosophy in the Republic of Moldova and the functioning of the probation system. We also correlate the response with the fact that the relationships of probation officers with representatives of other institutions are formal and strictly institutional, without a significant personal dimension. Based on these considerations, and on the observations made during interviews by the interview operators, we hold the view that probation services operate within a climate of *institutionalised insecurity*.

> *[...] revolts exist in our country too, but I think the courage [is lacking], because look, we still need to be united and we need to reach a decision, a change, something. In our country this courage does not exist, especially for those of us who are getting close to retirement, and you think that if you open your mouth they can tell you: 'Well, you can go and find yourself another job.' Anyway, in a country where the law is respected more, it means you can also have more courage, and I think that is why something was actually achieved (IMD03).*

The Influences of the Retributive Mentality on Probation Practice | The persons interviewed draw attention to the retributive mentality, widely entrenched among the general public. The convicted person is labelled, and a series of rights are denied to them, including those necessary for integration into society. Probation officers complain that they themselves suffer from this labelling, the public's lack of respect towards probation service clients being partially transferred onto the officers. In this regard, respondents indicate the need for changing public mentalities (IMD03; IMD04), but also for changes to the normative framework, in the direction of greater protection afforded to probation officers (IRO04). What is important in probation practice is that the judicial sentence be applied with respect for the rights of the convicted person, and first and foremost, for their dignity.

> *I have post-it notes everywhere; when I read a sentence, I read it very carefully, because if an error has crept in, we must request clarifications from the judge, so as not to infringe upon the person's rights, because at the end of the day that is the most important thing. They may have the status of a convict, but they have rights that must be respected (IRO04).*

The same hostile mentality towards persons who have committed criminal offences was mentioned by the Moldavian respondents, who indicate that among the most significant problems currently faced by persons who have committed criminal offences is the difficulty, even impossibility, of obtaining employment (IMD03). We note, however, a difference in discourse between the respondents from the two countries. Both categories of respondents agree that offenders must be punished, for reasons of retribution, for example to deter other offences. Moldavian respondents have a more intransigent attitude in condemning crime. The public mentality aimed at marginalising and rejecting offenders is justified by the harm they have caused. Here, the creation of a vicious circle of crime–harm–marginalisation–crime is identified.

> *[...] through their very attitude towards society, and that is why society rejects them. And if society rejects them, they will become even worse (IMD03).*

The Relationship between the Probation Service and Other Institutions Involved in the Execution of Non-Custodial Sentences | In the fulfilment of their professional duties, probation officers cooperate with a number of institutions, such as: courts of law, the prosecution service, the police, local social assistance services, public authorities, etc. Probation services prepare pre-sentence evaluation reports aimed at facilitating the judge's individualisation of the sentence to be applied to the offender. Romanian respondents indicated that one of the most significant achievements of probation officers was that, in many situations, judges adopted the solution proposed by probation services in the body of the sentence and in its reasoning. Moreover, until 2014, proposing a measure was not part of the duties of the probation officer preparing the pre-sentence report; the practice of many courts was to request such an opinion from the probation service and, if appropriate, to take it into account only if they considered it adequate. The frequency and effectiveness of this practice led to its institutionalisation through the New Code of Criminal Procedure. Also in connection with the relationship with the courts, respondents draw attention to the importance of this relationship from the perspective of the possibility of requesting clarifications from the courts regarding sentences (IRO08), regarding what the court meant when it issued a particular sentence (IRO05). The relationship with the courts is a privileged one, evidenced by the care taken to maintain constructive relations with the courts.

The relationship with the courts is an optimal and constructive one, because that is where our cases come from. [...] The care to maintain as constructive a relationship as possible with each of them is sustained throughout the entire period (IRO01).

Despite the care for the quality of the relationship between probation services and the courts, the relationship with them is ambivalent, with situations where certain county probation services register a discordance in the relationship with the courts, even a rupture.

With the court, there is a rupture. Each party looks after its own interests (IRO02).

Other respondents, although indicating that they personally have a close relationship with the courts, noted a distancing of the probation service from them, especially after 2014, when probation services were no longer administratively subordinated to the tribunals, nor did they have their premises within the tribunal buildings. Regarding the issue of premises, several respondents indicated that the probation service relocated after the separation from the administrative tutelage of the tribunal, with only one respondent indicating that in his county, the premises remained at the Tribunal, this institution making the space available to the probation service free of charge.

My relationship as a person is roughly the same with all courts, in the sense that we built the relationship with all these institutions from the very beginning of the service's establishment. Of course, in 2014, when the administrative link with the Tribunal was severed, the relationship became somewhat more distant. It perhaps also matters that before, we had our premises at the court and we spoke permanently with the judges. But my communication with the courts has continued; I have tried to maintain it because the activity is strictly linked to them – all activities are linked to them, whether through judges at the Court of Appeal or through the penitentiary (IRO07).

The lack of uniform practice on the part of Romanian courts is brought into discussion, which makes collaboration with the courts difficult. The relationship with the courts is managed, in some situations, by the head of the service, a person with extensive professional experience. For streamlining cooperation with the courts, it is considered necessary to consult with colleagues from other probation services across the country, and with the National Directorate of Probation. Practically, although the respondent indicates that the relationship with the courts is generally constructive, the mention of the need to consult the National Directorate and other services may lead to the interpretation that there exists an at least problematic relationship with some courts or magistrates.

> *[...] when it is necessary to consult the judges, we consult them. However, a small yet significant problem arises here because there is no uniform practice at the level of the courts. One judge may rule in a certain way in a given case, and at another time may say something entirely different. Consequently, we try to align ourselves generally with the needs of the magistrates. And at the level of colleagues, I direct the practice in collaboration with them; we consult with colleagues across the country on various documents, how one does it, how another does, and when necessary, we turn to the National Directorate of Probation, which provides us with an opinion (IRO08).*

The personalised relationship with the courts means that magistrates trust the opinion of probation officers, and if the latter succeed in presenting concrete and correct legal grounds, the courts take their opinion into account when issuing criminal decisions. A subtle note of professional pride transpires from the respondent's discourse, the judge's acceptance of the proposed solution being interpreted as a personal success. The possibility of discussing informally with certain judges represents, in the respondent's opinion, an indicator of the professional recognition he enjoys, based on his prior professional experience.

> *I have also encountered different opinions, but if you are well-prepared in the sphere of law and you speak their language, you give them the legal basis, because they are fixed on the legal basis, and you know how to frame the issue, you will always have their collaboration. I have judges who call me personally to ask about cases, with whom I can speak on familiar terms; I have judges with whom I must speak more formally (IRO08).*

The other respondents practically confirm the importance of the feedback received from the courts in the self-evaluation of officers in their capacity as professionals.

> *The relationship we have with the Court [...] is a very good one, because at this point we are able to pick up the phone and call any judge and each of them offers us support, which is wonderful. They know what we do, they know what we are engaged in, and for the court, our evaluation report, or any document we issue, is very important and greatly assists them, and this was communicated to us not by just one judge, but by very many judges [...]. I think first of all we have positive feedback from the courts, and for us that matters a great deal (IRO11).*

Collaboration with the courts depends on the relationship of probation officers with each individual judge. If the general relationship with the criminal courts is assessed favourably, this is due to the relationship built over time through ongoing communication. The same does not hold true regarding the execution courts, where delegated judges change frequently, each bringing their own perspective. The frequent rotation of magistrates who serve on the execution courts makes it difficult to establish a flexible and somewhat informal mode of communication.

> *There are two types of criminal judges: those who hear the merits of the case, and those who handle execution. On the supervision side, we collaborate with the execution judges, but they change constantly. Therefore, if you manage to establish a common ground, a way of working with a judge, you will have the surprise that within a year at most, that judge will change, and then you have to start all over again. That does not mean we have problems with them (IRO08).*

The generally good, or very good, relationship with the courts is the result of sustained personal communication with their representatives. However, where problems persisted and personal relationships with justice professionals did not yield results, intervention was sought from professionals at higher-level courts, in order to explain the importance of probation. This approach proved successful.

[...] the relationship with the court is a very good one, and where we had problems – I know of certain divergences related to certain approaches – they were resolved at the local level by accessing the competent higher bodies. For example, we had certain problems with the District Court of P, but we appealed to colleagues at the higher courts, and then it was explained to them and we were much better understood (IRO11).

Respondents observe a certain predilection on the part of Romanian courts to reject the revocation of suspended or deferred custodial sentences. The violation of conditional release conditions should lead – on the basis of the officers' reports – to the revocation by the courts of those measures and a return to stricter measures, including custodial ones. The leniency of the courts in applying sanctions for the violation of supervised release conditions somewhat undermines the activity of the officers, diminishing their capacity to enforce the sanctioning measures.

A Romanian specificity is that when a person violates the obligations and measures imposed by the court, and the officer reports this to the court, in very few cases is the revocation of the suspension or deferral actually ordered. And unfortunately, the persons under our supervision learn from one another that if they violate [the obligations and measures imposed], the court is likely to be very lenient and our work is in vain. If they knew that a violation leads to revocation and imprisonment, they would otherwise comply with the measures and obligations (IRO05).

The enforcement of sentences is carried out through the Criminal Execution Bureau, an institution where the delegated judge for executions also operates. This judge has jurisdiction over all decisions concerning the execution of sentences. Respondents indicate that although judges are the ones who establish the types of punishment that a defendant must serve, probation officers are the ones who monitor the activities for executing non-custodial sentences. This monitoring is carried out in close collaboration with the delegated judge. Although previous respondents indicated that there are communication problems with the execution courts, whose judges change frequently, respondent

IRO04 indicates that at the institutional level there is very good communication. We consider that this difference of opinion reflects distinct particularities at the local level, but also a difference between institutional and individual discourse. Respondents who refer to personal relationships with judges articulate possible communication problems that are somewhat related to the personality structure of those involved. When institutional communication is discussed, they acknowledge the interdependence between the two in the execution of sentences. The fact that both parties seek not to overburden each other denotes the existence of a personal note in institutional discourse, one that takes into account the needs of professionals.

> *Well, we have a fairly close relationship, especially with the Criminal Execution Bureau, because practically we are in constant contact with the delegated judge. Usually we establish the deadlines and the decisions concerning a case together, because the judges set the types of punishment, but we monitor and control all activities. And so we try, in a way, not to overburden them, and they not to overburden us, so we are in constant contact (IRO04).*

If Romanian respondents situate institutional communication within the sphere of interpersonal relations, with considerable informal resources employed, Moldavian respondents emphasize the formalization of communication and the maintenance of distance in the interpersonal relationship with representatives of other institutions, especially the courts.

> *It is a professional relationship and nothing more (IMD06; IMD04).*

> *An established relationship. But more of a formal one (IMD03).*

Good relations with the courts are the result of an effort to communicate as formally as possible, which is considered pragmatic in the relationship with the courts. The officers' opinions are taken into consideration by the courts, but the discourse of Moldavian respondents is more reserved regarding the capacity of the probation officer to influence the decision of magistrates through the arguments presented. Another institution with which the probation service interacts is the penitentiary. The criminal executionary system has practically two dimensions: the custodial one, represented by the penitentiary for adults and the custodial re-education centres for minors, and the non-custodial one, represented by the probation service. Representatives of probation services – from both countries – are mandatory members of Conditional Release Commissions in penitentiaries and of the commissions that decide on the temporary interruption of sentence execution – temporary leaves. As such, inter-institutional cooperation between probation and the penitentiary is a priority for both institutions. Respondents indicate that this relationship is a very good and constructive one (IRO02; IRO06; IMD02; IMD011). The opinion of probation officers is confirmed by the social workers in the penitentiary who participated in the focus group (FG).

> *We have a very good relationship with the penitentiary. That is, every time they need information, or we need their help, we always collaborate very well. We conduct the interviews there for persons who are in pre-trial detention (IRO04).*

Respondents belonging to other county probation services in Romania confirm the excellent relationship with the probation services, the probation officer benefiting from access in a climate of confidentiality to the persons in (pre-trial) detention whom they must interview in order to prepare the pre-sentence evaluation report.

> *We have worked very well with the penitentiary [...], on the basis of written requests because it is a closed environment, an environment with strict rules, and we have never had problems being denied access to the penitentiary to speak with a person. We were always afforded a climate of confidentiality and were able to speak face to face with the respective person, so it was an excellent collaboration (IRO05).*

Another respondent nuances the relationship with the penitentiary, in the sense that there is room for improving communication with the representatives of many penitentiary institutions. However, although the general framework of communication is limited by the total institution character of the penitentiary, examples are given of two such institutions that ensure all necessary conditions for the proper work of probation officers with persons in the penitentiary – for example, those in pre-trial detention. The emphasis is placed on personal cooperation between probation officers and the representatives of the partner institution.

> *The relationship with the penitentiary is a very good one, I can say, but, because there is a 'but' of course, penitentiaries have their own rules and many times you have to somewhat conform to their rules. More work should be done here. At the level of the penitentiary [in city B], I know the director personally because I collaborated with him when he was at [the penitentiary in city T]; I have no problem. When we need to, we enter when we conduct evaluations, we attend conditional release commissions – there are no problems (IRO08).*

Other respondents, while indicating that the relationship between the probation service and the penitentiary is very good, noted misunderstandings or even divergences that were resolved over time. The respondent was keen to specify that they – the probation officers of the territorial probation service they represent – consider themselves good professionals, and they demand professionalism and rigour from their partners (IRO11). Once again, Moldavian respondents provided less information, limiting themselves to appraising the relationships with the penitentiary as constructive.

> *[...] at least I see that this is a necessary relationship, and at least I see that at our level it is positive, because everything moves – it is like a chain that we cannot break; instantly [the custodial sentence] is applied. That is why the relationship from the outset cannot be something negative (IMD08).*

Once again, the formal and formalised relationship predominates, with respondents insisting on the strictly official character of communication.

> *[...] communication is strictly official – notifications, requests to which we strictly receive responses, but which in any case are along more general lines (IMD11).*

With other social institutions involved in the criminal justice system, respondents highlight a deficient communication:

> *With the other institutions involved in the criminal justice system, communication is quite weak. Jealousies related to salary arise (IRO02).*

Respondents indicate that the representatives of some community institutions involved in the administration of community service manifest prejudices towards persons convicted of criminal offences, labelling them and refusing to become involved in the process of assisting them. Practically, vis-à-vis the representatives of such institutions, probation officers carry out advocacy activities, trying to convince them that they are not merely enforcing a court decision, but are also performing a prosocial activity, supporting persons under probation in their social reintegration.

> *[...] the most difficult part is with the institutions that must provide community service under the New Criminal Code. There are institutions that do not want to receive them into the community, and we explain to them that they are covering a harm done to the community of their locality of origin, and they have certain rules that we establish, but the type of activities is established by them, and we explain that we cannot label them, and that these people need help. With certain institutions, not with all. There are other institutions where things are perfectly fine (IRO04).*

In some situations, respondents indicated refractory or even hostile attitudes on the part of the representatives of some of the town halls where supervised persons had to perform community service. However, the cases are isolated and seem to involve ill-intentioned individuals rather than an inadequate institutional attitude.

> *[...] there have been certain problems with the Town Halls regarding the obligation to perform community service. In the sense that we received information according to which the person responsible for community service either lost the list in which the number of hours was recorded, or did not report certain problems to us in a*

> *timely manner. In any case, we had certain suspicions regarding the veracity of the data recorded in the community service reports sent by the town hall (IRO05).*

Other respondents specify that this relative desynchronisation with the representatives of some community institutions was due in particular to the changes that occurred in the legislative framework, which introduced the compulsory nature of community service. The representatives of town halls reacted negatively in some cases to this situation, considering it an increase in the tasks incumbent upon them. Moreover, the reluctance expressed by them was based on possible prejudices, fears, or a lack of awareness of the legislative changes. Respondent (IRO11) indicates that the majority of these reluctances have been successfully overcome at present.

> *As regards the institutions in the community, we went through a more difficult period, which we call a transitional one, because they suddenly found themselves, with the entry into force of the New Codes, with certain responsibilities – that is, they had to receive convicted persons to perform community service, and this meant a very strong reluctance on the part of these institutions, because they had the impression [that it was not their responsibility, asking themselves] 'what?! but this is a convicted person, it's their problem – how can we receive them?! ... we cannot receive them' (IRO11).*

In order to overcome the reluctance of some local institutions to collaborate, probation officers conducted information campaigns among the representatives of the local institutions involved, including through personal discussions with their representatives. The information sessions addressed the role of the probation service, the characteristics of persons who have to perform unpaid work in the community, and their relatively low degree of dangerousness.

> *And then we had to go and discuss in person; so, first we addressed the problem at a personal level – discussions were held with each community institution, each institution was visited, everyone was explained what our role is, what we do, and above all, what profile our beneficiaries have. Because those who receive a suspended*

sentence, most of them do not have a very high risk of committing new offences, or perhaps the offence in question was a circumstantial one (IRO11).

Furthermore, respondent (IRO11) indicated that many of the persons sentenced with suspension, who are obligated to perform unpaid work in the service of the community, are persons who committed the offence circumstantially – the example being given of road traffic offences. The respective persons are socially and professionally integrated, often known in the community as good professionals and above all as trustworthy individuals.

We have a great many persons under supervision, especially in the last year to year and a half, who are [convicted] for driving under the influence of alcohol, for example, but they are bank directors, lawyers, social workers, police officers, anything else – dignified professions regardless of their nature. And then we had to go and explain to them: 'Sir, the convicted person, the offender you speak of, you know him – he works at such-and-such town hall, or at the DASPC, or at the hospital; he is not just anyone from the street...'; let us relate to the profile of the beneficiary, and then they understood. But there was a transitional period that, well, left certain marks, because we were also somewhat caught in the middle (IRO11).

Respondent (IRO11) described how the institutions where convicted persons must perform unpaid community service are selected by the courts – randomly, on the basis of a list of institutions that appears on the ministry's website. Among these there are also some semi-private companies – in which the state or the municipality hold shares. The respondent insists on the obligation to enforce the criminal decision exactly as issued, including with regard to the place where the convicted person must perform the unpaid work, even if the representatives of the institution do not wish this (IRO11). Another institution with which probation services interact is the police. This relationship is difficult, since a large number of police officers are involved, each with their own working style and mode of communication.

Well, of course [we collaborate] with the police too, but with the police it is a bit more complicated because

> *there are very many persons in the police. In each commune there are several police officers, in [the city] likewise there are police stations, at each station I don't know how many persons, and so it is a bit more complicated, but certainly as an institution, very good (IRO07; IRO08).*

A difficult relationship with police officers is also reported by Moldavian respondents, who compensated for the lack of communication with local police bodies through equally official, written communication with their hierarchical superiors. Collaboration with the Ministry of Justice is based on permanent consultation. This consultation is somewhat called into question by the respondents who indicate that in the relationship with the Ministry, one can detect a relative lack of involvement on its part, a lack of assumption of the methodological dimension of practice. This attitude of transferring responsibility to the territorial probation services entails difficulties in communication, especially in the management of funds. It is noteworthy that the respondent has a good reputation, being a former director in the Ministry. According to him, the officials in the Ministry take his opinion into account in the decisions made, but at a general level, communication and consultation are difficult, the respondent indicating the need for dialogue in order to streamline activity, in the sense of the voluntary adherence of officials to the tasks assigned to probation officers.

> *With those in the Ministry I have remained on very good terms. We consult permanently. What I continue to see, however, is that many in the Ministry do not assume elements of practice, do not take ownership of one thing or another. The good part is that they still take my opinions into account. So, years after having been a director, if I call and send messages and maintain my point of view, it is taken into account, which is a good thing for me. But it is very difficult when it comes to money. A machine executes; a person, you have to convince them to do something (IRO08).*

In general, respondent (IRO08) indicates that in the collaboration with any institution, the prior relationship between the probation officer/service manager and the representatives of the partner institution is very important.

> *I have observed that for them too, up to a point, it matters a great deal how you frame the issue, whether you know how to speak with them, how to find advantages for each – whether it is a judge, a prosecutor, or a penitentiary employee – you win their collaboration (IRO08).*

> *I very much rely on an informal relationship with the penitentiary, because having been in [city B] for years, I know them more easily, and it is one thing to pick up the phone and speak directly with the director of the Penitentiary, for example, or with a person you have known for a long time, and another to work through paperwork. I say it is easier (IRO08).*

The respondent notes that difficulties in institutional communication arise where personal relationships with the representatives of partner institutions are also absent. Strictly official institutional communication encounters the rigidity inherent to the internal rules of each institution — a rigidity that is overcome through direct interpersonal contact and communication between professionals. A mild criticism is even directed at the National Probation Directorate, which neglected to establish inter-institutional connections. Without such connections and without a set of communication rules, the professional sometimes feels that they are disturbing representatives of other institutions, even when the request is legitimate and well-founded.

> *The relationship with the other institutions involved in the criminal justice system, within the limits of their competencies, is good. Here, when probation was established, our superiors who lead us did not create that inter-institutional connection. The Police operates in one way, AJOFM [the County Agency for Employment] in another, the School Inspectorate in yet another. Each has its own rules. Instead of establishing a common rule for this category, each works within its own small domain, each has its own problems, its own caseload, and so, many times, you get the feeling that you are disturbing them — even though you are making a pertinent request that they should answer (IRO08).*

The relative difficulty of institutional communication is linked to the behavioural particularities of various professionals and, of course, to their professional workload. The respondent underscores the importance of each professional's individual decision, noting situations of professional cooperation with representatives of public institutions despite the disagreement expressed by their hierarchical superior.

> *Some respond with great difficulty many times, others respond easily. Some collaborate more actively; for example with the Police — in smaller towns we collaborate very well because they monitor our minors. At the Municipal level (...) it is more difficult. So, the heads of the respective bodies matter a great deal, but I have noticed that many times, if the boss says no, the subordinate has helped us — not personally, I mean professionally. His boss told him: "Don't do that." And yet we collaborated well with that person (IRO08).*

The importance of cooperation with the professionals directly involved is emphasised, despite the difficulties of relating to the official representatives of certain institutions.

> *For example, with AJOFM [the County Agency for Employment] we collaborate well, they help us, yes, but we collaborate precisely with the person, with the individual who helps us with the qualification course, we collaborate with the person who sends us the lists for job placements. If you go to the bosses, everything is lost (IRO08).*

Contrary to the consistent position of Romanian respondents regarding the importance of interpersonal relationships with representatives of other institutions involved, Moldavian respondents are consistent in highlighting the formalisation of communication and the greatest possible reduction of the counsellor's personal component in institutional communication. We consider that such an approach is grounded — whether consciously or not — in a premise according to which institutions predominate over individuals. Institutional pressure somewhat crushes initiative, generating obedience. The formal, almost ritualistic response corresponds to a professional heteronomy. Respect for the law transforms into a partial refusal of problematic situations and of problematisation itself. We consider it important to observe that the evolution of the Moldavian probation system is perceived in terms of *correctness*. Correctness is understood in terms of compliance with legality. We consider it a specific feature of Moldavian probation — a focus on the letter of the law, which appears to be motivated by the desire to avoid malpractice. Respondents consider that probation is primarily an *assistance-based practice*, the counsellor's role being to provide the supervised person with support in social reintegration: advocacy for employment, finding housing, etc. The continuous reference to legality may create the impression of a timorous attitude towards authority, resolved through a minimalist stance manifested as normative sufficiency. Contrary to the tendency to avoid confrontation with authority, there emerges an overvaluation of authority and its representatives. Political support was invoked for resolving the chronic personnel deficit in the probation services within the system. This support is considered to be at its highest level at present — throughout the entire 15-year history of probation in Romania. The respondent takes care to specify that, up to that point, no Minister of Justice had ever participated in any meeting of probation counsellors. This remark appears to indicate that respondents consider themselves ignored at the level of the Ministry of Justice leadership, under whose subordination the National Probation Directorate operates. This disregard extends to marginalisation, the respondent emphasising that from previous ministers they had received neither visits, nor official professional correspondence, nor even service orders other than those related to appointment to positions. The support that probation enjoys at the highest level of the Ministry is questioned, the respondent taking care to specify that the minister — in office at the date of the interview — belongs to a government with limited political support, and that only the government to be installed after the elections coming in a few months — autumn 2016 — would be legitimate (IRO11).

2.1.3. The Evolution of Probation Practice in Romania and Moldova

Referring to the evolution of probation practice in the two countries, the respondents point to its continuous development from the perspective of the improvement of working instruments.

From pilot projects to a public probation system

If, at the time probation emerged as a professional practice, specific working instruments were entirely absent, at present these exist and have proven their effectiveness (IRO07; IMD08).

Probation practice has evolved a great deal; first of all, it has evolved from the perspective of working instruments. I remember that at the beginning of my professional activity we had virtually no instruments. Of course, initially there were no instruments whatsoever; we created them along the way (IRO07).

The existing working instruments — modern, practical, and efficient — are the result of collaboration between Romanian and Moldavian professionals, as well as between these professionals and the academic environment. The development of the profession, especially in Romania, has benefited from the expertise of specialists from countries such as the United Kingdom, France, Norway, and the United States. Experience exchanges were carried out both in the creation of working instruments and in their implementation (IRO07). The most significant (visible and major) change, however, is represented by the evolution of the system in its entirety. Respondents indicate a substantial difference in the level of approach and in the professionalism of practitioners (IMD08). The history of the profession proves to be a (co-)construction of practice, a shared evolution of practitioners on both the professional and personal planes. The probation system is recognised as being not merely a gathering of institutions, but a gathering of all the professionals who constitute it. Once again, the personal dimension is evident. If, in the previously analysed category, the interpersonal dimension of practice was related to professionals from other fields, in the present case, the cooperation among probation counsellors themselves is brought into discussion. Furthermore, the respondent's discourse leads us to consider the emergence of a distinct professional identity, one that sustains the motivation for good practice.

It is about my professional evolution and personal development, which is in fact connected to the evolution of the entire system. An evolution that is noticeable, visible, and major. I am not speaking of the beginnings, but if the total is 15 years of probation, at any rate let us say from the midpoint of those 15 years until the present — if we compare the situations, the level of development, of approach, of intervention upon cases is very great, and so we formed ourselves together, in a way. In fact, the system is each one of us, a gathering of us all (IRO07).

Recalling the trajectory of probation counselling, in which the respondent has been involved from the very beginning, (IRO08) shows that there was an evolution from an experimental model managed privately through a network of NGOs. The transition from the private pilot initiative to the generalisation of probation as a public service encountered a limitation of resources, which entailed a more deficient remuneration in the initial stages, leading to a lack of motivation. There were a number of shortcomings that marked the history of probation in Romania, among which the respondent highlights the necessity of constructing instruments. The reform of the penal system and the broadening of probation counsellors' attributions mean that, at present, working conditions are more difficult than at the outset. The lack of vision concerning probation is signalled especially among representatives of the justice system and the political milieu, but not among probation representatives themselves. The respondent indicates that it is possible that representatives of the political milieu and of the justice system may not desire the genuine development of the profession and of probation practice itself.

> *We started from a private system, from an NGO in which you had resources, and with a vision you arrived at a state system in which remuneration was very poor at the beginning, people were not motivated, we had absolutely nothing, we had to build absolutely everything from scratch, and after 15 years of probation, it has become harder than at the beginning. And here I am not necessarily referring to working conditions, but to vision — we do not have people with vision in probation. I am not referring to those within the system, but to those in the justice system, among politicians, who do not want to develop this probation system (IRO08).*

The evolution of practice, from pilot centres to a national structure that is part of the penal enforcement system, is considered a significant evolution, both from the perspective of the institutions that now compose the system and from the perspective of the importance of the practice, especially in light of the modifications that have appeared in the Criminal Code — as well as in the Code of Criminal Procedure and in the law on the enforcement of non-custodial sentences (IRO09). The implementation of probation — its "invention" in Romania, according to the respondent

— was based on the British model and was carried out through a project that lasted 10 years. At present, a project based on a Norwegian model is underway, which operates on the basis of a different probation system, a different approach. The respondent considers, however, that the British model — already established and somewhat adapted to the Romanian specificity of the practice — continues to prevail. The importation of models means that the system functions on the basis of good practices that are not, however, entirely adapted to the Romanian legal system, nor to the mentalities prevalent among the population (IRO07). The same trajectory of practice is presented by Moldavian counsellors. The beginning of Moldavian probation was constituted by a series of private initiatives, undertaken by NGOs that aimed at establishing social alternatives to custodial sentences. The respondents show that probation is part of the Moldavian penal enforcement system, continuing the tradition of the conditional suspension of sentence. A series of systemic transformations of probation were carried out in 2003–2004 through penal reform, targeting the introduction of unpaid community work, special detention regimes for minors, etc. We observe, in practice, an almost total similarity with the evolution of the Romanian probation system from the perspective of the construction of its formal institutions.

> *Our history goes back a long way, from the 2000s onwards, beginning with the Soros Foundation, the beginnings of projects aimed at developing alternatives to detention. And from then on it started — there were projects, ideas concerning probation, unpaid work. And in this case too there were NGOs, Centres for the Assistance of Penitentiary Reform in 2002, and it was [under] the name "Institute for Penitentiary Reform," and to this day this organisation is still operating. And this Institute, through various projects with the Soros Foundation and Dutch organisations — if I am not mistaken, the Helsinki Committee was also involved, including UNICEF — was involved in alternatives to the detention of minors. And all of this developed. A mixed working group was also created, so to speak, comprising state, public, and non-governmental bodies. And in 2002, the "Department of Enforcement" was created, which included bailiffs, and a directorate was created for the enforcement of criminal sentences. What existed until then, if we take the general*

> *history of criminal sentences, had also been around in earlier times — that is, during the Soviet era, the conditional sentence was also applied, and in the 1990s this was within the Ministries of Internal Affairs, then in the Ministry of Justice at the Penitentiary Service. From 2002, it was demilitarised, becoming a civilian service within the Department of Enforcement under the name "Directorate for the Enforcement of Criminal Sentences," and I was appointed head of this Directorate, and I was involved in all these projects that needed to be developed alongside probation. The directorate for unpaid work had to be developed, as well as probation. And in 2003, unpaid work was introduced in the Criminal Code, and in 2005 it appears in the Enforcement Code, which also includes unpaid work, and from this point probation appears as well. And it developed starting from 2004; already within this Directorate, the function of supervising minors who are not in detention was transferred from the Police. And in 2007 the Government Decision comes out in January, and what was called the "Directorate for the Enforcement of Criminal Sentences" is reorganised into the "Directorate of Probation." And everything was done through these projects, including programmes for the detention of minors, the preparation-for-release programme, and all of this was done in parallel with various NGOs and this Directorate. And in 2008 the law on probation is already approved. After that, in 2010, the Department of Development is dissolved because bailiffs become private, and we were transferred [transformed] — this Directorate of Probation — into the "Penitentiary Department," and since 2013 we have been an independent structure within the Ministry of Justice (IMD08).*

Another direction in which probation has undergone transformations concerns the types of beneficiaries, as it has become increasingly frequent for persons with a high social position, with higher education, with public functions, and even representatives of political power and/or members of public administration to come under supervision.

And our role is precisely to implement this supervision, especially as we work increasingly with persons who hold important social positions, or persons who are involved in all manner of activities that have implications for all of us, at the community level — more and more lawyers, more and more persons from public administration, from the leadership of localities, of the country, and so on (IRO11).

The co-construction of probation counsellor practice

The enforcement of a non-custodial sentence is seen as a series of stages through which the person passes by most of the important actors in the community. In this chain of interactions, the role of the probation counsellor is that of a mediator between the court and the community. The respondent's discourse is strongly influenced by the restorative justice model, with significant responsibilities for the social reintegration of the offender falling upon society. The two poles — the court and the community — are symbolic representations of the two major functions of punishment: retribution — established by the judge — and rehabilitation — grounded in the community.

Because if we analyse the persons who have committed offences, from the moment they committed the offence until they finish serving their sentence, it is a chain in which all institutions and all pillars of the community play an important role. And we intervene at several stages. And I believe our role is very important because we represent a bridge between the court and the community (IRO03).

The respondent shows that probation is teamwork, with counsellors cooperating among themselves, discussing cases in formal or informal peer-supervision sessions, with the aim of identifying best practices for the benefit of the client, while respecting the client's rights and the legislation in force.

Even if it is not my case, I help my colleague; we help each other, we engage in peer supervision. No official correspondence goes out until we have studied the law very carefully to make sure we are not violating the law,

> *and secondly, that we are not violating the rights of the persons registered with the service. And moreover, we have the support of our superior, so we always consult with him (IRO04).*

The co-construction of probation practice is supported by other respondents, who reiterate the idea of peer-supervision sessions based on the cases being handled by each counsellor.

> *If we speak of the colleagues in the service, with whom I meet and have permanent contact, this can be seen both in the results and in the professional meetings and working sessions we hold. Because each one of us, in the working meetings we have, discusses cases, situations, and so, on the one hand, I see how they present the case and I also see how they explain their intervention up to that point. And for those in other services across the country, with whom it is harder to maintain contact because there is no time, I see the results they have obtained (IRO07).*

Communication with other probation services in the country is carried out, among other purposes, for the sake of a genuine exchange of experience concerning the caseload being handled, the personality types of the offenders under supervision, and especially the successes that each service has achieved in practice. Practice models constitute a resource of professional knowledge.

> *We have access to all the reports across the country, and so, among other things, I sometimes read a report from a service that is interesting from the perspective of having more cases — it is interesting that it has more cases involving, say, substance users, drug users, or they have cases with well-known underworld figures at the national level, and it is interesting how they intervened in their supervision — they have remarkable cases. And so we see that within the service, although they have very difficult cases, they have very good results (IRO07).*

In managerial activity as well, an important dimension is constituted by communication and collaboration, both at the level of one's own service and with the other services across the country.

> *We learn from mistakes; we try to collaborate among ourselves — the Heads of Services and colleagues across the country — but also at the local level; we have permanent team meetings in which we discuss various aspects (IRO08).*

Referring to their own expectations — from collaboration with other colleagues — the respondents indicate that these are generally very high, in the sense of adherence to the principles of good practice. The high demands placed on colleagues — subordinates — are balanced by equally high demands placed on oneself and one's own professional practice.

> *What I demand of myself, I also demand of others, only it is not necessarily offered to me in return. Expectations are high, but I expect others to see things as I see them — professionally. It does not always happen (IRO08).*

The interdisciplinarity specific to the profession translates, at the team level, into reciprocal learning among probation counsellors. This attitude places probation services within the sphere of knowledge-based organisations and of the *learning organisation*.

> *They are interdisciplinary teams and we always have something to learn from one another. I believe it is important for us all to be together and to learn from one another. We are all probation counsellors (IRO09).*

The diverse initial training of probation counsellors — social workers, psychologists, pedagogues, jurists — makes cooperation among colleagues and team-based learning necessary.

> *On the other hand, teamwork is very important, and in our case this exchange of information at the office level is very useful and we carry it out at any time. For instance, when I, as a social worker, am not very well*

> *versed in a certain legislative aspect other than the one I should know about probation — a judicial subtlety, a legal one, which, I don't know, I would not have learned or I don't know what a specific legal term means — then I go and ask my colleague. Just as my colleague tells me that they have a more reticent beneficiary, or one who does not speak, or "I don't know how to extract a certain piece of information," and they come and ask me what method to apply, or what technique, or they ask a psychologist (IRO11).*

The lack of visibility of probation as a social practice in the public sphere

The lack of visibility of probation as a social practice in the public sphere — not merely of one or another service — is linked to the specificity of cases under supervision, including public figures. Increased visibility of probation services would draw attention to the various cases under supervision, thereby compromising counsellor–supervised person confidentiality and exposing persons under supervision to risks of discrimination. The need for confidentiality runs counter to the need for public visibility of probation as a professional activity, as a representative of restorative penal philosophies, and of a distinctive vision of punishment from the perspective of human ecology. The lack of visibility of probation is a real problem when it comes to institutional communication and cooperation with other institutions in the system. Precisely in order to reconcile these two needs — the notoriety and credibility of the profession on the one hand, and the confidentiality of the territorial services' activities and of the beneficiaries on the other — the task of promoting the profession and probation as a social practice should fall to the National Directorate. In practice, however, the promotion of probation generally falls to the territorial services, with counsellors being compelled to carry out lobbying activities with other public institutions, which burdens their work.

> *We tried not to make ourselves known in the community precisely because we tried very much to preserve this character of confidentiality with regard to our beneficiaries [...] we realised at a certain point that perhaps we were wrong. Romanian society does not know what probation means; not only does Romanian society*

> *not know what probation means, [but] there are decision-makers at the level of the Ministry of Justice who do not know [what probation is], and it is very difficult because when you are a young system [the probation system] and you struggle to have your role known, it is frustrating, because you as a probation counsellor should be doing your work, your job, but it is frustrating and difficult to also have to lobby other institutions or within your own Ministry, so that you become recognised or so that someone there — a decision-maker — realises that you have needs that must be met in order for the work to be carried out under normal conditions and as well as possible (IRO11).*

The lack of visibility of probation is compounded by a deficient image of this profession, through its association with the practices of the *probation officer*. It is important to underline that, although respondents indicate that this image of probation officers who come to work armed, and whose activity more closely resembles that of prison guards, is not applicable to the Romanian probation counsellor, there have been appreciative references to the usefulness of changing the professional title from *probation counsellor* to *probation officer*, a designation that confers an aura of authority through association with the military connotation of the term *officer*.

> *When you say probation, if you are a person who has read even a little in their life, your mind goes to American films in which the probation officer sits somewhere in an office with a gun at his belt and the individuals come in and "if you don't behave, I'll send you back" (IRO11).*

With a view to increasing visibility, examples are given of joint actions with other state institutions, such as the penitentiary. These activities, conducted jointly with penitentiary staff, concern the promotion of conditional release as a reintegration measure, in which the two institutions of the penal enforcement system collaborate. Persons released on parole from the penitentiary are not simply sent into society but are supervised through probation services.

> *Perhaps we have also been invited to various activities that the penitentiary has organised, and then we had a certain visibility in the sense that there is a connection between those who leave from there under the supervision of our service, because everyone complains that they leave prison and no one takes care of them — well, that is not true; they leave prison and someone supervises them. But have you looked into it — do you actually know that no one takes care of them? And when you tell them about probation, even the word itself does not seem like a Romanian word (IRO11).*

Highlighting a series of contradictions linked to the lack of appreciation for the difficulty of the work performed and the effort expended, the example is given of the absence of a cleaning person employed within the service, which makes it necessary for employees to pay out of their own pockets the salary of the person who carries out the cleaning.

> *I do not believe that anyone is aware of how difficult it is to work with people. Only someone who has such a socio-human activity can realise how difficult it is to change them, to make them responsible, to make them autonomous [...]. We do not have a cleaning person; we pay for one out of our own money (IRO11).*

The respondents are optimistic regarding the increase in professional visibility, noting that this requires time and sustained efforts to present the social importance of the profession and the benefits it brings to society.

> *I consider that the majority of society still does not understand the importance of our activity. But nevertheless, education and re-education are of great significance, and they will realise that it will yield results; it just takes a little time. [...] Perhaps more information [is needed], because many institutions do not know what probation means (IMD02).*

> *I believe more roundtables are needed, and we need to communicate more about what our purpose is (IMD06).*

Moldavian respondents are more optimistic than their Romanian counterparts regarding the appreciation that this profession enjoys within society. A study conducted by the Institute for Penal Reforms is cited, which showed an upward trend in the population's positive attitude towards probation.

> *And people do change, and paid work is applied as well; he [the person on probation] observes that this work is performed in order to return the physical, financial harm that he has caused to society. And people understand that, yes, more or less, this is something positive (IMD08).*

Also in the direction of the Moldavian respondents' optimism regarding the increase in visibility and the positive public image of probation, there are a number of responses that detail the promotional activity of the profession: television appearances and media presence of probation counsellors more generally, the organisation of seminars, informational sessions, etc.

> *A very important role [is played by probation], because people know us, they know what probation is; we often go out — perhaps not very often, but quite well — we appear on television, we write in the newspaper, we inform minors, we organise camps, meetings, all kinds of activities, and I believe that society knows the role of probation (IMD05).*

Attributions removed from the competence of Romanian probation services. Victim–offender mediation

In general, respondents indicate that, following the reform of the Penal System in Romania, the professional attributions of probation services have grown exponentially. Attributions were introduced in the domain of supervising unpaid community work and the enforcement of non-custodial measures, as well as additional attributions concerning the conditional release of detainees. Victim–offender mediation, a professional attribution of probation counsellors in many legal systems, was removed from the Romanian system starting with the New Code of Criminal Procedure that entered into force in 2014. Respondents indicate that these attributions require specialised training, which only some of them possess. In addition, this practice requires a long-term approach, for which probation counsellors currently lack the time. Some respondents (FG) indicate that such a practice is not only difficult and time-consuming but, in many cases, carries a heightened potential for re-victimisation. This practice can be effective from the standpoint of restorative justice only when the meeting between the victim and the offender does not cause the former additional stress or even trauma.

> *Yes, but I was trained at a course at the Mediation Centre in Iași, and do you know what it means — it means time; somehow there should be an office that deals with this. I can do [victim–offender mediation] but I do not have the time, and I am not even allowed to, [because] we do not do mediation. It requires a great deal of time, which we no longer have, especially in cases involving family, mother, minor — to sit and listen to them separately — I would enjoy it, but I do not have time for it. And they are beneficial, indeed (IRO04).*

The potential for holding offenders accountable through the victim–offender mediation process is accepted by respondents, but they draw attention to the fact that, at present, this restorative practice lies outside the professional competence of probation counsellors.

> *It would lead [to holding offenders accountable], but it is not within the attribution of the Probation Service (IRO09).*

Neither do Moldavian counsellors advocate for the extension of victim–offender mediation practice, except in certain cases, such as domestic violence. Moldavian counsellors have more attributions in the sphere of penal mediation than their Romanian counterparts, from whom the criminal legislation has now removed this attribution. For example, respondent (IMD05) indicates the existence of counsellor responsibilities regarding the verification of reconciliation between the offender and the victim, which is mandatory for conditional release from the penitentiary at the halfway point of the sentence.

2.2. Thematic Axis II. Human Resources Development

2.2.1. The attributions of the probation counsellor in relation to the types of beneficiaries

Within this category, information was included regarding the specificity of the activity carried out by probation counsellors. We were able to identify in the respondents' statements a number of major directions in which probation activity is effectively carried out: pre-sentence evaluation, with the role of supporting the court in the individualisation of the sentence; supervision of persons sentenced with suspension under supervision; supervision of the enforcement of non-custodial educational measures for minors; participation in the conditional release committees for persons in detention; and the implementation of social reintegration programmes for persons who have committed criminal offences [237, 238]. We present below a synthesis of the work tasks assigned to probation counsellors in the Republic of Moldova, which are similar in the case of Romanian counsellors, with the exception of certain specific elements of social assistance based on providing/ facilitating access to community resources — finding employment, housing, social benefits, and occasional support.

> *When our Probation Service was created, we had many visits, many trainings, practical and theoretical study of materials, and as a result it was done according to our law, let us say, which includes more activities — or all of them — apart from mediation, which exists in some countries, and victim assistance, which also exists in some countries. On the other hand, in our case there is the entire spectrum of activities, beginning with supervision and ending with social assistance, pre-sentence reports — let us say the types: the type of pre-sentence probation, which includes the preparation of the pre-sentence report, and now we have started from the 15th [of the month] also the pre-sentence assistance, or psycho-social assistance at the pre-sentence stage. Second, sentential or community probation, which according to the latest modifications includes the supervision of persons who are on probation, their assistance, and counselling. Then there is the penitentiary [stage] with preparation for release, and the post-penitentiary [stage] with post-penitentiary assistance.*

In each of the 42 Offices we have persons who deal with these activities. But here I want to draw attention to the fact that in our system, criminal penalties are separated from probation, because with probation one is released from punishment, so to speak. But in our case there are two situations: the enforcement of sentences, which is established by the Criminal Code as punishment — unpaid work and deprivation of rights. Probation has as its purpose re-socialisation, and this re-socialisation includes supervision, assistance, counselling, and all necessary activities (IMD08).

The preparation of evaluation (pre-sentence) reports

The preparation of pre-sentence evaluation reports is mentioned by virtually all respondents as a current activity in the practice of probation counsellors (IRO04; IRO01; IMD01; IMD04; IMD06). Current Romanian legislation requires these reports to contain proposals and recommendations that allow judges to individualise the sentence. In the Republic of Moldova, although the legislation does not mandatorily require such recommendations, they are customary, and courts generally take them into account if they are correctly and legally argued. Pre-sentence evaluation may be carried out at the request of the police or the prosecution during the investigation and/or criminal pursuit phase, or by the court during the trial phase. Psycho-social evaluation can only be carried out for defendants, and cannot be requested for other participants in the criminal proceedings (IRO07).

Supervision activities

Probation services supervise the implementation of non-custodial educational measures in the case of minors. At the beginning of the experimental implementation of probation programmes, in both Romania and the Republic of Moldova, the majority of these targeted the identification of social alternatives to incarceration, especially for minors.

But if we are to discuss a minor, we meet much more frequently and much more often draw the attention of a minor who has committed, for example, a theft offence, and who is at heightened risk and already has a second, a third conviction, or the parties have reconciled because the injured party has forgiven, and there is the order to initiate criminal proceedings (IMD05).

As such, probation counsellors with seniority in the system have extensive experience in the supervision of non-custodial measures for minors. Educational measures may be custodial or non-custodial. Only the latter fall within the responsibility of probation services. The modifications that have appeared in the normative frameworks of practice are underlined by respondents, especially by the Romanian ones, who have confronted this situation of task overload more recently than their Moldavian colleagues. The expansion of tasks assigned to probation counsellors, and implicitly the increase in the degree of stress and professional demands to which they are subjected, is considered a source of professional demotivation and of possible errors.

> *And regarding supervision, under the old code we had less work, but under the New Code we have a great deal of work, especially with persons who have suspension under supervision [...] (IRO04).*

Supervision activity is described as being particularly complex, involving the verification of information received from the persons being monitored through fieldwork, home visits, and interviews with persons in the supervised person's social environment, the carrying out of observations in the supervised person's living environment, etc.

> *[...] exercising control over the enforcement of the sentence for persons released from punishment and to whom a coercive measure has been applied (IMD01).*

In addition, community supervision involves verifying compliance with the deadlines regarding the activities that the supervised person must carry out in order to reintegrate into society. This activity also entails monitoring and case management.

> *[...] The supervision of the person must be permanently monitored. From my point of view, persons under supervision are the most demanding for me, because minors are the least aware, and so it is also very difficult to work with them (IRO04).*

Supervision activity includes working with persons whose sentence has been suspended under supervision, as well as supervising the performance of community service work — including by persons who have received a criminal fine converted into community service work.

The respondent insists on the supervision of compliance by persons on probation with the measures and obligations imposed by the court.

> *In short, those who are conditionally sentenced come to me for supervision (IMD02).*

Alongside the monitoring of compliance with the measures imposed by the court, case management (IRO12) involves the social reintegration of offenders and the assistance offered to them in order to avoid recidivism.

> *The second fundamental activity is that of supervision, which consists of supervising persons sentenced to imprisonment and not only, and also [those sentenced to] the criminal fine converted into community service work, whose sentence has been suspended under supervision. [...] We monitor the manner of compliance with these measures, but we also deal at the same time with their social reintegration, with helping them somehow not to reoffend, not to commit other criminal acts (IRO07).*

Supervision activity is based on the conduct of interviews that take place during supervision meetings. The interview is likewise the fundamental technique in the preparation of evaluation reports and in the interventions carried out according to the evolution of the case. The activity of probation counsellors and case management also entails statistical activities, record-keeping, and the preparation, issuance, and dispatch of documents to various institutions (IRO07).

> *So, I, as a psychologist, try to understand the motive for committing the offence, and if a lack of financial resources is identified, we travel to the home, we speak with the parents. There are cases where we have no one to speak with, because the parents are in a state of perpetual inebriation, and we turn to everyone, starting with social assistance, the town hall, and ending with the church, because the priest also carries great value in the village, as well as the police inspector in the given sector. And we try, besides explaining the negative side of the offences that he has committed and is likely to commit, we forewarn him about what can happen to him and we try to find what he needs (IMD05).*

Also within the framework of supervision activities, there are those carried out with persons conditionally released from the penitentiary (IMD05), who must comply with the obligations imposed by the court. Violation of the measures imposed by the court must be reported by the probation services to the enforcement courts, and depending on the severity of the violation, may lead to the revocation of the person's release.

> *Plus, more recently, those conditionally released also come to us, after they finish serving [their sentence]; as such, it is a new attribution — until they serve the entire term of the sentence, until their detention end date, they will come to the Probation Services and will comply with the obligations imposed by the Court (IRO04).*

Participation in the conditional release committees in penitentiaries

Although Romanian probation services do not have attributions in the development of educational measures within penitentiaries, probation counsellors are required to be present in the establishment of the detention regime for incarcerated persons, in granting them temporary leave to interrupt the enforcement of the sentence, and even in the process of evaluating them with a view to conditional release before term from the penitentiary.

> *I worked for 5 years in B., and having a penitentiary unit, I participated there in everything that involved the establishment of the detention regime, because there are 4 types of regimes. If the person in the penitentiary unit wanted to take leave because they had health problems or a death in the family, a probation counsellor also had to participate — that is, we had other attributions as well (IRO04).*

Moldavian counsellors carry out probation activities within the penitentiary, particularly those related to preparation for release or conditional release (IMD08).

> *If there are penitentiaries in the sector, then there is a more restricted collaboration because one also goes to the committees for the release of persons from detention before the end of their term. But here we do not have a*

penitentiary, so communication is strictly official — interpellations, requests to which we are strictly given answers, but which in any case are along more general lines (IMD11).

The implementation of reintegration programmes

A particular activity of probation counsellors in both countries is the implementation of individual or (IRO11) group reintegration programmes for persons under supervision. These programmes can be implemented in Romania only after specific training in which probation counsellors must participate, training organised by the National Probation Directorate.

[...] I am trained only for group reintegration programmes, which means we run courses with several young people at once, and it is very exhausting. That is, if in one day you work 5 hours with 13 persons, the next 3 hours you can already say you are beside the point [exhausted, ineffective] (IRO04; IRO07).

Reintegration programmes, both individual and group-based, aim at the construction of social skills intended to prevent recidivism, through the acquisition of a new mode of consequence-oriented thinking and a self-reflective attitude. There are also a number of programmes designed for violence control, especially in the case of juvenile offenders. Other programmes target the development of skills for avoiding undesirable behaviours related to alcohol and/or drug consumption, including driving under the influence of alcohol (IRO06).

The Motivation for Change programme. This programme is in the process of implementation; we are trying to implement it, but it is very difficult (IMD06).

Providing reintegration programmes is an obligation of the Probation Directorates, as some of the persons under supervision are required by court order to attend such programmes (IRO03). Respondents are partially reluctant regarding the implementation of these programmes:

I hate the programmes. They seem useless to me, at least in our case (IRO02).

(...) I am in charge of a programme: Motivation for Change, but it goes rather poorly, because there are many shortcomings, starting with the room, with the time — there are several factors that prevent us from carrying it out successfully (IMD03).

Another respondent highlights the benefits that programme participation brings to supervised persons, especially minors.

So, what I liked was that we were able to awaken another characteristic in the minor's personality, to see positive things as well, not just the negative in them. And they already became friends among themselves. I believe it was a very good project (IMD05).

Respondents insist on the effectiveness of reintegration programmes, especially in the case of juvenile offenders. The delivery of such programmes, respondents affirm, can only take place after the minors have been fed, enabling them to concentrate on the programme content.

The Prevention of Juvenile Delinquency is a programme that lasted 10 hours. It was conducted by me in collaboration with another Probation Office from the neighbouring area of [N]. There were minors registered with the Office in [U] together with the Office in [N]; it took place here in this office. The minors were gathered, brought by car; here, every time, we served them tea and a sandwich, because if the minor has not eaten anything since yesterday, everything I discuss is worthless, because he is only thinking about his empty stomach, and we make an effort to serve them, to feed them, after which we begin the programme of activities (IMD05).

Respondents note that, due to the heavy workload of probation counsellors, it is very difficult to implement such reintegration programmes repeatedly, as they require a longer period of time.

I cannot say — yes, I work more on supervision, because as a trainer on a particular programme I only manage to deliver it once, because we have several programmes and so we try to deliver them all (IRO11).

Everyday activities and work routine

Romanian respondents indicate that all categories of activities falling within the obligations of the probation counsellor are equally important, as there is not yet a clear differentiation of probation service activities:

> *We are professionals in everything. In the future, we should be organised into offices — a supervision office, a reports office, and a programmes office. We do everything. I try to do everything well; now the inspectors also evaluate us — they come and review the documents. And there is still more work to be done on the documents, from my point of view; there is a great deal to be done (IRO04; IRO03).*

Moldavian colleagues have a clearer division of tasks, with one counsellor designated to work in the penitentiary with detainees during the preparation-for-release period, and another designated to maintain contact with the court. The majority of respondents indicate supervision activity and the conduct of various interviews as the activities that occupy the most time in the working schedule of probation counsellors.

> *The 8-hour working day begins with supervision activity, when we have cases, when we schedule supervised persons for the first meeting or for the meetings carried out within the framework of supervision activity, or the assistance and counselling activities that we have scheduled for the delivery of work programmes with them, or the activities carried out in the penitentiary with detained persons (IRO01).*

An ordinary working day is materialised in the conduct of meetings both with persons under supervision — considered straightforward by respondents — and meetings with persons newly registered with the probation services. In addition to meetings, the counsellors' activity is supplemented by the preparation of correspondence with collaborating institutions and with the courts.

> *I very much enjoy discussing with convicted persons, giving them correct guidance, seeing where their shortcomings are — that is, in life, in society — and we strive as best we can to help them, within our possibilities (IMD04).*

The first meetings with a supervised person involve informing them of the obligations imposed by the court and, at the same time, preparing the documents relating to the enforcement of judicial decisions (IRO01).

> *Today, for example, I have scheduled certain persons who must come for a meeting; we speak by telephone with some persons if they cannot come, or we set another date. The minimum duration of a meeting is 15 minutes (IMD06).*

The specificity of probation service management activity

The management of probation services is not a separate activity, distinct from that of the probation counsellor; persons occupying head-of-service positions retain their counsellor competencies, which they carry out alongside their managerial duties.

> *As head of service, I have never compromised on my attribution as a probation counsellor; as such, I continue to handle cases [...] I prepare evaluation reports for the courts and prosecution offices, I have supervision cases with convicted and sanctioned persons — fewer, in any case, than my colleagues, since I also have other attributions. I have participated in Conditional Release Committees at 4 penitentiary units and in everything that constitutes probation work as provided for by law, but the focus is more on the management side (IRO08).*

In addition to the specific counsellor competencies, persons with managerial attributions at the level of probation services are responsible for the legality and correctness of the documents issued by the Service, as well as for its proper functioning.

> *According to my job description, I have the following: ensuring collaboration with public administration, ensuring the legal framework, ensuring probation activity. (...) In addition to the attributions of deputy head, which I fulfil in the absence of the head, I also have supervision work with convicted persons (IMD02).*

The management of the probation counsellor team entails attributions of representation and coordination, but these tasks do not individualise service managers and do not transform probation management into a standalone occupation within the field (IRO09; IRO08).

> *My activity is more complex. Since I have been working at the Ministry of Justice, I am the Head of the Probation Service in [B]; therefore I also have the capacity of manager and coordinator of the probation team in [B], and I [temporarily] represent the institution as PR (IRO08).*

When asked to describe their own activity in the capacity of manager, respondents who simultaneously hold the status of probation counsellor and service manager underline their assumption of administrative attributions, among which are listed the registration of documents received by the Service, alongside the activity of endorsing documents issued by the Service, the allocation of cases to each counsellor, and representation activities in relation to the Ministry of Justice, the courts, etc. (IRO08; IRO09; IRO10; IRO11; IRO12; IMD01; IMD05).

> *First of all, at least for a period of time, I register all the documents that enter the Service, so I am also a kind of secretary. Case allocation. Entering cases into the Service databases. Discussing cases with my colleagues, on a case-by-case basis; endorsing documents — everything that concerns documents leaving the probation service. Maintaining contact with the Ministry of Justice, with local partners, with probation colleagues across the country. We speak on the telephone permanently because our legislation is very ambiguous, and so we consult one another, especially on the New Criminal Codes. Reading and endorsing Evaluation Reports for the judicial bodies; supervising convicted persons; supervision activities; registering convicted persons in my cases or in the cases of my colleagues who are temporarily absent from the service; preparing the records of supervision sessions; preparing correspondence related to probation or even to my own cases (IRO08).*

The same communication management activity is described in a somewhat similar manner by a Moldavian respondent:

> *Supervising all persons, guiding and verifying the counsellors in their probation activity. I am also a driver, a secretary, a cleaner, and a counsellor (IMD05).*

Managerial activity also entails a number of immediate administrative activities, such as identifying suitable premises for the Probation Centre, in the case of the interviewed manager (IRO09).

> *Allocating cases to counsellors or to myself, as the case may be. Allocating evaluation reports. Working with the service's beneficiaries. Countersigning documents and, of course, the analysis associated with them — some are simple correspondence, others are more elaborate documents such as the preparation of the evaluation report, which requires a more detailed analysis; verifying probation files; procurement if necessary; requesting quotations. We maintain permanent contact with the National Probation Directorate, through which we inform them, and conversely, what they transmit to us I bring to the attention of my colleagues. I try very much to pursue a participative management approach, so that colleagues are permanently informed with the information coming from Bucharest, and when I make a decision, I take into account the opinions they hold. And in this sense, we organise periodic meetings that also include case peer-supervision — for example, when there are more complex cases from a legal point of view or more complicated cases, we discuss the respective situations as a team, of course with the preservation of confidentiality. But at the same time, the more important decisions are also taken within these team meetings (IRO09).*

2.2.2. Professional socialisation

Within this category, information was gathered regarding basic and continuing professional training, including the outcomes of professional training in terms of the professional competencies necessary for the effective exercise of the probation counsellor profession, the mode of career entry, and the motivation for choosing this career.

Career entry

Career entry into probation counselling is achieved, in both countries, through a public competition, in which persons with training in the fields of social work, psychology, sociology, pedagogy, or law may participate, provided they are medically and psychologically fit, have no criminal or fiscal record, have a good reputation, and have a good command of the Romanian language. No prior work experience is required for participation in the competition. Being a position of public interest, the regulations in force require that posts be filled exclusively through a competition organised under conditions of maximum transparency and promoted at the national level. Respondents indicated that, in their case as well, access to the counsellor position was achieved through a competition, both in Romania (IRO01; IRO03; IRO05; IRO06; IRO10; IRO11) and in the Republic of Moldova (IMD01; IMD02; IMD06; IMD07). The competition is described as:

> *[...] a very serious, rigorous examination, when I passed it (IRO06).*

Participation in the competition was motivated by the fact that:

> *[...] I always wanted to work with persons who had violated the law in one way or another (IRO05).*

> *In total I have 30 years of work. I worked as a bailiff, and afterwards, seeing how things were going in probation as well — that is, I took an interest — it is a welcome thing, I would say, for the integration of convicted persons into society. That is, something is being done which is also welcome for convicted persons. I like the work and I strive to do it according to the law and instructions (IMD04).*

> *I worked at a school and I was left without work, and it happened that I was hired, and I liked it, and I stayed here (IMD02).*

In the case of some respondents, participation in the competition was preceded by a period of volunteering:

> *[...] For a period of 3 months I volunteered within the service. Subsequently, I considered that it is a profession in which I can work and I identify myself as a professional within it, and I went further to the competition when the posts were opened (IRO03).*

Some respondents were involved in the development of probation from the period of the pilot programmes.

> *This year marks 17 years [of activity]. I worked from 1999 to 2001 in the Experimental Probation Centre, which was financed through European Projects. In 2001, Probation was established at the national level and I came to [B]. So I have 15 years in the Ministry of Justice and 2 years at ... (the organisation implementing the pilot probation projects) (IRO08).*

> *In my case, the story is also long, because I have been there from the beginning, since 2002, when the talk about probation first began. I participated in all the seminars (IMD02).*

Professional training

The professional training of respondents is diverse, covering practically all the fields — social work, law, psychology, pedagogy — permitted by the probation law. Some respondents mention a dual specialisation:

> *The training I had at that time was the Faculty of Philosophy, Social Work section, followed by the Faculty of Law. At that time I did not yet have my degree; subsequently I also completed the Faculty of Law, but at that time I was hired on the basis of my social work studies, and at the same time a preparatory school was being held in Arad for two weeks, in which we were trained to become probation counsellors (IRO01; IRO07).*

> *At present I have studies in the field of international law, psychology, psycho-pedagogy, and I am completing a master's degree in anti-corruption (IMD05).*

Respondents, both Romanian and Moldavian, highlight the importance of psychological training for the activity of the probation counsellor; in their case, this is complemented by legal training.

> *My personal opinion is that the most important thing is to have studies in psychology — not necessarily the entire faculty, but at least courses. And a counsellor also needs the other two, but to a lesser extent (IMD02).*

> *I have a dual specialisation as well; it seems very important to me to also have psychological training, because for the person who comes to you, you truly need to know how to interpret a sentence, to see certain legal aspects (IRO05).*

The majority of respondents have professional training as social workers, in many cases followed by a master's degree in the field of probation, organised within faculties of social work. All respondents attended probation courses at the national level, both in Romania and in the Republic of Moldova, organised through the National Probation Directorate — in Romania — and the Central Probation Office — in the Republic of Moldova.

> *At the Central Probation Office, a course was held for probation counsellors that lasted approximately 2 months, covering legislation and normative acts, as well as service-related matters (IMD12).*

Postgraduate training courses were the solution for supplementing the initial training in social work:

> *I am a graduate of social work in Iași and I have three postgraduate courses in several fields: criminal law, probation, and social management (IRO08).*

Being an interdisciplinary profession, entry is made from various spheres of initial professional training, with professionals attending, after employment, a series of specific training courses.

Motivation for career choice

In the career choice of future probation counsellors, a number of factors played a role, such as: the novel and attractive character of the profession, the absence of the requirement for prior professional experience, participation in volunteering activities, and the implementation of programmes in the field of restorative justice (one of the theoretical models of the first probation programmes in Romania). The attractiveness of the profession, even in the absence of knowledge about its exact significance, led respondent IRO04 to choose the career of probation counsellor:

> *I completed my law degree and studied the law, and at that time it sounded like something completely different to me. Probation — evidence, proof in a case — something completely different, but I have remained in the system for 14 years. I completed the Faculty of Law [...] (IRO04).*

The absence of a requirement for initial experience, and the non-recognition of volunteering as professional experience, contributed to the career choice in the case of IRO02:

> *It was the only job where experience was not required. I had been out of university for a year and everywhere experience was required, and volunteering at that time was not considered experience (IRO02).*

Initial contact with probation during the university period and the preparation of the bachelor's thesis on this topic led to the choice of probation counselling as a career opportunity for respondent IRO08.

Continuing professional development

The initial training of probation counsellors is followed by specific preparation, within which the professional acquires the competencies specific to the conduct of their principal activities: supervision, the preparation of evaluation reports, case management, participation in conditional release, and the implementation of educational programmes for persons who have committed criminal offences. Continuing professional development targets, in addition to the acquisition of the competencies necessary for carrying out these activities, the updating of knowledge according to the evolution of the specific normativity, the development of professional standards and requirements, and the evolution of international practice. The continuing development of professionals — Romanian respondents specify — has also benefited from an international component: until 2013, primarily British, and more recently Norwegian (FG). This international component has partially left its mark on the specificity of Romanian practice, although some elements specific to the British and Norwegian models, respectively, are considered incompatible with the Romanian legislative and institutional framework: the overloading of Romanian probation counsellors' activity, who have up to 250 cases in progress, as opposed to their Norwegian counterparts, who work with approximately 30 cases, thus having more time to devote to each case (FG). Legislative elements are also particularised; since 2014, for example, victim–offender mediation has been removed from the attributions of probation counsellors (FG), an element specific to restorative justice used predominantly in the United Kingdom. Nevertheless, training together with international specialists is seen as beneficial (FG), bringing an additional degree of professionalism to probation counsellors. In turn, Moldavian respondents highlight the involvement of their Romanian colleagues in their professional training. With respect to continuing development, both through participation in courses and training programmes and through self-improvement, respondents display a heightened interest, being conscious of its necessity for the proper conduct of their activity as professionals:

> *I participate in the courses that are organised for us at the initiative of the Directorate. I also document myself personally and individually in the field in which I carry out activities, because there is no other way, since cases are very complex and require thorough preparation (IRO03).*

The interdisciplinary nature of the practice requires a high degree of professional training:

> *From all [perspectives] (social worker, psychologist, or jurist), as much information and as much training as possible is needed, because this profession involves activities from all these professional spheres (IRO06).*

Initial professional training is considered insufficient, which is why continuing development after entry into the system is absolutely necessary:

> *What you lack in theoretical training before entering the system, you subsequently perfect through trainings, through professional development courses, through preparation, and through the individual study of each person using the materials available in the service (IRO07).*

The need for additional training

The majority of respondents feel the need for particularised professional training that would correspond to the high degree of inter- and transdisciplinarity that probation practice presupposes. This is probably also the reason why many of the respondents have pursued multiple bachelor's and/or master's degree fields, with one respondent even holding doctoral studies in the field of sociology, on a topic related to probation (IRO08). The majority of Moldavian respondents highlight the benefits of initial training in assistance-oriented professions — social work, psychology — motivated by the fact that the ultimate objective of probation is the social reintegration of the offender.

> *Psychologist and social worker, and the choice is because in this segment, probation specifically provides for re-socialisation and not the sanctioning of the person. Therefore, for re-socialisation to be as it should, a psychologist and social work are needed, because our task is primarily that they do not commit further offences. So here, certain psychological measures and social assistance are needed so that they understand why we carry out the evaluation. For example, a minor who took a telephone to show off, and who is fully provided for by the parents, or who works, or who took the telephone in order to eat something. These elements are very important; that is why the psychologist must evaluate and then the social worker must implement (IMD08).*

Among the training needs identified by respondents whose initial training was in the assistance sphere is the penal dimension of the practice — integrated within the sphere of penal enforcement law, probation is grounded in the legislator's vision regarding the functions of punishment, the gravity and social danger of offences, and the legislator's vision regarding the social reintegration of the offender.

> *[...] It would have seemed helpful to me if, in the initial training, emphasis had been placed on what the penal side means — someone to explain at least in broad terms, but there are certain subtleties that you need, and perhaps it would have been much simpler for me if we had initially had training from people who have worked and who understand what we are confronted with (IRO02).*

The deepening and consolidation of competencies in the socio-human fields are felt as equally pressing needs for continuing development, beyond initial university and postgraduate training and the courses organised by the National Probation Directorate. Results similar to those exemplified below are found in relatively similar forms in other interviews conducted: (IRO02; IRO03; IRO04; IRO07; IRO08; IMD08; IMD11; IMD04; IMD05).

> *I believe that one should have a profound consolidation of knowledge on the socio-human side, from all fields [...]: you need to be empathic, and this is something you most often learn in social work; you need to know how to listen and to make yourself understood, and this is something you usually learn when you graduate from the faculty of psychology; but you also need vast and solid knowledge regarding rights, freedoms, and laws, and this information you most often acquire from the field of law (IRO11).*

> *Here you need to be mixed, because being only a psychologist, or only a social worker, or only a jurist does not really help you. As a psychologist, from the very beginning it was very difficult for me to orient myself in legislation, because I see the problem that the person has from a different angle. Whereas a jurist seems to have blinkers on when it comes to the subject of probation — does he have money or not, he must come to the meeting; if he violates the law, one must immediately go to court because he does not comply with the law, and so on. But I believe that, in any case, a different approach is needed (IMD11).*

Another training need felt by respondents is that related to the specific programmes for working with persons under supervision.

> *[...] I have only heard about them from colleagues — [probation programmes] DAS, Stop! Think and Change, OTO, and so on. But I have only heard their names and have never participated in a session (IRO05).*

Regardless of the initial field of training, respondents consider that, in practice, each of the probation counsellors currently in the system — at least within the Directorates from which the respondents come — possesses competencies in all the constitutive spheres of probation, having psychological, counselling, assertive, and assistance aptitudes, as well as the capacity to understand and apply the normativity in force. This is due to the continuing development in diverse facets of the profession from which each counsellor benefits. In our view, the current absence of an office-based organisation of Romanian probation services — of the type involving pre-sentence evaluation offices, supervision offices, monitoring offices, conditional release offices, etc. — also contributes to this multidimensional specialisation of probation counsellors.

> *I do not believe that in our service, at least [...], there is anyone who would say that they are good only in a particular area. Over time, we have developed professional skills in several fields through the professional training seminars that we hold almost every year; we are trained in certain professional areas. We have tried to develop ourselves precisely where we consider that we do not master the subject matter very well (IRO11).*

The importance of transcending the theoretical and methodological framework acquired during initial training is frequently underlined — not because this training would be insufficient, but because, by virtue of the profession's specificity, major changes in professional practice occur almost continuously.

> *I participated in various trainings that took place at the beginning; I attended courses, I have certificates from courses; I am also a trainer in unpaid work, which was also done through the National Institute of Justice; I also attended a course for judges and prosecutors who in the*

> *future will nevertheless apply these procedures and will need to be familiar with them (IMD08).*

The typology of persons under supervision changes continuously, as society itself is in a constant dynamic; therefore, there is a permanent need for professional self-actualisation.

> *[...] if you intervene with methods that we learned 10, 15, 20 years ago, at university, with modern, new personality types, controlled according to society, to the dynamics of society, [at present] you are no longer effective, and then you are no longer a professional, and if you are no longer a professional, you are no longer a probation counsellor (IRO07).*

Empathic capacities, as well as capacities for analysis and synthesis, are considered absolutely necessary for good practice as a probation counsellor (IRO12). Continuing development is based on the experience of those with seniority in the system. Persons who were initially trained become trainers in turn; thus, professional experience spreads within the probation services, which, from the perspective of human capital, can be described as falling within the type of knowledge-based organisation, as well as a knowledge-producing organisation — generating know-how, proprietary methodologies — and a learning organisation, drawing from external trainers, from experienced persons within the system, and from colleagues through the system of peer education and peer supervision.

> *First I participated, then I taught my colleagues, and then many of them in turn became trainers. I participated in various trainings that took place at the beginning; I attended courses, I have certificates from courses; I am also a trainer in unpaid work, which was also done through the National Institute of Justice; I also attended a course for judges and prosecutors who in the future will nevertheless apply these procedures and will need to be familiar with them (IMD08).*

> *We learn every day; we consult the specialised literature; we participate in various programmes, in workshops (IMD01).*

2.2.3. The professional identity of probation counsellors

Professional identity is analysed from the perspective of probation counsellors' self-perception regarding the status of the profession, the perceived or self-perceived social importance of the profession, professional recognition and the recognition of the profession, the operational definition of professional success, and what it means to be a good professional and/or to achieve professional success. The most significant problem highlighted by the majority of respondents is the insufficient staffing of probation services and, stemming from this, the task overloading of probation counsellors, which entails a bureaucratisation of practice and a reduction of the time available for working with each individual person, with risks of diminishing the quality of the services provided.

The perceived importance of the profession

Respondents recognise the social importance of the probation counsellor profession, which makes continuous professional self-improvement necessary. Romanian respondents in particular displayed an enthusiastic attitude towards belonging to this professional category, demonstrating professional optimism despite signalling — almost as a leitmotif — the high degree of daily task overloading. Moldavian respondents also report a high degree of task loading, with the figures they mention — between 110 active files (IMD04) and 400 active files per year (IMD06) — being comparable to those declared by their Romanian colleagues, between 150 and 300 active files. Respondents bring into discussion the network of interdependencies among professionals as a key element in the social construction of the probation counsellor profession.

> *To be a probation counsellor means, first of all, to be a link in a chain (IRO03).*

The social importance of the profession is doubled by the personal importance accorded to the profession, a strong identification with professional values, and generally a heightened self-esteem with reference to one's own professional identity.

> *[to be a probation counsellor] It is a very important and primordial thing. To be a good professional, I believe each one of us makes efforts in this direction. We attend courses; we are self-taught (IRO03).*

For me, this was a dream — that is, I have been working for about 30 years in this field (penal enforcement); imagine, I have never changed my job, I work and it is fine, thank you — it means that for me it is a great deal. It means something, a fruit, especially when we receive certain files — that is, certain convicted persons who have positive results — and I see that they understand, that they are interested. I am glad that, yes, I work, and it means that a result can also be seen, a fruit of the labour (IMD04).

Respondents insist on the personal importance attributed to the profession.

For me it is very important, but that does not mean I am in a position to capitalise on this (IRO02).

I like it; I want to be useful; I want to help persons in conflict with the law to be better off, to find a purpose in life, to stop committing offences (IMD03).

The interviewees indicate that they are conscious of the professional responsibility and the risks involved in exercising the profession.

It is a profession with very many risks and with very great responsibility (IRO05).

Professional recognition

The professional prestige enjoyed by probation counsellors derives from the recognition that the profession enjoys among other professions in the assistance sphere, as well as those in the sphere of justice administration. Adequate professional training finds its recognition through professional status and the remuneration received. Nevertheless, respondents draw attention to the fact that the volume of work constitutes a factor that reduces motivation towards professional excellence.

Why not acknowledge that there is a certain recognition of certain studies — at least for me, with special psycho-pedagogy — perhaps I would not manage to obtain the same status or the same remuneration at another institution. On the other hand, most of us lose

> *much of our enthusiasm, because it is one thing to feel satisfaction with your work, and another to feel that no matter how much you try, you do not succeed — because here it is no longer even a question of salary; it is effectively a question of how efficient you are [...] the problem is the volume of work, which exceeds our capacities (IRO02).*

Regarding the significance accorded to professional practice, one respondent considers it a long-held aspiration that has been fulfilled. This response, along with similar ones, confirms what was mentioned previously regarding professional optimism and the strong attachment to professional values (IRO05; IRO07; IMD02; IMD03; IMD04). Professional recognition is linked to the effectiveness of practice and to the recognition received from other categories of professionals, especially from the justice administration sphere. The fact that their professional opinion is solicited — initially in an unofficial and personal manner by judges regarding the individualisation of sentences for offenders — is considered an achievement that denotes professionalism. The fact that this practice of proposing to the court, through the pre-sentence evaluation report, the solution considered optimal by the probation counsellor has been incorporated into legislation represents evidence of the growing social importance enjoyed by probation counsellors within the criminal justice system. The absence of any lack of clarity regarding the solutions proposed in the pre-sentence evaluation reports, as well as in other documents submitted to the courts, is considered evidence of the professionalism and good professional reputation enjoyed by probation counsellors.

> *And I want to say that in the 15 years I have been working, there have been no lack of clarity. On the contrary, judges have called me to ask my opinion, what they could give, because until 2 years ago the probation counsellor could not recommend to the court an institution of punishment or educational measure. At present, under the New Criminal Code, we can. And then it is very difficult to recommend something to the judge based on risk and need, but for the most part the courts take our opinions into account; there have been no situations in which we have received complaints or queries from judges or prosecutors (IRO07).*

The good professional

Probation counsellors define professionalism as being result-oriented, with work efficiency being designated according to results. It is important to note that a series of ethical values, such as dignity and responsibility, are included in the definition of the professional. These values make possible a particular attitude on the part of the professional that allows them to guide the supervised person towards results (IRO01). A series of qualities of the good professional are defined: involvement, organisation, devotion — which can be considered professional virtues — alongside personality traits such as rigour, the capacity to clarify the obligations incumbent upon the supervised person, etc., considered necessary for being a good professional.

> *The qualities that recommend a good professional in Probation are: adequate involvement, organisation, planning, devotion, rigour, clarification of the measures and obligations incumbent upon the supervised persons, etc. (IRO01).*

Respondents make reference to the most exact observance of the legal framework for the conduct of probation, including the facilitation of compliance with supervision deadlines by the persons with whom the counsellor works.

> *[professionalism] It means, from my point of view, doing your job well, within the limits of the law, respecting your deadlines and the laws of the state in which you operate (IRO01).*

> *A professional, I consider, is the person who carries out their service functions carefully and in accordance with the law (IMD02).*

Motivation for success and the capacity to overcome professional obstacles are considered defining elements of the good professional. Involvement in the activity, dedication to the profession and to cases — even despite obstacles — represents a correct attitude that the professional should adopt permanently. The capacity to overcome professional obstacles and an optimistic professional vision are conditions for success in probation practice.

> *[...] a good professional dedicates themselves to what they do, regardless of the impediments behind them — because if we were to analyse it, there are impediments in every profession — but overcoming all these obstacles, to manage to do your job and to see beyond the barriers that are placed before you (IRO03).*

Another characteristic of the good professional is professional experience. Experience must be complemented by the acquisition of a set of competencies relating to professional practice.

> *A competent person who knows their obligations and, of course, the rights of the citizens of the Republic of Moldova (IMD06).*

Experience allows the adaptation of practice to the particularities of the supervised person, a certain degree of empathy and flexibility of practice within the limits of good practice guidelines.

> *We have good practice guidelines, but you also adapt practice according to the person you are working with. Now, it also depends on experience. That is, if an interview used to take me more time [at the beginning of my practice], now, after 14–15 years, just by looking at the person — the eyes are the mirror of the soul. That is, I respect the good practice guidelines, but ultimately you approach the person according to the individual you have in front of you (IRO04).*

Professionalism is seen as going beyond the mere fulfilment of legal obligations. It is necessary to *put one's heart into it* — that is, to adopt a proactive attitude, to make efforts to bring the supervised person to an awareness of the significance of their actions and the necessity of prosocial behaviour.

> *From the standpoint of probation, we do not think only about producing the documents that the law requires, to do them just to cover yourself; you must make efforts so that the person under your supervision understands what the consequences and benefits of adopting prosocial behaviour are [...] beyond doing what the law says, you also need to put a little heart into it (IRO05).*

Responsibility is invoked by several respondents as an exceptional operational value for the activity of the probation counsellor.

> *[professionalism] For me it means being a responsible person. Responsible with yourself, with others, and in everything you do, to put your heart into it. To do everything correctly. To do everything for people. What defines me is that even if the laws are poor, I am the kind of person who respects the rules and the law (IRO08).*

The good professional is a team player. The mutual help that probation counsellors offer one another is considered by the respondent to be a good result in itself.

> *That is, we help each other as a team. We often work as a team, which is also a good result in itself (IMD04).*

Good relations and communication with supervised persons are considered conditions of professional success and of the probation counsellor's professional status.

> *I believe that the bond between the convicted person and the counsellor — I believe I can sense it by now, from practice. That is, if there is a connection between the counsellor and the convicted person, that is the most important thing (IMD03).*

A series of other ethical values are invoked, their practical realisation being a sign of professional success and an achievement that can qualify the probation counsellor as a good professional.

> *One must be, first of all, informed; secondly, one must be patient, punctual, and still have some experience in the field (IMD03).*

> *Optimism and courage (IMD07).*

The significance of the expression "resolved case"

The idea of a "resolved case" is linked to the social reintegration of the supervised person. For a case to be considered "resolved," the supervised person must fulfil a series of conditions, of which the most important are those related to the avoidance of recidivism, good collaboration with the counsellor, and compliance with the conditions of supervision as imposed by the court. All these defining elements of success are correlated with a change in the supervised person's behaviour and the acquisition of a cooperative, prosocial attitude (IRO08; IRO01; IMD02; IMD03; IMD06; IMD07). An interesting perspective on the significance of the concept of a resolved case is one according to which this term includes the resolution of problems of the supervised person of which they are not themselves aware. Making clients accountable for their own problems, especially those of which they are unconscious, leads to a more efficient and rapid social integration of the person, reducing the risk of recidivism. If in other assistance-oriented professions the identification of the client's problems is carried out jointly with the client, the specificity of probation counselling may consist in making the person aware of the problems that led to the sanctioned antisocial behaviour, the assumption of responsibility, and the autonomous decision (the moral agency of the subject) to change. The involuntary character of the supervised person's participation in probation counselling creates a special situation related to the necessity of transforming the supervised person's mandatory compliance into a genuine *therapeutic alliance* between the counsellor and their client [152, p. 57–70]. Such an approach of medicalising the probation relationship after the model of psychological counselling [142, p. 203–214, 143, p. 21–24, 151, p. 832–847] transfers this relationship from the sphere of retributive supervision to the restorative co-construction of social equilibrium. Viewed in this way, probation counselling becomes a sociotherapy of social reintegration. Although the attitude of respondents (IRO04; IMD03) is somewhat paternalistic, discussing the identification and resolution by the counsellor of certain client problems, the reference is in fact to the co-construction of the subject's reintegration trajectory.

> *A resolved case would be if I manage to identify [resolve] some problems identified by me and not only by them. I give the example of drug use. They generally see that they have financial problems, but I also identify other problems. Somehow, if they are in the pre-contemplation stage, you cannot make the person aware, but through motivational interviewing and by calling them to meetings more frequently, I somehow make them — I do not force them — on their own to realise that I am offering them*

> *support, I give them institutions, I offer them my support, and somehow I help them to become aware that they have a problem and to resolve it during the supervision period. That seems to me a resolved case (IRO04).*

> *I consider that a case brought to a good conclusion is one where the convicted person no longer commits offences, no longer reoffends. We help them, we discuss, we guide them. We help them find accommodation in cases where they have no employment. We advise them where they can resolve their questions (IMD03).*

In attempting to respond to the question regarding the significance of the term "resolved case," respondents also refer to the specificity of other probation activities. From the perspective of the preparation of pre-sentence evaluations, for example, a resolved case is one in which the judge uses the respective evaluation in the individualisation of the sentence, taking into account the solution proposed by the counsellor.

> *Well, a resolved case, for example from the perspective of evaluation activity, means when the report that you have produced, that you have prepared, helps the judge in the application of the sentence. Some of the reports we prepare are cited in the judicial sentence, and then we consider it a well-made case, insofar as the judge has also accepted our proposal and idea as an evaluation, and when we see that the sentence applied by the judge coincides with what we supposed or suspected or estimated for the respective case (IRO07).*

Inter-institutional cooperation is considered essential for the successful resolution of cases under the supervision of probation counsellors (IRO08; IMD05). A particularly important aspect signalled by the respondent is the durability of results. It is not sufficient that, during the period of enforcement of the non-custodial sanction, the subject does not reoffend and does not violate the measures imposed by the court. It is important that a lasting prosocial attitude be constructed, so that the risk of recidivism is very low for the entire remainder of the supervised person's life. As such, the results obtained in probation must be lasting — they must be sustainable.

> *I relate to results; the results refer to the concrete changes that you observe in the beneficiary, and they are fewer now because the very large volume of work does not allow an adequate intervention for each beneficiary, and neither is the relationship what it should be [at present] [...] but over 15 years I have indeed had absolutely remarkable results — that is, changes that were almost unexpected, produced by very good feedback from beneficiaries, very powerful moments of awareness even during an evaluation interview, during a one- or two-hour meeting (IRO12).*

Another important dimension of the co-construction of probation practice is precisely the counsellor's relationship with the supervised person. Successful cases are those based on trust, in which a therapeutic alliance is formed that transforms supervision into a form of sociotherapy aimed at social reintegration. The experience of supervision becomes transformative for the beneficiary. The respondent indicates that, at the end of the supervision period, some beneficiaries express that they now consider the collaboration with the probation service as a stage of personal development, regarding the supervision period as a beneficial event in their life from the perspective of their own social integration. The transformation of the enforcement of punishment into the beneficiary's personal development removes probation as a social practice from the retributive sphere, placing it fully within the restorative domain. In this situation, the probation counsellor considers themselves an agent of change. A significant part of probation activity is seen as the exercise of motivational and transformational leadership vis-à-vis the supervised person. The idea of the learning team also transfers to the counsellor–supervised person relationship, with trust and good communication generating a genuine behavioural, attitudinal, and lifestyle and thinking change.

> *I believe that, as a probation counsellor, satisfaction lies in working with the beneficiary. When they come and say: "I have understood something," "look, I am finishing my supervision term," "I never imagined how important it was that the police caught me using drugs, but now, at the end of my supervision term, I realise how much I was wrong," "now I have completed a university degree," "I am an engineer," for example, "I am about to get married,"*

> *"the fact that I came here to you" for 4 years, or however long the supervision term was, "was for my personal development and it is very good that this happened to me." And then the satisfaction of the probation counsellor is that they motivated a person to change their life (IRO09).*

> *When a person who is under supervision has arrived on their own at the idea that they have certain problems and tries to resolve them on their own (IMD01).*

> *When, after committing the offence, the convicted person realises what they have done, feels regret, and has a different vision of life, a different interest, a different purpose. When they stop stealing and start working, start a family — even the one who has returned from the penitentiary and truly believes that this is it, life ends here — starts all over again and even changes their surname, remarries, no one knows about what they have committed, goes to another district and lives — in other words, starts everything from scratch. I consider that this is a good outcome (IMD05).*

Professional success

Professional success is seen in correlation with the number of resolved cases — defined strictly as supervised persons who have completed the supervision period, fulfilling the obligations imposed by the court and managing not to reoffend.

> *When the convicted person commits [an offence] once and no longer repeats it, and understands and says: "I have understood; I will strive in the future not to commit such offences again" (IMD04).*

A minimalist definition of success is the absence of complaints or grievances from supervised persons or from other institutions — courts, prosecution offices — or other professionals involved.

> *[...] And as long as there is no complaint against me, neither from the judge, nor from the prosecutors, nor from the supervised persons, then it means that I do my job responsibly (IRO04).*

Respondents underline the small number of cases that have reoffended or failed to comply with the obligations imposed by the court, actions that led to the revocation of the non-custodial measure and the incarceration of the person. The extremely low rate of recidivism among persons on probation is compared with the significantly higher rate of recidivism among persons who have served a custodial sentence (IRO04; FG). This difference, although among its explanations is the difference in the criminogenic profile of persons — at the level of statistical averages — who have undergone custodial and non-custodial sentences, clearly demonstrates the effectiveness of probation as an alternative system of sentence enforcement, as well as the individual success of the counsellors involved in case management. Indeed, the assessment of the risk of recidivism, and implicitly of the person's criminogenic profile, is a task of the probation counsellor within the framework of the pre-sentence evaluation.

> *[...] there are people who can be helped; now I do not have statistics, but as proof, from my cases I do not know if they have reoffended — out of 220 files I do not know if I have 3 or 4 files; the rest are integrated persons, they have families. So, practically, they maintain the same lifestyle — the family, the workplace — they are free and they also contribute to the expenses of the state (IRO04).*

> *[...] in almost one year, out of 400 files I have only 3 recidivists; I believe that our calling also plays a role in this fact (IMD05).*

Referring to the effectiveness of probation within the penal enforcement system, respondents indicate that, at the national level (Romania), 350 probation counsellors supervise over 40,000 cases, whereas in the penitentiary system, in which 12,000 detainees are incarcerated, 15,000 employees work. The savings in resources that the state achieves through the application of non-custodial sanctions are immense. Moreover, beyond the public material costs of operating a vast penitentiary apparatus, the generalisation of non-custodial sanctions leads to the avoidance of the social costs of incarceration (IRO11). Respondents insist on the role of the team in professional success. The team is united, the relationships among its members being characterised by mutual assistance and permanent cooperation. Cooperation within the team is complemented by hierarchical cooperation with representatives of the National Probation Directorate, on whose support respondents rely, in their capacity as managers of territorial services and as professionals (IRO09; IMD04).

> *I consider that these achievements could be fulfilled through teamwork, and now, both in the capacity of counsellor and in the capacity of head, I consider (...). I could not see myself as head of service in any other team than the one I am in now, and I could not (...) make the machinery run (...) if my colleagues did not help me. That is, if things work, it is because I am helped by this unitary whole that is the team (IRO09).*

The greatest achievement of respondents as probation counsellors

The majority of respondents indicate that their greatest professional achievement is linked to continuing development and the improvement of professional competencies.

> *[the greatest achievement as a probation counsellor] Involvement in programmes. It is a field that I appreciate very much, and I believe that in this area I have obtained some good results (IRO06).*

Respondents also highlight a personal, emotional dimension of professional success, which consists in the creation of a bond of trust between the probation counsellor and the supervised person. This bond, when maintained after the conclusion of the supervision term — even through the simple fact that the person who has exited supervision remembers the counsellor and greets them in the event of a chance encounter — is considered a personal success of the counsellor. The therapeutic alliance is thus validated, the former supervised person confirming that, beyond the strictly institutional relationship, there existed an interpersonal solidarity, within the limits of the obligations imposed by the supervision process. The simple gesture of greeting, and especially if it is continued with conversation after the conclusion of supervision, confirms to the counsellor that the supervised person perceived them also as a resource of support for change, and not merely as a jailer tasked with strictly verifying the enforcement of a criminal sentence.

The greatest achievement [is] that I have seen people I have worked with — I am referring to convicted persons who, after completing their supervision, have integrated and still remember me and greet me. That is, I considered that it was fine. Sometimes I still meet them and they ask me one thing or another. Yes, it is a great achievement (IRO08).

Our achievements — the successes of the convicted persons and as little recidivism as possible. 2. As close a collaboration as possible with the persons registered [with us]. When a person comes and has trust, and discusses more, and is much more open — I believe that this is very important (IMD06).

Moreover, one respondent considers not only that the normal relationship between counsellor and supervised person is one of collaboration, but that this is in fact the situation in the majority of cases administered in the probation system of the studied area. The effective and efficient relationship is considered a characteristic of the counsellor's professional activity. Once again, we note the professional optimism that probation counsellors display.

[...] the fact that at the end of the supervision period you see that the respective person has not committed any further offence, has found employment, has married, has children — so everything has followed a normal course — and at the end they tell me: "Madam, thank you — we had a very good relationship with you and everything was wonderful." I believe that this characterises my professional activity (IRO11).

Professional success is defined, on the other hand, in terms of participation and involvement in the development of the working methodology within the probation service. The fact that a counsellor, whether or not they also hold a leadership position in the system, can contribute to the methodological development of the services provided is considered a symbolic recognition of their own professionalism and, implicitly, of their professional prestige (IRO08). Success in the capacity of manager of probation services is linked to teamwork.

As a manager, I have managed, I would say, to keep my team more or less united; that we have very good collaboration with the institutions — and here it truly is a team effort, and people are very difficult at other institutions as well; that we have no complaints, no grievances, no dissatisfaction from people, even from people who have not behaved well (IRO08).

Motivation for practice and professional involvement

The optimism of the majority of Romanian respondents is explicable through the high degree of professional involvement. The motivation is intrinsic to probation activity, stemming from the specificity of the practice and the prestige it can bring to the professional. The high degree of motivation (IRO10) is considered by the respondent as a source for successfully overcoming the phenomenon of professional overloading. The capacity to cope with professional stress is considered by the respondent a constitutive dimension of the good professional in the field.

[...] the entire system is overburdened and the caseload far exceeds European standards, and if we were not good professionals we would have given up, and we probably would have sought an alternative, if we did not enjoy probation. As long as work continues beyond regular hours — it is, as I said, intense — but not by chance; the pace is very brisk, and if we were not professionals, no one would withstand this rhythm (IRO09).

Motivation produces a dynamism at the level of the work team, enabling them to carry out activities that exceed current tasks — activities oriented towards the development of the service and of probation in general.

I have managed to have an extremely motivated team, committed to doing other things besides current activities — such as European projects, programmes that we implement with our beneficiaries — so we are an extremely united team (IRO10).

2.2.4. Dilemmas and professional problems in probation practice

A number of respondents also noted the existence of problems that probation counsellors encounter in practice. In general, the problems relate to the overburdening of tasks assigned to them.

The professional overloading of probation counsellors as a source of disappointment

The disappointment generated by the failure to resolve problems relating to overloading erodes the enthusiasm and motivation for practice. Although these remain high, respondents indicate that disappointment with working conditions is beginning to appear — a fact that could redirect the attention of professionals towards other fields. Significant with regard to this possible shift in motivational status and career decisions is the professional status attributed by other professionals — how much probation work actually matters to others.

> *I have been here for 2 years; I am relatively new in the system. I came with enthusiasm, I came with the hope that we could bring about changes in the thinking of supervised persons, I came with fresh energy. Unfortunately, we are beginning to be disappointed with the conditions offered to us, and we wonder whether we should not perhaps go elsewhere, where what we do would also matter to others (IRO05).*

> *I have up to 120 persons under my management. We do not have sufficient staff; most of them leave (IMD12).*

Respondents draw attention to the fact that professional overloading risks transforming probation counsellors into mere civil servants, with effective time for communication with evaluated or supervised persons being absent. Yet it is precisely the inter-human dimension that is seen as fundamental to probation practice. The degree of professional loading far exceeds European standards.

> *The schedule is restructured differently [...] when you have hundreds of files, when you end up being a mere civil servant, when you no longer have time to work with the person, to work on a programme with the person, to work on changing their behavioural attitude (IRO08).*

Additionally, respondents from the Republic of Moldova indicate that low salaries constitute a source of dissatisfaction and a lack of professional motivation on the part of counsellors.

> *The salary, first of all, is very low and the volume of work is very large. For example, in the districts it is different — there, yes, work gets done, they manage, they have fewer persons under their management — and here, being in the capital, you can no longer manage to run around, to look for them (IMD12).*

The lack of involvement of state institutions in the social reintegration of offenders

Another source of dissatisfaction highlighted by Romanian respondents is the lack of support from state institutions for the social reintegration of persons under supervision. The desirable support would be the creation of a framework in which, for example, professional training programmes could be conducted for persons who have committed criminal offences and who lack education. Enrolling them in such courses, especially for those who have no professional qualification whatsoever, can constitute a powerful form of societal support, diminishing criminogenic risk and discouraging the choice of illegitimate career opportunities.

> *And the state does not come, as in other European legislations, to help the convicted person — for example, a facility for employment, a facility for a qualification course — because many in our case, for example, have no education, even if you want to help them (IRO06).*

The same lack of state involvement partially transpires from the discourse of Moldavian respondents, though it is not formulated explicitly. We attribute the absence of this mention to the fear that some Moldavian respondents expressed — that, should they formulate criticisms of the system, they could lose their jobs. Discrepancies were signalled between the various applicable normative frameworks. For example, it is specified that, through the criminal sentence, some persons under supervision are required to attend qualification courses. This is, however, impossible if the person has not completed the 8 compulsory school years, which in some situations leads to difficulties, or even to the impossibility of enforcing the measure imposed through the criminal sentence.

[...] many sentences come with the obligation for convicted persons to attend a qualification course; [but] how can they attend a course if the law states that without a minimum of eight years of schooling you cannot attend an employment course? And in our case, approximately 80% are without those 8 years of schooling, and so you are somewhat blocked by your own legislation (IRO08).

Some respondents draw attention to systemic deviations from what was expected of the probation system in the early stages of its implementation. The expectations of professionals who have been in the system since the beginning of the practice in Romania point towards a practice system centred on working with people, oriented towards the social rehabilitation of the offender, rather than the mere — bureaucratic — supervision of the enforcement of sanctions. For probation to constitute an agent of change, respondents consider that time and specific instruments based on communication are needed.

Probation is no longer what we wanted it to be, and it is heading in that direction. But if those who lead us do not ultimately understand that the person is important — returning them to society. You no longer supervise a ton of offenders, who in any case will commit or not commit the offence if they want to; [...] my role is in fact to produce change; to produce change I need time, I need instruments — [but] I cannot create the instruments myself. I am not allowed, for example, to collaborate with institutions that are not accredited. I am not allowed to effectively implement empowerment programmes if they are not accredited by my directorate, and if those there produce this thing and I do not have the necessary time, I do not have the necessary space, my work amounts to what a clerk does — I come in nicely, do my formal paperwork, and that is essentially my work (IRO08).

Respondents insist on the discrepancies between the conditions of probation practice in the countries from which the current normative framework was adopted — the United Kingdom, Norway — and the Romanian framework within which the practice takes place. The reform of the probation system should have been accompanied by a modification of the frameworks for the practice of the profession, including the resources — especially human resources — involved in the functioning of probation services.

> *I do not believe they are necessarily favourable [the adoptions from other legislations], because when good practices were imported, the background from those countries was not also adopted, and I refer here to the fact that, from the entry into force of the Criminal Codes and related laws in 2014 until the present, the corresponding background has not been ensured. That is, I believe that somewhere we have far fewer resources than the countries from which the practice models were imported (IRO09).*

The dominant retributive mentality at the level of Romanian society

Another obstacle confronted by professionals is the Romanian mentality of social rejection of persons who have suffered convictions for criminal offences. Romanian society at the present time is quite vindictive, the commission of a criminal offence leading to the almost automatic social exclusion of the person. It is signalled that certain reform measures in the probation system are adopted from the legislation of other states without being coherent with the specifically Romanian mentality and without being practically adequate to the needs of the Romanian penal system. There thus exists the risk of transforming probation into a new bureaucracy of the type described as *forms without substance* [192].

> *In order to implement what the English, the French, or other peoples have implemented over years and have arrived at something concrete, [an open mentality is necessary]. Practically, a system was taken and applied in Romania without being realistic [adequate] for the Romanian system (IRO08).*

Another criticised situation is the lack of public visibility of probation as a social practice. The measure of conviction with suspension, for example, is widely known to the public, but not the institution responsible for carrying out the sentence, and especially not the philosophy behind probation — the reasons why non-custodial measures are more effective from the perspective of the social reintegration of the offender, the risk of recidivism, the avoidance of stigmatisation, and deviant re-socialisation in the prison environment. The fact that some respondents complain about the lack of public visibility of the profession does not contradict what was identified previously regarding professional prestige. This prestige comes above all from the profession's belonging to the penal enforcement system, which itself enjoys prestige. But the visibility of probation within the penal enforcement system is considered deficient. Some respondents draw attention to the fact that the obligation of confidentiality constitutes an impediment to the public visibility of the profession. At the present time, public figures are serving non-custodial sentences, including politicians — serving senators and members of parliament from whom the right to hold a position of public dignity was not withdrawn by sentence. In such cases, greater visibility of the Probation Services would implicitly bring to the attention of the mass media the presence of public figures as supervised persons, which would constitute a breach of confidentiality and an undesirable exposure with discriminatory consequences (FG).

> *It is frustrating for us that when suspension is discussed, no one says what happened during that period of suspension. Sir, that person is not just suspended like that; they do not remain suspended in a void. Yes, they go to an institution; there is an institution that has responsibilities and obligations; that person has things to do; they must perform community service work; there is a counsellor who carries out an evaluation. There is someone who goes and checks every day — paperwork at the police, and goes into the field (IRO11).*

Other respondents nuance their view regarding the public recognition of the profession, showing that it is on an ascending path but can be improved. The Romanian mentality centred on punishment and its exemplary character is underlined. The public mentality regarding punishment places emphasis on the severity of the sanction and the control of sanctioned persons, without taking into account the dimension of social integration and the social rehabilitation of offenders. This situation is set against a background in which the public perception primarily envisages a corrupt political milieu, marked by incompetence and clientelism.

> *The disappointment that all probation counsellors across the country share is that we have not been recognised at our true value, not even now — or let us say that now we have a beginning of recognition. [...] we have*

not been sufficiently supported, because the Romanian mentality is very focused on punishment, control, and less on the idea of reintegration, which is poorly understood, and on the fact that in our country the political climate is marked by incompetence, corruption, and interests that do not refer to the interest of the community but to personal interest. [Probation] Presupposes very complex work, unrecognised and unrespected (IRO12).

Critical experiences in the exercise of the profession

There were not very many expressions of negative experiences in professional practice relative to the success experiences of probation counsellors. The disappointments mentioned — regarding the high volume of work, the excessive bureaucratisation of practice, and the relative lack of visibility of the profession — are nonetheless kept within moderate limits.

I have not had great disappointments (IRO06).

Respect for the activity of probation counsellors is a sensitive point, inasmuch as this activity, especially in its restorative dimension, enters somewhat into contradiction with the ideas existing in the public mentality regarding persons who have suffered criminal convictions. The respondent underlines the incompleteness of the legislation, which is in the process of being refined.

[...] we need to change mentalities first of all. Because if you go to an institution to take that person to work, they tell us: "Why are you coddling them?" We are not coddling them, but even the judge only individualises the case; [...] So somehow, mentalities should be changed and support should be ensured for us first of all. We have a legislation that is not yet finished (IRO04).

A number of dysfunctions were highlighted in connection with the functioning of the probation service as an institution for the enforcement of criminal sentences. Although the average dangerousness of persons sentenced with suspension is lower than that of those serving custodial sentences, the profession of probation counsellor remains one with a high degree of danger. Under these conditions, respondents consider it unacceptable that there is no specialised security whatsoever, or control at the entrance to the institution.

We do not have a gendarme because it is not written in some document or other, even though we are a state system and we are not a greengrocer's — we do not sell doughnuts and tomatoes. We work with persons who have committed offences; granted, 10% have a very high risk level, but I know one of those who does not have a very high risk level — today he comes frustrated and angry, something happened to him on the way, and he comes here very angry, and he does not like what I am telling him, or he does not like my face today, and he grabs me by the throat. Can I prevent such behaviour? Do I have a panic button somewhere? Does anyone search him at the entrance to our premises to see whether he might have a weapon? (IRO11).

Among the causes of professional disappointment is also the attitude of supervised persons.

These [disappointments] come from the persons of whom I have higher expectations, who have a certain level of understanding and who do not comply with the measures (IRO04).

Inter-institutional cooperation represents another source of professional dissatisfaction for probation counsellors.

I am struggling with a person who has to perform community service work, and I have some difficulties in obtaining a medical certificate to attest whether or not they are fit (IRO06).

Even in situations where the performance of community service work is mandatory and community institutions sign protocols with the probation service, difficulties continue to exist in the assumption of supervised persons for the performance of community service work or of other imposed community sanctions.

Non-custodial sentences have been given as much as possible in accordance with European legislation. [...] I want to integrate the person; very many persons come, but I do not have the necessary levers, I do not have the necessary collaborations, because signing a protocol does not mean that you [effectively] collaborate with the respective institution. They encounter certain legislation, a certain budget. [...] I want to employ persons, and then I encounter the mentality of the Romanian who does not want to hire such persons. [There is] reluctance to find a solution for this category of persons — [since] we want them to attend school; but at the school we were told that they do not want juvenile offenders in school. Well, wait — there is still an anti-discrimination law; if I notify the anti-discrimination office, you as a school will have very serious problems (IRO08).

The degree of professional loading (with tasks) of probation counsellors

A leitmotif of the interviews with probation counsellors is the exposition of problems raised by the degree of professional task loading. The number of cases per counsellor exceeds 150, with situations of loading with over 250 cases also existing, according to the respondent's statements. We will not dwell on the responses in this category, as the implications of this professional overloading have already been discussed above. We will merely reproduce a few of the respondents' statements that clarify their perception of this degree of loading. Adopting a constructionist approach, we will trace the significance that professionals ascribe to the high degree of case loading — namely, the increased risk of human error with a negative effect on the quality of the counselling and supervision process, especially in its subjective dimension.

At this moment I have 182 files and participation as a counsellor in the conditional release committees at penitentiary units (IRO01).

Now I believe I have somewhere around 260–270 cases [cases in progress] (IRO06).

In supervision I have 105 cases, and as for reports, from the beginning of the year until now I have prepared 5 evaluation reports. I have participated in the conditional release committees at the penitentiary (IRO07).

2.3. Thematic Axis III. The Probation Officer–Supervised Person Relationship

2.3.1. The Specificity of the Probation Officer–Supervised Person Relationship

The relationship between the probation officer and the client is considered to be one of trust and assistance, grounded in the fact that the supervised person recognises the effective help provided by the officer, while the latter observes the beneficiary fulfilling the obligations imposed by the court.

> *As long as the person sees that they benefit from my help, a relationship of trust and mutual assistance is established. I have trust when I see that they respect the measures and take steps in that direction, and they, simply by seeing that they need my legal help—because that is all I can offer—or that they benefit from an institution's assistance. And the fact that they see they are being helped and are treated as a person and not as a convict, that matters enormously to them (IRO04).*

A certain reluctance on the part of supervised persons regarding participation in rehabilitation programmes is noted, motivated by a lack of information about the meaning and utility of such programmes. Nevertheless, the respondent—a probation officer—indicates that some of those under supervision ultimately express satisfaction with the programmes they have attended.

> *At first, some of them display a certain reluctance because the notion of a programme is somewhat unfamiliar to them. They do not know exactly what they are getting into when they are about to follow a programme. The beginning is harder, but afterwards they come to feel so good in some of the programmes that some of them—not all—regret that it has ended and would like to continue further (IRO06).*

The respondent notes that, in the course of working with supervised persons through reintegration programmes, surprises may emerge on the part of the beneficiaries. An instance is described in which a person, despite coming from an anomic environment, participates in rehabilitation programmes with openness, involvement, and a desire for knowledge and self-knowledge.

> *Yes. Right now I am working on a one-to-one programme, as an obligation imposed by the court. It is a person who has surprised me in a positive way. Why? Because I have observed that she has very good potential. Unfortunately, she grew up in a less than beneficial family environment, and yet she has a willingness to learn, to discover new things, to acquire new information. I notice that she has a very good capacity to make connections between pieces of information, and I often realise how much influence the family environment can have on a person's development. And she surprises me positively every time; whenever she comes to the programme with a rather low level, she nonetheless shows great openness towards learning, knowing, recovering, and evolving. It is one case, but there are others as well (IRO06).*

Analysing the nature of their own relationship with supervised persons, the respondent—a probation officer—considers it a professional one, based on empathy, understanding of the context of the offence, and the absence of any evaluative judgement regarding the supervised person and their actions. The officer–supervised person relationship is symmetrical, with the officer regarding the individual as an equal. Central to the relationship are the objectives aimed at the offender's reintegration into society. The moment when the offender becomes aware that all the probation officer's actions are carried out in the interest of the supervised person constitutes a moment of professional satisfaction for the officer.

> *My relationship with the persons under supervision is a professional one, in the sense that I understand the criminogenic needs of the persons under supervision, I try to understand the criminal context in which the offence was committed, and I do not judge in any way. I try to maintain an equidistant relationship, so that it is neither one of closeness nor one of defiance. I consider the person an equal, in a way, and I try to have a relationship based strictly on focusing on certain objectives. And our objectives are reintegration into society. The more they understand that everything we do is for their benefit, that is a moment of satisfaction for the Probation Officer as well (IRO01).*

Respondents consider communication to be the key element of the relationship with supervised persons. Communication must transcend any labelling or resentment regarding the offences for which the person was convicted.

> *I try to cope with the situation at the moment. Before, I would have said that I try to form as accurate a picture as possible of the person's situation, beyond the personal, beyond the circumstantial, because by understanding the person you can also communicate differently with them. Regardless of what they have done, regardless of how they ended up with you, if you fail to open a channel of communication, you achieve nothing (IRO02).*

The respondent emphasises the importance of communication in the implementation of probation, bringing into discussion intercultural communication—with reference to communication with members of Roma communities. Their cultural particularities are described as manifesting a reserve towards communication with persons outside the community, a high degree of adherence to community values, and group unity. The lack of communication skills may entail a series of professional risks, including provoking violent reactions from interlocutors.

> *I think that, just as I have said for myself, one should communicate well with the people one has on record, communicate well with those one meets in the field. We also go into Roma communities, where—without any snobbery, racism, or anything that could be considered as such—they have their own culture, they are very reserved, very united, and when you go to talk to a family, you find yourself surrounded by an entire community. And then, if you do not know how to communicate with them, they can very easily feel offended, and you may feel threatened, in a certain sense endangered. It has happened; if you know how to manage the situation well, fine—if not, you risk leaving in a compromised position; it happens (IRO02).*

The planning of communication is based on a certain degree of empathy, described by the respondent as a sound evaluation of the person and an estimation of the communication style appropriate to each interlocutor.

> *(improving communication with supervised persons) To evaluate the person very well. That way, I believe, you can better estimate how you can communicate with them. To communicate with each one as required (IRO02).*

The ethical and behavioural values necessary for a good relationship with supervised persons are sincerity and consistency. In their absence, the chances of a successful intervention are considered null.

> *Consistency, sincerity. If you are not sincere, you have no chance (IRO02).*

Respondents consider particular communication competencies to be necessary when the officer addresses sensitive topics, especially in dialogue with offenders convicted of violent offences.

> *If I may mention here, there are persons under supervision who have committed violent offences or offences of a sexual nature, and here there is a very wide range of offences, and these persons must be approached with a certain strategy when speaking with them. And you have to be somewhat prepared for that; you cannot just anyhow and at any time address delicate subjects (IRO03).*

Describing her own relationship with supervised persons, the respondent indicates that it is based on mutual respect, equality in the interpersonal relationship, assertiveness, and empathy. In the course of the counselling process, the officer seeks to motivate the beneficiaries to adhere to the required measures, to become aware of the offence committed and its consequences. The effectiveness of the helping relationship in probation stems solely from the existence of the supervised person's need for change; in its absence, the intervention is virtually futile.

> *It depends on the sentence, because I want to bring all the cases I have to a successful conclusion. The risk of recidivism in cases has increased compared to previous years, but I monitor, so I try, through the interview I conduct with the person, to motivate them, to seek all sorts of barriers to prevent them from committing offences in the future, and I rely very much on the communication relationship. If a relationship of communication and trust*

> *is established—I never treat them... I am the officer and you are... There is respect, and somehow I treat them as equals. I am assertive with them so that I can get closer, and then they communicate much better when they see that they are being helped. And here there is a trap, because sometimes you help too much and they no longer know how to make decisions on their own. That happened to me at the beginning; now I only channel my energy towards persons who are in the contemplation stage—that is, when they become aware that they have a problem. So those who want to be helped, I help; those who do not, I cannot help. All motivation starts from within (IRO04).*

Another respondent highlights the primacy of compliance with the law in their activity. Their relationship with supervised persons is one of respect and equality—in the sense of symmetrising the relationship—with beneficiaries, but only in the context of reciprocated respect. Regardless of the supervised person's level of education, their rights must be respected, without emotional involvement, especially of a negative nature. The relationship is maintained within professional limits, without being transformed into one of camaraderie or friendship.

> *I am a person who, first of all, respects the legislation. But I am also a person who behaves well, respectfully; I impose certain... That is, I have certain expectations: if I respect you and treat you as an equal, I expect the same from you. But there are also people who have no education or who speak in a different dialect, and even if I am at maximum capacity that day, with the persons in front of me I respect their rights and try to control any impulse, even though I am an impulsive person; I go and vent elsewhere, and nothing can be read on my face. I effectively do my job and try to respect the deadlines imposed by judges, not to deviate. You see how it is now, you have to be very careful about who you talk to, what you say, how you say it, because things get interpreted. It is an officer–supervised person relationship and nothing more; we are not friends, not comrades, or anything else (IRO04).*

Conversely, in the relationship with supervised minors, the respondent adopts a friendly attitude, on the condition that the obligations imposed by the court are respected. An open, communicative attitude combined with an authoritative one only when necessary is far more effective than a formal authoritarian posture.

> *I like to tell the minors that I am a sort of second mother to them. I come down to their level; I am a friendly person and they relax much more, and they are more likely to come if you are authoritarian—because indeed I am also authoritative when it is called for—but rather, a sweet word brings much. I even tell them: 'I can also be your friend, but at the same time, respect the obligations imposed by the court' (IRO04).*

Mutual respect in the officer–supervised person relationship is a priority for several respondents—probation officers. Other ingredients of the officer–offender relationship include trust, empathy, sincerity, and the officer's commitment to what they communicate to the supervised person.

> *(The relationship with beneficiaries) It is based on mutual respect. I try not to disappoint them, in the sense that if I have said something, I take responsibility for what I have said. I try to have all the facts of the matter, in the sense of not promising something I cannot subsequently deliver (IRO05).*

Empathy should not be merely formal but genuine; the officer should not merely pretend to understand the offender but should truly understand them. Empathy must be conveyed to the beneficiaries, who must be able to perceive it in the officer.

> *I put myself in their shoes, I empathise with them, I give the impression that I understand their situation—and I do not merely give the impression but actually try to understand the situation they are in (IRO06).*

The construction of the officer–supervised person relationship is achieved gradually, on the basis of trust. Trust rests on the results progressively obtained by the beneficiary in implementing the imposed measures and in changing their behaviour. Trust is also founded on confidentiality, which creates a safe environment for the beneficiary.

> *There is a principle of confidentiality that we must respect. We bring it to the beneficiary's attention from the very beginning, and this creates a sense of security; subsequently, this state of mutual trust is built. It is built gradually through the interventions that occur along the way, through the fact that we come to accustom ourselves to one another, through the fact that the person also sees that they have achieved or made certain accomplishments on a personal level. So I believe these things are built over time (IRO06).*

The importance of confidentiality in the relationship between the officer and the supervised person is also underlined by respondents from among the latter: *What we discuss stays right here (IBM5)*

A good probation officer–supervised person relationship is also viewed from the perspective of thorough and complete information of the offender regarding the officer's expectations. The imposition of authority is also an ingredient of an effective probation relationship when supervised persons are more recalcitrant.

> *In general, it is a good relationship (the relationship with persons under supervision), in the sense that I try to speak kindly with them, to give them the right information, so that they do not leave unclear about things, so that they know the consequences of their behaviour and the extent of my professional and human limit in that relationship. There are also situations—I do not know if you have heard of the good cop–bad cop approach. There are colleagues who have more recalcitrant persons under supervision, who do not understand, who are more aggressive, and then one thing is for the gendarme to intervene—because that also happens—but then the idea of imposing authority arises (IRO08).*

Also important is the establishment of the limits of communication. A communication standard exists for both the evaluation stage and the intervention stage. In their capacity as case managers, officers oscillate between the minimum and maximum of communication. Unlike other respondents, officer IRO08 expresses distrust in the importance and even the possibility of empathy in the relationship with beneficiaries—persons under supervision. Instead of a relationship based on empathy, the respondent proposes one based on assertiveness, grounded in authority, with the officer as the representative of the state. The helping relationship is one of respect, based on the clear establishment of boundaries.

> *I do not discuss more than what needs to be discussed. We have a standard for talking to a person during evaluation, for each interview. The officers under me, being also case managers, each oscillates between the minimum and maximum so as not to be exhausting; but otherwise, you have to be a little assertive. I do not believe in empathy, but you have to be a little assertive; you have to see the person's situation, but you must always remind the person, very carefully, that you are the authority, that you represent the state, and the counselling operates within this limit, in the sense of: 'I help you, we talk, but we respect each other'; we do not become chums, we are not friends—I have to report to the judge what you do. Because ultimately, if I determine that you are in violation, I send you to court, or I give you one more chance, depending on your behaviour. And so you do not shout, you do not yell, but you must know exactly how to establish the boundary (IRO08).*

2.3.2. Case Management Between Supervision and Counselling

Each probation officer is designated as the case manager for the persons under their supervision, being the one who establishes the objectives and intervention strategies within the limits of the law and the conditions imposed by the court.

> *In general, in my files, I am the case manager, but I always respect the legislation in force. In a way, I am autonomous, but I am also responsible at the same time. After all, I comply with sentences imposed by the court; I do not decide—the judge decides—only I manage my own case file (IRO04).*

The key to case management in probation lies in compliance with the law. Only in this context can the counselling relationship become an assistential one, a helping relationship. The support offered by the probation officer consists of mediating access to resources—primarily informational ones—that the supervised person needs for the reconstruction of their social integration. For example, the officer provides information regarding the rights to which the person is entitled, the institutions they need to contact to obtain them, how to approach these institutions, how to draft a request, and so on. The sole necessary condition for supervised persons to benefit from the probation officer's assistance is to request it, and for the request to be within the bounds of the law.

> *We comply with the legislation in force. We are the persons who help people after they go through a trial phase that is quite costly—and you can imagine, being in a courtroom where you have to present your offence, the issue is not exactly easy. The fact that they come here—they see this as support on our part. And I consider that, having reached us, they are more helped than other persons who have not committed offences. I, for example, have a law degree, and I recognise that I have more skills on that side, and so everything related to legal matters—drafting an appeal, institutions to contact—they learn from us. They need support: how to pay the expenses, where they can file a request, how to draft a request—so they benefit from our support. They only need to ask for help. That is, I cannot offer to someone who does not want to be helped. And we comply with the legislation in force—that is clear (IRO04).*

Time management is considered extremely important, especially under conditions of overwork. Thus, although documenting all of the officers' actions is necessary—which requires the production of a large number of documents—this activity is time-consuming, both for the officer and for the courts.

> *Well, first of all, I myself look for all sorts of documents, papers, so that my efforts are visible, but somehow my activity has to be monitored somewhere, because we too are inspected in turn. But given that there are very many cases, we have to practice time management. So somehow I strive to give them the necessary attention*

> *while also leaving room for another colleague of mine—because you can see how we carry out our activity—especially since we also overburden the courts (IRO04).*

Activity planning and time management by the probation officer are essential for the efficiency of their work. In the first part of the day, the respondent schedules the most demanding interviews, usually the initial interviews with newly supervised persons. At these first interviews, an initial assessment is carried out, and the supervised person is informed of the measures, obligations, and restrictions they must respect, while the relevant restrictions are communicated to other institutions in the community. In the second part of the day, meetings are planned with persons who have been under supervision for a longer period and who have acquired a certain degree of social autonomy and moral agency, making the interviews less difficult.

> *In general, in the first part of the day I conduct the first interviews. This means I have to carry out an initial assessment for each person. Normally, I used to have one person per day. Now I see as many as three. At a first interview, you have to inform the person of the measures, obligations; if there are restrictions, you have to make sure you send the relevant notifications in time—such as to the border authorities, to Interpol, all sorts of things. That is, it is very demanding. And in the second part of the day, I see the persons who already know me, and the interviews are no longer as demanding. Only if situations arise, such as I have today, for example—a case in which a young woman committed a violation during the probation period, and here there is much to discuss because she is at risk (IRO04).*

Time management and the officer's availability are adapted as much as possible to the needs of the supervised person, to their engagement in communication, and so forth. The respondent notes that this practice of allocating time resources according to beneficiaries' needs contrasts with the practice in other probation systems, where the time budget is standardised and calculated in advance.

> *We discuss at interviews; there are the pre-established interviews, and I am at their disposal for as*

long as necessary. That is, I do not have a rigid time limit. I have seen this with foreign practitioners—the time they allocate. And we have this time and we discuss. It is an adaptation of time according to the person I am talking to, because there are persons who open up with more difficulty, and there are persons who are more communicative. And so I adapt my availability according to the other person (IRO09).

The professional relationship is described as involving two facets: one of monitoring and control of the implementation of the sanctions and measures proposed by the court, and another of support and counselling. Decisions concerning case management are made together with the beneficiary, as much as possible.

A professional relationship, and when I say this I refer to a relationship that involves both a monitoring and control component and a support component. Although it might seem, or it might be said, that the Probation Service focuses primarily on the control aspect—that might perhaps be said from the outside—we offer, at least I in my work with the persons who are our beneficiaries, this possibility of expression. I discuss with them before making a decision; I see, analyse, and evaluate each person's situation, and we make decisions together (IRO06).

A strategy for working with more difficult beneficiaries involves appealing to the authority of the head of the probation service—a kind of good cop–bad cop strategy. Generally, collaboration with the supervised person is achieved solely on the basis of good communication and the clear transmission of instructions.

When the officer often cannot manage such a situation, they call me in, knowing that I see things differently, not knowing the person—not exactly harsher, but more authoritative. I try to tell them what the situation is, and then there arises the scenario in which the officer is the one who also supports the person, but the supervisor comes and says: 'Look, my supervisor says this; I have told you so many times to do this, but you have not done it, and I can send you to court. Look, my supervisor told you very clearly; he has also given you

> *one more chance, but things are not going to change.' Yes, I do have situations of this kind, in which I am the bad cop. But I do not shout at them, I do not yell at them, I do not behave badly with them; on the contrary, I have more patience with them, and people come and ask me, 'but what do I do here?, but how do I do this?'—and ten times over. It is tiring at a certain point, but after all, we work with people. At some point, someone you know might come in, and you cannot not speak kindly with them (IRO08).*
>
> *An important activity is the assistance and counselling activity, because when the premises exist for a negative development—a recidivism more concretely, or a violation by the persons on my record—of the judicial decision, or the commission of new offences, it is very important for bringing the case to a successful conclusion and achieving the objective to have a targeted, concrete, case-specific intervention in assistance and counselling, through programmes or individual intervention, individual counselling (IRO07).*

A professional virtue of the probation officer is patience. Asking open-ended questions allows the beneficiary to open up to the officer and recount the experiences they went through at the time of committing the offence and prior to it. The supervised person's accounts must be cross-checked with data obtained from other sources, in order to avoid potential manipulation that the beneficiary may attempt. Time management is also a component of case management in probation practice.

> *Many of the supervised persons speak with great difficulty, are very closed off, do not want to relive certain moments, do not remember. You have to be patient. Ask open-ended questions. See where you can press further, press; where you cannot, do not. You must always have information so that you do not allow yourself to be manipulated by that person, because there are persons who manipulate very easily verbally. The tone must be appropriate. And I try to practise time management (IRO08).*

A situation that probation officers face is the supervised person's misunderstanding of the specifics of a suspended sentence under current legislation, whereby the supervised person must report to the officer at a set interval, respecting a series of measures. Supervised persons confuse conditional liberty with the absence of any constraint, sometimes being advised in this direction by their lawyers. The role of the officer, at least during the first meetings with the supervised person, is to explain these measures and to make them aware of the obligations incumbent upon them.

> *Lawyers tell them: 'Oh, you have supervision, do not worry, from now on you are free.' And many come here with this idea: 'But my lawyer told me I am free—why do I have to report that I am leaving for more than five days? Or why do I have to bring documents here? The judge told me I am free now; I can do whatever I want.' And you try: 'Hold on, sir, it is not like that'—you have to comply, you have to bring documents, you have to do things, you have to do community service; you gave your consent (IRO09).*

The same issue is raised by respondent IRO11, who shows that it falls to the probation officer to explain the sentence the supervised person must serve and to motivate them to comply with the measures required by the court.

> *And you, as a probation officer, have to sit and explain and motivate the person, so that they accept their sentence. This is more difficult, and here there is a great deal of work, because the person comes in with the impression: 'Yes, I am free.' Yes, but you are not quite free—you have certain obligations to fulfil. And that is why it is hard work (IRO11).*

It also falls to the probation officer to verify the fulfilment of the accessory obligations imposed by the court and the civil obligations imposed by the sentence of conviction, as well as the good faith of the supervised person in fulfilling these obligations. For example, the officer must verify whether the house in which the beneficiary resides is their property and can be legally capitalised upon for the payment of damages and other expenses imposed by the court, or whether they merely reside there while the property belongs to someone else. In order to verify the ownership status of the person's assets, in the absence of documentary evidence, the officer must contact various other institutions to confirm the supervised person's financial situation.

> *They tell me they do not have a house—OK, I can believe the house is not theirs but their mother's, and they have no means to pay because the house is their mother's. I, as a probation officer, have the obligation, six months before the end of the supervision period, to inform the person who has civil obligations to pay that they must pay them; three months before, I must notify the judge whether or not they have paid. If they have not, I must verify good or bad faith. How am I, a probation officer, to know, if the person in question does not bring me documentary proof that the apartment is or is not theirs, or belongs to the mother, or the father, or...? I have to verify somehow. And rather than sending formal requests and waiting for them to respond—thirty days maximum for a reply—is it not simpler for me to go online, click, and verify? Yes, sir, look, they have a house in their name; they should have capitalised on it, given that they know they have to pay, because civil obligations are civil obligations (IRO11).*

In the event that the supervised person does not cooperate with the probation officer and does not comply with the imposed measures, including the non-payment of civil obligations, the court may revoke the supervision measure.

> *The court can revoke the supervision; it can revoke the deferral of the application of the sentence for non-payment of civil obligations, even if you came in calmly for two years of supervision. Otherwise, I have no way of verifying the person's good or bad faith (IRO11).*

The management of a supervision case involves several stages and the application of specific methodologies for each stage: notifications and summonses in the initial stage, the initial interview, the supervision plan, communicating the measures and obligations imposed by the court to the supervised person, requesting documents and information for estimating the risk of recidivism, subsequently applying measures to monitor the degree to which the supervised person complies with the court-imposed obligations, and cooperating with various community institutions for the implementation of measures and the monitoring of obligation fulfilment. In subsequent stages, systematic meetings with the supervised person take place, during which the implementation of measures is monitored and actual sociotherapeutic work is carried out. If the person does not comply with the imposed measures, reports are filed with the court, which may even lead to the revocation of the non-custodial measure. If everything has proceeded well, the obligations have been fulfilled, and recidivism has not occurred, a series of case-closure reports are prepared.

> *A supervision case. From the moment such a case is assigned to you, notifications are made to summon the person to the office of the service; subsequently, a first interview is conducted with the person, the supervision plan is drawn up, the person is informed of the manner in which supervision will be carried out, of the measures and obligations established by the court; subsequently, documents and certain information are requested to estimate the degree of recidivism risk. Then, all sorts of steps are taken to see whether the person complies with the measures and obligations imposed by the court. Collaboration takes place with the police, town halls, and other institutions, in order for the person to perform community service or fulfil whatever other obligation the court has imposed. There are periodic interviews with the person, during which their socio familial situation and behaviour are constantly monitored; we try to have a clear picture of the risk they present of committing further offences. In the event that they do not comply with the measures and obligations, self-referral reports are drafted to notify the court of the violations committed by the person. The payment of the civil obligations imposed on the supervised person is also monitored. And if everything is in order, we conclude the supervision process at the end of the supervision period and the final reports are prepared (IRO05).*

2.3.3. Stages of the Probation Officer–Supervised Person Relationship

Regarding the evolution of the officer–supervised person relationship, it passes through different stages depending on the depth of the offender's assumption of responsibility. In the initial stages following conviction, the offender accuses those around them for their actions, projecting blame onto society. Gradually, they partially assume responsibility for what they have done. In this way, the probation officer–offender relationship also deepens.

> *Let us take, for example, a person who is at the beginning and accuses everyone—everyone is guilty—and as you work with that person, they come to realise that part of the fault is also theirs, and not just the society from which they come (IRO05).*

Another periodisation of the officer–supervised person relationship is presented by respondent IRO06. They indicate that the first stage is an evaluative one, which may last several sessions. At the beginning, the officer forms a general picture of the supervised person. For a more accurate evaluation, the officer allows the supervised person a certain degree of freedom of expression, consisting in a lack of strictness regarding the time at which the person must report to the officer, regarding the timely submission of certain documents, and so forth. In this way, the respondent observes the beneficiary's behaviour and the degree of responsibility they manifest on a day-to-day basis. After the evaluation phase, the approach towards the beneficiary becomes stricter, in order to make them aware of the obligations incumbent upon them, and together with the internalisation of these obligations, a process of responsibilisation emerges.

> *Well, in general, my relationship with people differs. In the initial stage, while I am still evaluating the person's behaviour, I personally cannot evaluate them after just one meeting—totally and definitively. Of course, I form an image of them, but the evaluation for me extends over about two or three meetings. And when I evaluate them, I give them the freedom to behave naturally so that I can assess them. I am not very strict about the time they should arrive, and that in itself means something to me—that is, I see whether they can respect the time without my*

> *telling them, or whether they cannot respect it even when I do tell them; that means something. The same with bringing certain documents within the legal timeframe. Of course, if the law says thirty days, I will tell them fewer days, and some manage well within thirty, but I see how quickly they react, what kind of documents they bring, and so on. After the evaluation phase in which I let them behave freely, I approach them much more strictly, because otherwise they get used to it, and if I lose control, they no longer understand whether it is mandatory or not; they may consider that everything is permitted, and then we can no longer continue the activity professionally (IRO06).*

The support relationship is phased: at the beginning of the intervention, the relationship is closer, with more frequent meetings, and the frequency of meetings decreases as the person becomes autonomous, taking ownership of the decisions made in the direction of change.

> *A support relationship. It depends. If they are persons at the beginning of the intervention, we pursue a much closer support relationship, in the sense that we meet much more often; then, as the case evolves and things are in order, we try to become independent (IRO10).*

The first meeting is regarded as a power game, an establishment of the communicational equilibrium between the two parties. The offender—in many cases—seeks to portray themselves as an innocent person, the victim of a judicial error, of the environment from which they come, or of a necessity beyond their control. The officer must make themselves known to the beneficiary as the representative of a public institution that implements the sanction received. This struggle for symbolic power will conclude either with the acceptance of the officer's authority or with a possible failure of the counselling process.

> *At the first meeting, it is somehow a game of power roles. So the person maintains that they have done nothing, does not take responsibility—most of the time very few assume the offence for which they are here—and you have to see. And if at the beginning you fail to make yourself understood and the person does not realise that*

> *you are a representative of a state institution here—that is, you are not just anyone off the street—the relationship cannot work, because then you transfer power to the supervised person: they come when they wish, however they please; your evaluation will no longer have the necessary objectivity, because they will tell you certain things and you are focused on believing those things without analysing further beneath the surface, and then it remains at a superficial level where, OK, I understood you, but you also have to understand me—I am doing my job, and that is all. That is why it is very important that this initial interview takes place, in which you, as a probation officer, establish very clearly the role you have here, because the actual criminal proceedings have been concluded (IRO11).*

Following the evaluation carried out at the first interview, an action plan is drawn up at the second interview, which includes the estimated risk of recidivism and measures to counter it.

> *It is difficult for me after a single evaluation, because we schedule a first interview and at that first interview we carry out an initial assessment. On the basis of that initial assessment, at the second interview we issue a supervision plan. In that supervision plan, the risk of committing new offences or the risk of recidivism is recorded (IRO11).*

2.3.4. The Probation Officer–Supervised Person Relationship as a Therapeutic Relationship

Respondents emphasise the dual dimension of probation practice: in addition to the supervision and monitoring of the execution of the non-custodial sanction, officers also carry out counselling activities and provide effective support in resolving the problems that led to the commission of the offence or that could lead to new antisocial acts in the future.

> *Probation, besides the legal dimension, also has a practical social dimension, because in addition to supervision, any person under supervision has the possibility of requesting assistance and counselling from*

> *the probation officer, so that the criminogenic needs of the supervised person will be supported through a counselling process, enabling the supervised person to work through those problems that led them to commit offences and to focus on the objectives of reintegration into society (IRO01).*

Counselling and supervision are seen as activities that overlap and reinforce one another, with the ultimate aim of the offender's integration into society and the elimination of the risk of recidivism.

> *Both [counselling] and [supervision]—that is, we have used them together and they work very well together. It is very difficult to differentiate them because the final objective is reintegration into society. Both through supervision and through counselling programmes, we reach that social dimension of reintegration into society; so we do two in one (IRO01).*

The respondent places particular emphasis on the dimension of supervision, while other respondents privilege the counselling and supportive dimension. In the respondent's view, supervision leads to the construction of the supervised person's self-responsibility and moral agency.

> *I consider supervision more favourable to reintegration, because in addition to the therapeutic dimension of following a reintegration programme, the supervised person is made aware that they must comply with certain measures and obligations, which can foster self-discipline. The measure of self-discipline, which runs in parallel with self-help, I consider more effective from this point of view (IRO01).*

The probation officer–supervised person relationship is viewed in its therapeutic dimension, centred on trust—both in oneself and in the officer. Trust constitutes the premise for rehabilitation, as it leads the beneficiary to understand the sanctioning measures and the obligations imposed by the court, collaborating effectively with the officer in implementing the supervision measures.

> *Trust is very important in any therapeutic relationship, and I mean here that in the officer–beneficiary relationship as well, one can speak of a helping relationship, or a counselling relationship if not a therapeutic one. And the way we build the relationship with our beneficiary will lead us, will guide us to the chance of successful reintegration. Having trust, the supervised person will understand much more easily the measures and obligations placed upon them by the judge and will cooperate much more efficiently for their own benefit and for the benefit of reintegration into society. They will be able to trust in their own strengths, in their possibilities for rehabilitation, so that the benefit will be social reintegration and the prevention of recidivism (IRO01).*

Trust constitutes the key element of the officer–supervised person relationship as a social intervention. Without this trust, empathy and genuine knowledge of the supervised person are not possible, regardless of the level of professionalism the officer may consider themselves to have attained.

> *Well, I believe that trust is the most important element in communication and in making the intervention and probation activity effective. Because without trust, you can understand that you cannot know the person. If they do not trust you, you cannot know them, no matter how knowledgeable or professional you are (IRO07).*

For establishing the relationship of trust, the respondent indicates that sincerity and the proper establishment of the boundaries within which the relationship will operate are needed. An important element in the respondent's view is the offender's awareness that change comes from within and not from the officer, who is neither obligated nor responsible for the offender's cognitive-behavioural change.

> *What do I do (to establish the relationship of trust)? I try to be sincere, I try to establish the boundaries between myself and the person, and to make them aware that, in fact, the change comes from them. I am not obligated and I am not responsible for their change (IRO08).*

The establishment of boundaries is carried out on the basis of a limited willingness on the part of the officer to engage in the relationship. Nevertheless, the willingness does exist, including the willingness to communicate with the supervised person beyond the strict confines of scheduled counselling sessions, including by telephone if necessary. The respondent notes that this practice is widespread at the level of probation services.

> *But of course, it is not an unlimited willingness, because if a person comes along who does not know when to stop, then we move to a guided interview and we stop where necessary. And the fact that we can talk by telephone, if they have questions or uncertainties—I consider that a good thing. It is a general practice across the entire service, not only as far as we are concerned (IRO09).*

As a communication strategy, the officer adapts their message to the communicational particularities of the supervised person in order to achieve the desired effect.

> *Well, we try to reach their level of understanding and to make sure that our message arrives where it should and in the form in which it should (IRO10).*

Effective communication with the supervised person must be grounded in quality, conciseness, and determination. The supervised person must become aware that they are serving a sentence, but that the execution takes place in the community, in their own living environment, and not in prison. The conditions imposed by the judicial decision must be fulfilled; they make the offender aware of the sanctioning nature of these conditions, and compliance with them enables the person to be rehabilitated at the end of the supervision period.

> *Effective communication with the supervised person must have clarity, conciseness, determination, a certain respect for the law and the legislator; it must be well understood that it is a conviction that the person is serving in their own living environment, in society, in the community. Communication based on respect and on the fulfilment of duties and norms in society. That is, if the person has been required not to leave their domicile*

without notifying the probation officer, they will understand that this is a sanction, and the manner in which they comply will lead them, at the end of the supervision period, to understand that this conviction has come to an end and that they can be rehabilitated (IRO01).

Working with the person—the actual counselling activity—is considered essential for the success of the social reintegration of offenders. The counselling activity aims to identify the traumas the individual suffered prior to committing the offence, their environment of origin, the influence of their social circle, and so forth. Awareness of the sources of antisocial behaviour can lead to its change, more so than simply appealing to various state institutions.

The actual discussions and working with the person. Not necessarily referrals to institutions. Actually sitting down with the person, discussing, explaining what the advantages and disadvantages are, how they ended up there, because very many of them come from disorganised families or come with a trauma from the past and do not realise where the cause originated—not just the effect that led to the commission of the offence. Many of them do revise their behaviour (IRO05).

Within the counselling activity, emphasis is placed on developing an appreciative attitude on the part of the beneficiary, focusing on their strengths and positive thinking. As an example, the respondent recounts a counselling sequence in which they propose that the beneficiary enrol in vocational training courses in order to obtain employment. The respondent underscores the role of the officer as an agent of change for the beneficiary, enabling them to think in perspective and to make decisions for the future.

To teach the offender to think positively, to highlight their good qualities and use those, and to leave the lesser ones there until they wither and die. But to do something with them. Whom do you tell this to? They come to you: 'I have no job.' OK, let us enrol in a qualification course; look, you can learn something new—what do you like? 'Nothing.' But look, really nothing? Let us think of something; look, here is something new... What are you doing now? 'Well, I work as a day labourer,' and how much do you earn? 'Fifty lei a day.' And do you like it? 'Well, look, it is hard,' and I say: OK, this will work until you are thirty; when the body starts to deteriorate, you will no longer be able to do this. How will you manage? We are generally not taught to think in perspective. We see the here and now. Look, go to school because it is important; you have to try to convince them, to open a door for them. I was just talking the other day with a young man under supervision who had completed ten school years and wanted to go abroad to work. And I said, OK, look, I have a friend who left Romania a few years ago, came back, and so on, and I kept insisting, and he went to school. You go to school twice a year, you submit assignments, you talk to the teachers, but look—you finish high school. You have better chances with a high school diploma to find something better to do. 'Yes, I had not thought of that.' They need to be taught to think, because in the family nobody teaches you to think. That is the greatest human tragedy. I was watching the Americans a few years ago when Bush was president. People were doing interviews on the street, and what impressed me about them was the lack of stage fright—regardless of whether it was a person taken from the gutter or anyone else, they spoke well, fluently, coherently. Not like here, where you see educated people or politicians who cannot command their discourse. Brother, say it nicely in your own words, without shouting—say your opinion. People have no opinions. People borrow opinions and go to the ends of the earth for other people's opinions, but if you ask them what they themselves want to do, they do not know what to do. Well, that is what I see (IRO08).

Respondents emphasise the importance of establishing a communication relationship from the very first counselling sessions, when the conditions of cooperation between the two parties, the role of each, and the extent and limits of communication are clearly established.

It is very important that when the officer has the first interview, it should ideally be the one who takes over the case, because it is the first moment when the supervised

> *person comes into contact with a representative of our institution, and then the role of each party is established very clearly: the manner in which you convey the information from the official report, what exactly you emphasise, what you identify as being important for the person, how you evaluate them in that interview, what information they provide you and the way in which they tell you, what attitude they have towards you, how you react to their attitude (IRO11).*

Among the social reintegration programmes with a therapeutic role described by respondents, the following are mentioned:

– *One to One* – an individual counselling programme aimed at preventing the risk of recidivism, based on the analysis of one's own behaviour from the perspective of its consequences;

– *Stop* – a group intervention programme aimed at raising awareness of the consequences of the offender's own actions;

– *Drink and Drive* – a programme for raising awareness of the risks of drink-driving;

– *Civic Training Stage* – a group counselling programme for minors who have received as a mandatory educational measure the completion of a civic training stage;

– *DAS* – a programme for the development of social skills;

– *STOP. Think and Change!* – a programme for awareness and behavioural change.

> *I have applied and am currently applying several programmes. One of them is an individual programme, One to One; it is a one-on-one programme with the beneficiary, the aim being the prevention of the risk of recidivism. The basic idea of the programme is to support the beneficiary in developing consequence-oriented thinking—that is, to better analyse their behaviour before making a decision, before acting; that is roughly the purpose of this programme. Then there is another programme, Stop. Stop and Think!, which closely resembles the One to One programme, except that it is a group intervention this*

> *time, pursuing the same objectives as the previous programme. I also apply a newer programme, Drink and Drive, which is a programme for persons who have committed road traffic offences while under the influence of alcohol; it is also a group programme. And there is another programme for which I was recently trained—the civic training stage—for minors who have been sanctioned with educational measures involving a civic training stage. I have not yet applied this programme so far. I am curious to apply it and see how it goes (IRO06).*
>
> *Individually, we have the OTO programme (one to one / face to face) in which twelve sessions are conducted with the person. As group programmes, we have the development of social skills—DAS—and we also have Stop. Think and Change. Usually there are between seven and twelve persons who work with the entire group. All of them have the same ultimate purpose: awareness of behaviour and behavioural change (IRO08).*

All these programmes originate from the field of cognitive-behavioural change practice, and probation officers must be trained in order to apply them.

> *These are the programmes in which the probation officers have been trained. They are cognitive-behavioural programmes, for the development of social skills—I am referring to the group programmes—and Stop, Think and Change, and One to One, which is an individual programme (IRO08).*

The therapeutic dimension is validated by respondents who are beneficiaries of probation services, in the sense that they positively appreciated the role of the probation officer in their own social reintegration.

2.3.5. Stories from Practice

A narrative approach to practice is presented by one of the respondents, who highlights the importance of peer groups in the deviant socialisation of offenders—especially juvenile offenders—and the importance of the communication relationship with the officer as a resource for changing the convicted person's behaviour. The case described involves a fifteen-year-old minor from a criminogenic peer group, with a brother who has a criminal record, who enters probation following the commission of an offence together with his brother and members of the latter's group. The officer recounts that communication with the minor was difficult in the initial stages but gradually improved, with the young person ultimately completing the supervision period successfully and reintegrating into society, despite the difficult start and the resistance to change displayed in the early period.

> *A child, around fifteen years old, had an older brother—a brother with many criminal records—entered his brother's circle and committed an offence, a robbery. Interestingly, I remember very well, because he actually finished his supervision this year. He had entered a circle of well-off youngsters; he was the least culpable, and if you read the indictment, it is clear that his contribution was minor. But he had the disadvantages: firstly, of coming from a less accomplished family, and secondly, of having a brother known to the court, and so he received the longest period among those involved. And I had a great deal of struggle with him at the beginning. He refused to cooperate, and it is interesting that somewhere, beyond objectivity, I agreed with him. It was clear that there had been social considerations at play. Well, the point is that he managed to finish—even with an extra year compared to the others—in conditions where, at our service, there is a maximum of two warnings, and he received his in the first six months; the probability of him completing the six years was minimal, and yet he did, and I am very proud of him. Now he has been away for about two years, working somewhere in Italy with an employment contract. I was very pleased when he came the last time—he was talking on the phone with his girlfriend. These are minor things for us, but for a person who had every chance of ending up badly, the fact that he understood—that is what I struggled with the most. I cannot change what happened; I can change what will happen from now on. And he understood, somehow. I do not know why the beginning was terrible, but it is well—now it is well (IRO02).*

Another significant story concerning the officer–supervised person relationship is mentioned by respondent IRO02, who narrates their communication with a minor client who was somewhat emotionally overwhelmed by the situation, and who managed to find resources for change precisely in the communication with the probation officer. The success of the intervention was grounded in a focus on successful reintegration and the client's strengths—an appreciative approach—rather than an exclusive focus on the offence committed, which the minor initially denied.

> *He did not have a mother, and the fact that we are somewhat close in age, the fact that someone showed interest in him, that someone did not deny that the reality he saw was—let us say—perceptible to others as well. He did not come to me to complain about these things, and I did not tell him, 'Oh, that is not true, you do not know what you are talking about,' as had happened before. I simply told him: I cannot change what happened. Fine—what do you want to do from now on? End up in a care centre?—the father was devastated by the loss of his wife, did not really have contact with him in the sense that he went about his own business—Or do you want to succeed and for things to be well? (IRO02).*

One of the respondents shows a correlation between their own professional development and the breadth of practice, recounting a supervision case from the period 2002–2003—before the entry into force of the current probation legislation. The offender was also a social case, and the success of the intervention depended on the application of specific social assistance measures, which consisted in enrolling the person in a programme for individuals who had dropped out of school, called *A Second Chance*. In order to procure textbooks, the officer resorted to providing financial assistance from their own funds. The case was a success: the person completed the supervision period without recidivism or other incidents and achieved optimal social reintegration.

> *Well, that sense of achievement relates to the stages I myself was at in terms of professional and personal development. At the beginning, for example, in 2002—actually it was finalised around 2003—I had a case, a minor, whom I remember constantly, and of course the*

> *legislation at that time was much simpler and so on. He was from P., and he was also a social case in everyday life. And I remember that I went with him—one of the objectives I set for him was to resume and continue his studies. He was seventeen years old and had completed four years of schooling. It was quite difficult, shall we say, from the system's point of view, but there was the option for him to continue at A Second Chance, on a reduced-attendance or distance-learning basis. And I went with him to buy textbooks in the city of I.; he was from the town of P., but I wanted to be sure he actually bought them. I went with him; he did not have enough money, so I helped him with money, which his father later returned to me. And I know that he finished without committing other offences, although at that time recidivism was quite high. He also enrolled in school, and I considered it a professional achievement. Subsequently, achievements became of a somewhat different calibre (IRO07).*

Another account from practice concerns the process of producing evaluation reports. Within the limits of existing resources, officers go into the field to the person to be evaluated, or the person is requested to report to the probation service. The evaluation interview covers information about the person's criminal history, education, health status, family situation and relationships within the family, and the offender's perspective on the offence. The interview with the offender is supplemented by other data sources: the family and the community are investigated. Precisely in order to achieve a higher degree of objectivity, especially in the case of pre-sentence evaluations whose purpose is to assist the judge in the circumstantiation and individualisation of the sentence, it is recommended that this inquiry be conducted effectively in the field.

> *I will refer only to evaluation reports, because supervision can last up to eight years—to know what happens over eight years is too much. We receive the request from the court; if at that moment we have the necessary resources, we go into the field. If we do not have the necessary resources to go into the community to the person, we send them a summons. The person, together with their family, is called to our office on a*

> *certain date. There are some difficulties, because you always have to check the portal to see if you have a room available—if not, it is difficult. They are called here. If the person shows up, an interview is conducted. In that interview, information is requested regarding criminal history, the family environment, health problems, the person's education, the education within the family, and aspects related to the offence—it is essentially their point of view. Do they acknowledge it? If they acknowledge it, what was the context and their involvement? What ultimately led to their implication in an offence? Beyond contacting the family and the person, community sources are contacted. Sometimes they are much more objective. Sometimes—not always. Sometimes in the sense that the family, no matter how difficult the child may be, tends to cover for them; I presume every family does that, and so we also contact the community, the school, the town hall, the police—and that is precisely why it is recommended to go into the field. It is not always possible (IRO02).*

The respondent complains that, following the entry into force of the New Criminal Code in Romania in 2014, the workload of probation officers increased substantially, to the detriment of practice quality, making field visits no longer always possible. The situation in which an officer effectively loses an entire working day to attend the hearing of a minor who reported late to the court but was granted clemency is criticised. The occurrence of such situations diminishes the number of field visits by probation officers.

> *Practice, at least since the new Criminal Code came into force, has dropped to about twenty per cent, I believe, which affects our work. It is not a matter of lack of will; it is the inability to go into the field. I will give you a concrete example. Yesterday we were supposed to go for the enforcement of a sentence; I had a case in the city of M. and the enforcement was at the court there. I went with a colleague, and unfortunately the minor announced that he would arrive two hours late, and the court granted him clemency—I lost an entire day. Losing an entire day in the field for a case you did not even find, because the minor had left for Italy, greatly limits what I could have done at the office. And so, clearly, we choose much more carefully*

> *the moments when we leave, or we try to contact community sources beforehand and thus make sure that the minor is at their domicile when we go. That does not always happen (IRO02).*

Conducting evaluation reports at the premises of the probation services diminishes the quality of the evaluation, since the chance of obtaining references from other community sources regarding the offender's everyday behaviour is reduced. The respondent indicates that a series of details about the offender cannot be identified through a telephone interview or any other form of communication apart from the field interview.

> *For a minor, when you call them here, from my point of view the image you form is already distorted, given that here most of them come with that parent or that relative who more or less supports them—you get a different image; they come with a purpose. They are told: 'Behave well.' When you go to their doorstep and a neighbour appears and intervenes, saying: 'Sir, they are not exactly a model citizen.' Because everyone portrays whatever looks best, whatever appears best for others. Well, when you go into their environment, things change a great deal, and I had the surprise, at the first interview with a minor, of them seeming an extraordinary child who just happened to be caught in a set of circumstances, and the surprise, subsequently at a second report, of having the opportunity to go into the field and to see that they were a sort of small-time local strongman who terrorised everyone—something that nobody tells you by telephone; at the town hall, if you are not face to face with the person and you do not see them, it is, 'Well, you know, a teenager, as they are.' The image changes a great deal (IRO02).*

2.3.6. Strategies for Balancing Power

The respondent brings into discussion the involvement of the judge delegated with execution, who in a sense supervises the activity of the probation service and who may revoke the non-custodial measure if the court-imposed conditions are not respected. For the officer, it is very important to make those supervised persons understand that the sentence can be modified towards a custodial penalty up until the very last moment of its execution.

> *Until the moment when the person exits supervision, we still report to a judge—called the judge delegated with execution. OK, you have been given a sentence, but from now on there is another judge; I am the intermediary; I have to monitor certain things; if you do not do this, I notify the judge. It is very important for them to understand this (IRO11).*

2.3.7. Working Instruments

The routine of working with clients on a typical working day involves a series of initial interview sessions, during which the measures and obligations imposed by the court are communicated, and on which occasion the official record of the enforcement of the sentence is drawn up.

> *Last week, on Thursday, I had three sessions scheduled for first interviews—cases at the first interview to whom I communicated the measures and obligations imposed by the court upon the convicted persons, drawing up the official record of enforcement of the supervision sentences (IRO01).*

For the production of the evaluation report, a series of specific procedures exist: the person is summoned to the probation service for the purpose of drawing up the evaluation report. In the event of non-attendance, the parents are summoned in the case of a convicted minor; and in the event of continued non-attendance, measures for compulsory appearance are taken. The evaluation report is produced on the basis of an evaluation interview.

> *If we take the re-evaluation side, if we have been asked for an evaluation report, bringing it to a successful conclusion means producing the evaluation report. In this case, there are specific procedures. First of all, we summon the person to appear at the probation service for the interview necessary for drawing up the report. If the person does not appear, and if they are a minor, we summon them together with the parents; if they still do not appear, then we take other steps, in the sense that we go to their domicile ourselves or draft requests to the police for them to be identified and directed to appear. Then the*

interview is conducted and the document is drafted (IRO03).

The initial evaluation aims to determine a baseline situation as a starting point for the offender's reintegration process. It seeks to assess the person's strengths and weaknesses, and the need to contact other specialised community institutions, such as community psychiatry services. Since some of the reintegration programmes are conducted within the probation services, the outsourcing of services is carried out only when it is deemed strictly necessary.

> *Well, first of all, an evaluation of the person's situation takes place, so that we know exactly where we are starting from—what the point of departure is. After we have established the strengths and weaknesses of the person, we begin to work. We also collaborate with community institutions where there are problems that exceed our areas of competence, and here I refer to those persons who have problems of a psychological or psychiatric nature. There are also programmes that we run at the level of our service, and so we can work with such persons within the service as well. We outsource services only where we feel that we cannot work, that we lack the competence (IRO06).*

Particular methodological emphasis is placed on conducting the interview with the supervised person. The methodological rules for conducting the interview include: comprehension of what the beneficiaries report, providing feedback, and verifying the information from other community sources where possible. Communication with the beneficiary is based on a direct approach, requesting their point of view regarding their attitudes and behaviour, on the basis of an open and sincere approach to communication.

> *It is about the way the interview is conducted—to make sure I have understood what the person communicates to me. To always provide feedback. To verify the information when I have reports from the community that the person displays certain behaviours or has violated certain measures. I always ask for their point of view, so that things are explained to me from the other*

perspective as well—how that behaviour came about. I rely heavily on communication, and we address the subject openly and directly (IRO04).

Another responsibility of probation officers for which standardised methodology exists is the delivery of social reintegration programmes. These programmes are generally considered welcome, but they are implemented by a smaller number of probation officers who have been specially trained for this purpose. A number of respondents among the probation officers consider that these programmes, although effective, are quite difficult to implement, requiring a longer period of time—time that is lacking due to the heavy caseload of probation officers.

> *In addition to what I said earlier, I should add the delivery of social programmes, because we have this responsibility as well. And for those for whom the obligation to follow a programme within the probation service has been ordered, we have such programmes (IRO03).*

> *Principally, working techniques adapted to the typology of our beneficiaries, because we have an extremely varied typology compared to other European systems—ranging from level of education, area of interest, risk of recidivism, to educational background (IRO10).*

Failure of the Probation Officer–Supervised Person Relationship

A situation of failure in the officer–supervised person relationship is recounted by one of the probation officer respondents. The failure of communication is attributed by the respondent to the fact that they did not build the probation relationship from the very beginning, the case having been taken over from another officer who had left on maternity leave. The communication relationship is established from the outset and is strengthened over the course of the probation relationship's development. The difficulty of reconstructing the relationship is due to the personal style of the officer and the different expectations of the beneficiary.

> *I consider it a good one. I had only one case in which the supervised person requested a transfer to another officer, but it was not a case I had from the*

beginning—it had been transferred to me as a result of the responsible officer's departure on maternity leave. It was a rather difficult person. I like it when I establish a certain relationship from the beginning. It is harder when you take over cases after a certain period, in which a relationship has already been established between the supervised person and the probation officer responsible for the case. It is harder because, well, you have to see how malleable each person is; some have certain expectations, some have certain wishes. And the personal style of the officer is different—some are more relaxed, some are more focused on responsibilities or on responsibilising the person, others are very focused on motivation for change—and then, if the relationship between the officer and the supervised person is focused on a certain aspect, and you, when you take over the case, focus on something entirely different, even if initially you relate only to those measures, there comes a point where we cannot get on the same track (IRO11).

Probation Officers' Expectations of Supervised Persons

The respondent indicates that there are a series of expectations on the part of probation officers regarding the involvement of supervised persons in the process of their own reintegration. As an example, enrolment in vocational training courses is cited, where the supervised person is expected to go and enrol on their own, without being accompanied by the probation officer, who has, however, previously completed all the documents necessary for the supervised person's enrolment in the course.

As long as there are more cases, then our effort is even greater, and so if before I used to assist them more—we also make written requests—but I expect them to go on their own as well. Not to go hand in hand with them to the qualification course. I have given them what they need: the brochure, the institution, the phone number. So at least this much I expect—that they go on their own. I draft the formal requests, and their only task is to go and request enrolment. I cannot hold their hand; as such, I have certain expectations of them (IRO04).

2.3.8. Changing Attitudes Towards Society and Normativity

The respondent indicates that the labelling and stigmatisation of persons who have suffered a criminal conviction represents an obstacle to their rehabilitation. Stigmatisation operates at the level of self-esteem and constructed self-identity, such that the subject comes to identify with the public perception of themselves: *if the world says I am a thief... then I am a thief.*

> *In general, people tend to label, and the person who is labelled and assumes that stigma will never change. 'Hey, if I am a thief and everyone says I am a thief, then I am a thief.' So the mentality and the labelling by those around a person who does not benefit from community support—that is a person who will never change (IRO04).*

Against stigmatisation, as might be expected, respondents from among the supervised persons also speak out: *If a person has made a mistake once, I do not think society should judge them, because every person has the right to make a mistake (IBM02).* One of the respondents recounts their own experience: after having secured employment, when the employers were informed that they needed to send a monthly character reference to the probation service, they simply cancelled the person's employment.

> *I mean, I came here, I said look, I got a job, and a character reference was requested from the workplace. I went to work, to the boss, and said, look, this is the situation—I need a character reference because I sign in every month. 'Well, why did you not say so from the start? We will check with the higher-up boss.' And the boss called me about two days later and said: 'I am sorry, but we cannot officially employ you.' How so? You ask me to get officially employed, but you do not want to take me on. They could not tell me the reasons, and so I did not work any further—I only worked half a month (IBM07).*

The social effectiveness of probation is also highlighted from the perspective of the risk of recidivism. Respondent IRO04 demonstrates the efficiency of the probation system, starting from the perspective of the number of cases on record at the national level (Romania), amounting to 40,000, relative to the number of 300 probation officers. The recidivism rate for persons under supervision is 6–7%, far lower than that obtained for incarcerated persons, which reaches as high as 100% in some penitentiaries.

> *Well, the recidivism rate in the probation system—at our last review, there were some forty-odd thousand persons on record and 300 probation officers, so it is an enormous effort to do something for them. The recidivism rate was somewhere below 6–7%. There are penitentiaries where the recidivism rate in the prison environment reaches 100%, and so I cannot say that probation is entirely ineffective; rather, I, as a professional for whom probation is a passion, tell you that I feel disappointed (IRO08).*

2.4. Thematic Axis IV. Value-Centred Probation. The Theoretical-Ideological Dimension of the Social Construction of the Probation Officer Profession

2.4.1. Constitutive Values

Respondents underscore the discursive parallelism between probation officers and other professional categories involved in the act of justice: prosecutors. Discussing a *prosecutor's mentality* with reference to retributive discursive emphases, the respondent contrasts it with a discourse in which the emphasis falls on reintegration, suspending any reference to punishment, which is placed exclusively within the purview of the judge. Such a discourse highlights, in our view, a series of constitutive values—values that make necessary the emergence of a profession, and generally of a social institution—specific to probation, which are centred on reintegration. The social reintegration of the offender represents the social action generated by the professional body's adherence to the constitutive values of the profession, values from which the necessity of reintegrating persons who have committed offences derives. In practice, the constitutive values of probation practice originate from the sphere of humanism, the emphasis being on the (moral) value of the individual in themselves, beyond that of their actions. Retribution and rehabilitation are thus two central values that delineate two types of particular professional discourses, specific to two directions of society: social control and the repression of illegitimate practices—considered by the respondent as specific to the prosecutor—and concern for the individual as a bearer of dignity and, in general, of humanist values, even beyond responsibility for their actions—a discourse specific to the helping professions, among which, according to the respondent, probation is included. One of the discursive strategies specific to probation, derived from humanism as a constitutive value, is the separation between the negative value of the antisocial act and the unconditionally positive value of the offender as a human being. There is a difference between the person and even the personality of the offender and their act, which occurred within a particular juncture of their life. Trust in the unconditionally positive value of offenders as human beings is doubled by trust in their capacity to adopt socially desirable behaviour, to become morally good. The respondent underscores the role of the officer in the offender's rehabilitation trajectory, as well as the fact that the officer's professionalism determines the personal and social development, and ultimately the reintegration, of the offender.

> *That is the mentality of those who more or less know what probation means. I had to explain to my daughter what I do, because she spoke about professions at kindergarten. I told her: Mummy talks to people who have made mistakes from a legal point of view, who have broken the law, who were bad at a certain moment, but who are going to become good. But I think that I can give this explanation to any other person, regardless of age. Only someone who goes through such an experience can understand our role. Only someone who comes here can understand that my decision determines whether they can continue their profession in the country or abroad, that it depends on my decision whether they end up in prison or not if they do not respect their measures, that I have to verify good or bad faith. It depends on me that they perform community service at a certain institution—because at one institution they might be well and at another they might not. And so, only for those within our system is what we do important (IRO11).*

Respondents indicate that the individualisation of the sentence should be based on the social danger of the offence, and not on social resentments towards the offender or the offence. The sanction must be humanised through the identification of alternatives to imprisonment.

> *They committed an offence, but the punishment should be applied, from my point of view, according to the degree of social danger that was committed. I am a woman, and I have a problem with offences of a sexual nature—I control myself, but it consumes a great deal of energy; on that day I am no longer myself. Somehow, sentences need to be individualised; not all persons should end up being convicted. Great care must be taken. That is, it is a very great responsibility on the shoulders of the judge when they convict a person. Indeed, it is so—you committed an offence, you pay—but somehow you can pay not necessarily by losing your freedom, but through other methods and means, and that is why we are here (IRO04).*

The social reintegration of persons who have committed criminal acts responds, in our view, to a centrally constitutive value of probation, shared with the other helping professions, namely society's responsibility towards its members. This responsibility stems from the social consciousness—latent or manifest—of a (co-)responsibility of society in general towards the actions of its members, which to some extent transcends the individual responsibility of each person for their own acts. This individual responsibility is not ignored; on the contrary, as we shall see further, its construction represents one of the operational values of probation practice, the conscious assumption of responsibility for one's own acts being one of the objectives of probation practice. However, responsibilisation cannot be substituted by holding the offender accountable, the latter being within the purview of the judge.

> *I do not think that is the thinking of a probation officer. I think that is the thinking of a prosecutor. Somehow, with us, the emphasis falls on reintegration, and the punishment is applied by the judge. That is the judge's prerogative—to impose a sentence. We merely enforce it (IRO09).*

Responsibility—for the other—as a constitutive value of probation takes two directions: responsibility towards the individual—the offender—and towards society itself as responsibility towards non-presence. We construct the idea of responsibility towards non-presence drawing upon the ideas of Karl Otto Apel [127, pp. 9–29, 197, 198, 199], who shows that in post-industrial societies, the (individual or collective) capacity to do harm exceeds the boundaries of spatial and temporal immediacy; therefore, responsibility must be extended from that towards the Near Other to that towards abstract entities that are non-localised and non-localisable in space and even in time. The officer transposes responsibility as a value existing at the societal level, directed towards a significant Other—individually the offender and collectively the community—into a social-professional practice aimed at the social reintegration of the offender, that is, precisely the social construction of responsibility at their level. We shall see that a significant Other within the offender–victim–society triad, the victim, although a key element of the discourse on probation at the global level, is excluded from the major concerns of Romanian probation owing to the specificity of the legislation. The discourse of Moldavian probation officers, on the other hand, includes concerns for victim–offender reconciliation, at least in cases of early conditional release (IMD05).

> *One purpose of punishment is to protect the community from the person who has committed an offence (IRO09).*

The respondent considers that a characteristic of developed societies is the emphasis on the community and its interests, rather than on the traditional punitive and retributive system. It is the community's role to (re-)establish the society–victim–offender equilibrium. The particularity of restorative justice lies precisely in the pursuit of this equilibrium: the community is, on the one hand, interested in the existence of homeodynamics at its level, and, on the other hand, society is morally responsible both towards the offender—through the illegitimate opportunities that were possible due to a certain degree of societal passivity in the educational process, in the exercise of social control, and so forth—and towards the victim—whose harm, although caused by the offender, was made possible by the community's passivity.

> *Every trend, and I am referring to developed societies, has this triad (offender–victim–community) very well managed, in the sense that the judicial system is more focused on the community than on the institutional penal system. The re-establishment of the equilibrium among the three evidently starts from the community, and the victim–community, victim–offender, offender–community relationships—this means that the*

community has the primordial role of re-establishing this equilibrium. The community will have to take steps and make efforts to find the most effective levers for re-establishing this equilibrium, for helping both the offender and the victim to reintegrate into the community framework (IRO01).

The relationship between social image and the perceived place of the individual in the community is brought into discussion. The individual's positioning in the community—their social panorama [72]—the way in which they are regarded by the community represents a possible predictor of prosocial/antisocial behaviour. Nevertheless, responsibility cannot be considered exclusively individual. The co-responsibility of the community for the individual's eventual antisocial trajectory is thus indicated. The lack of sufficient and accessible legitimate opportunities, of public trust, and of the fostering of the social construction of the individual's self-confidence, family involvement in the individual's socialisation [56], and the construction of attachment [75] can all be social causes of antisocial behaviour. Equally important, in the respondent's view, is the individual's responsibility towards their own social image, the effort they invest in the direction of their social integration. This effort leads to a change in the community's attitude towards the individual and constitutes one of the keys to the resocialisation process necessary for the integration into the community of the person under supervision.

Most of the time, social image matters a great deal because it identifies the place we currently hold in the community. If you, as an individual, have not managed to have a self-standing, comfortable, balanced place in which all your neighbours, relatives, and persons in the community see you as a resource, it is clear that somewhere, someone has failed. And I do not consider that every time it is only the individual who has failed. I believe that the community from which the individual comes has also failed somewhere—either it did not grant them enough trust, or it did not grant them enough opportunities, or their family did not invest enough in their development as an individual. But I also believe the individual should make a certain effort towards building their own image, and then, if you care about this, you try

> *to respect the rules; and if you respect them, it is impossible for people not to change their opinion about you (IRO11).*

2.4.2. Operational Values of Practice. Retributive Justice Versus Restorative Justice

The retributive discourse is present in the approach to probation from a social perspective: retribution compensates social equilibrium through the social sentiment that coercion exists, the antisocial act itself generating the need for retribution. Punishment is personalised through the limitation of certain rights, a limitation made necessary by the existence of the act, with coercion being necessary—for both society and the individual. Society should see that the individual is attempting to re-establish the equilibrium, through the payment of damages, through community service, and so forth. The retributive discourse is somewhat associated with the restorative one; restoration—the restoration of the social equilibrium that existed prior to the commission of the offence—is not possible, in the respondent's view, outside of retribution.

> *If, on the other hand, it is an offence of lesser gravity—let us say someone drove under the influence of alcohol—I think they should also be punished, because OK, nothing happened now, but there is the possibility in the future of doing something even worse. Punishment in itself means the limitation of certain rights. If you have committed an act, some of your rights must be limited—that is my opinion. And somehow society, the community, must feel that you are trying to remedy the situation, whether through community service, through paying damages, or through fulfilling certain obligations—but there must be a certain coercion (IRO11).*

Another perspective is the reflection on the meaning of retribution. Punishment should be reframed as a positive element, a life experience. Such an approach should lead to the elimination of stigmatisation. In this regard, we concur with the idea that, no matter how grave an act may be and no matter how great its consequences, the act in itself is limited, and therefore the sanction should also have a limited character. This includes the stigmatisation generated by incarceration, which often extends beyond the completion of the sentence.

> *Yes, I agree that those who err must pay, but this should also be given a positive connotation—that is, you did wrong, you pay for what you did, but that does not mean you are stigmatised for the rest of your life. You must also see something positive in this part of the punishment (IRO06).*

The assumption of the consequences of one's actions also appears in the responses of supervised persons (IBRO1).

> *The rehabilitation of the individual, for the most part. To realise that they made a mistake, and that is it—they have to bear the consequences (IBRO01).*

Restorative and retributive justice are correlated, depending on the specificity of the damages produced by the commission of the offence. The specificity of the retributive discourse is given by the phrase *you must pay*, followed by argumentation of the necessity of this payment through the damage caused and eventually the suffering inflicted upon the victim. Retribution in itself represents a part of restoration—of the social equilibrium that existed prior to the commission of the act.

> *The nature of the offence matters a great deal, because if an act was committed against a person, if it brought harm to life, or to a possession, to a right that a person had, then I consider it necessary for this punishment to be somehow reflected. You hit them with your car, and then you must pay, because that person suffered damage. Or somewhere, someone lost a mother, a father, a brother, and then you must pay (IRO11).*

Supervised persons place emphasis on the specificity of the offence and especially on its degree of social danger, indicating that there is a clear difference between offences depending on their consequences—for example, driving a vehicle while intoxicated should not be treated similarly, from the perspective of punishment, when no accident occurred and when there were accidents with significant damage, just as other offences, such as homicide, are differentiated according to intent (IBRO01).

> *Everything is arranged in such a way and should be balanced with what was committed, and each offence individually should be able to mitigate, to set the person*

> *straight. You know how it is, there is a thing here—we all end up in the same pot according to the criminal code. For example, they caught you drunk—done, you have been convicted—but they do not look at the consequences. Well, hold on a moment; let me give an example: this one pulled out of a parking space, did not hit anyone, had no problems—how can I be classified together with someone who smashed three cars or killed someone? For instance, just as for the offence of murder there is murder, manslaughter, attempted murder, and so on. Well, here too there should be mitigating factors. Not just—you caught them drunk, hit them over the head (IBRO01).*

Trust, a Constructive Value of the Probation Officer–Supervised Person Relationship

A particularly important ethical value in probation practice is sincerity. Sincerity is seen by the respondent in correlation with other operational values of probation practice, such as dignity, professional integrity, and consistency. The establishment of the relationship with the beneficiary is greatly facilitated by the existence of a series of personality traits of the officer that are consonant with the mentioned ethical values. In practice, mere adherence to the idea of professional integrity, sincerity, or consistency is not sufficient. These must be internalised by the probation officer at the level of behavioural constants.

> *To establish the relationship of trust—that means being sincere. You must be sincere, be honest with yourself; what you say, you must also do, including when it comes to applying certain sanctions or going to court. You must maintain your direction, your backbone. The moment the convicted person knows that you are the person who says one thing today and another tomorrow—no, the same person—you automatically establish the personal relationship with them (IRO06).*

Trust—of the officer in the supervised person—should be grounded in frequent verifications of the beneficiary's claims, whether through direct observation, such as an unannounced visit to the person's domicile, through the solicitation of relevant data from other state institutions, and so forth. The responsibilisation of the subject—considered part of the trust relationship between officer and beneficiary—is accompanied by the verification of their statements and actions.

> *Trust is also important, but this trust is also verified, to an extent, through collaboration with partner institutions, because we cannot rely solely on trust in the relationship with the beneficiary—otherwise it would no longer be a professional relationship. It is obvious that we must also verify information, conduct an unannounced visit, make a phone call to the police, visit them at their domicile, maintain contact with the family. So we responsibilise them, but at the same time we draw their attention to the fact that what they communicate to us can be verified, and it is our duty to verify it (IRO09).*

Mutual trust between the officer and the supervised person is considered extremely important, especially when grounded in mutual respect.

> *Extremely important. It is based, in principle, on respect (IRO10).*

From Social Responsibility to a Responsible Society

Responsibility as a value of practice can be viewed from at least three perspectives: the responsibility of the probation officer towards the supervised person and towards society; the responsibility of society towards both the victim and the offender; and, not least, the responsibility of the offender for their own actions and for the consequences thereof. The officer's responsibility is seen as directed towards the prevention of the offender's recidivism and their social reintegration. To this end, the officer should mobilise the normative and educational resources available at the community level for the purpose of facilitating the offender's social reintegration. This situating of the officer's responsibility as an operational value of practice places probation within the sphere of social assistance practices, as a particular form of social work. The community is held responsible for the creation and maintenance of the legitimate opportunities for the offender's reintegration and social functioning. This invocation of the community's responsibility refers to the practice of probation in the context of community-based rehabilitation [113] of the person who has committed a criminal act. The offender's responsibility concerns their active engagement in the process of social reintegration, through the mobilisation of their inner resources as well as those related to their own social and family context—the offender's contextual resources.

> *Responsibility is a term employed by the probation officer, the community, the offender, and perhaps the victim as well. So the responsibility of the probation officer resides in finding those levers and mobilising the community's internal, educational, and legal resources available at a given moment, so that the offender avoids committing new offences and reintegrates into the community. Likewise, it falls to the community to assist them in the process of integration and the preservation of these prerogatives for as optimal a reintegration into society as possible—that is, to support them in finding employment, in keeping employment in the community, so that the supervised person no longer comes to commit new offences. Similarly, the offender has the responsibility to engage as optimally as possible in this reintegration process, to mobilise their inner and contextual resources, including family resources if applicable, for successful integration into the community (IRO01).*

Society functions repressively, rejecting those who have committed an offence and denying them the right to education, employment, and social development. Moreover, society does not prepare these individuals for a culturally autonomous life. In practice, the construction of the cultural autonomy of the person under supervision constitutes a component of the social intervention that the probation officer carries out, compensating for the elements of community-based rehabilitation [113] where this is impossible or precarious.

> *Society no longer accepts them, no longer understands them; the educational system does not prepare them adequately, does not develop them socially—mentally speaking, I do not mean knowing how to read; I mean how to learn to manage on my own, to learn to speak, to work, to learn to start from zero and climb on my own through my own labour (IRO08).*

Society is responsible for the antisocial conduct of some offenders, because it fails to construct the elements of an autonomous life for individuals, and they fail to build their quality as moral agents and as responsible social actors. The failure of socialisation processes leads to the individual's positioning in a situation of conflict with the law, for which they are incorrectly considered solely responsible. The respondent recounts a situation from their own professional practice, when, upon inviting a supervised person to find employment, they received a negative response: *"But why should I work?" (IRO08).* This rejection of proactive and prosocial conduct is seen as deviant anticipatory socialisation, due to the failure of the social legitimation of desirable behaviours.

> *When society, the family, does not teach you this elementary thing—it is called independent living for children; I would call it social life for adults—when it does not teach you elementary things, you automatically end up in conflict with the law. Because, look, we say there are no jobs, but there are jobs; I know of jobs, and I said to one person: 'Look, come and work,' and the answer was: 'But why should I work?' (IRO08).*

The respondent indicates that Romanian society experiences an extremely high rate of voluntary unemployment, associated with the absence of job-seeking. In the absence of legitimate sources of procuring the resources necessary to satisfy individual needs, and the refusal of underpaid work—the only kind readily accessible on the labour market—individuals resort to illegitimate means of accessing resources, including the commission of antisocial acts.

> *I heard on a programme that in Romania there are five million adults who are not even looking for a job—not that they are unemployed and searching for work; they simply do not want to be interested in a job. Now, speaking of Maslow's pyramid, there are needs; if I do not have the money to satisfy my needs, I have to find a source to satisfy them. Whether I stay at my mother's and she supports me, or I go and work in the fields and they give me fifty lei a day and cigarettes, or I go and hit someone over the head—these are choices. It is a choice to go and work at the bakery across the street twelve hours a day and be paid the minimum wage (IRO08).*

The respondent views Romanian society as being "handicapped" from the perspective of sociability, the assumption of prosocial behaviour, and social solidarity. A series of offences are committed—in the respondent's view—on a daily basis, from accepting undeclared work to the incomplete declaration of income for tax evasion purposes. The social legitimation of such behaviours, and the failure of perpetrators to acknowledge them as illegitimate, leads to difficulty in working with persons convicted of such offences, considered to be widespread throughout society. Society generally promotes a series of illegal behaviours—considered minor offences but offences nonetheless—with the values of honesty and upright, moral conduct lacking at the societal level.

> *The trigger is a mental one. Our society is a handicapped society, or has been desired to be handicapped, precisely so that people cannot manage. That, from my point of view, is what drives people in communitarian and social terms. They do not know how to manage, they do not assume their behaviour, they find the easiest ways to live—not necessarily to be honest. You see, very many commit offences; even the day labourer who works undeclared, all the priests who took money without issuing a receipt committed offences, but from my point of view it is not [seen as such] (IRO08).*

Comparison with the acts of others reduces moral guilt. The respondent emphasises the role of membership groups in the socialisation of offending. The encouragement within the membership group, or even reference groups, of antisocial behaviours leads to their legitimation in the consciousness of the offender. Especially when a certain antisocial behaviour is not only not considered reprehensible by the collective mentality but is somewhat appreciated—*the individual manages*—this reinforces the behaviour and renders resocialisation on the basis of morally and socially accepted norms particularly difficult.

> *Well, that is the second problem—the fact that people deny their own behaviour, considering that what they do is not as serious as what others have done. The moment you make such a comparison, you minimise your responsibility. And if in your group you also have people who encourage this form of expression, of awareness, it*

> *automatically leads once again to even more serious things—from thefts to robberies, to rapes, to murders, and so on (IRO08).*

The respondent raises the issue of imitation as a source of antisocial behaviour: if others have committed criminal acts, it is considered legitimate to commit them as well. Another justification for criminal behaviour is the perception of corruption at the level of society and the state, which, in the opinion of some offenders, justifies antisocial behaviour. This justification of antisocial behaviour through acts of resistance to state corruption can also be attributed to the mentality remaining from the communist period, during which anti-communist resistance, although constituting a criminal offence, was considered a legitimate act of political resistance. A series of acts considered antisocial by the communist regime indeed represented acts of anti-communist dissidence and contestation of the political regime. The communist state was regarded as the real enemy of individual freedom, which legitimated, in the view of the majority of the population, a series of antisocial acts, especially those of a petty corruption nature. In the immediately post-communist period, the common mentality was that *the Romanian manages*—in the sense that one could circumvent the rigours of an arbitrary and morally illegitimate legislation. The perpetuation of this mentality justifies, in the minds of some offenders, a series of acts of corruption, including grand corruption, the enemy no longer being the communist state but the corrupt state with an illegitimate government, albeit democratically elected. The respondent indicates that the acknowledgement of guilt and its acceptance represent the necessary premises for behavioural change. The acknowledgement of the act must be genuine—that is, accompanied by an awareness of guilt—and not merely declarative, expressed solely for the purpose of avoiding incarceration.

> *Because many say, 'I committed the act because someone else committed it,' or, 'Look, the state is corrupt, and I did this thing too.' You must not justify yourself through others or through something else. The first point is to acknowledge. We have these stages—contemplation, pre-contemplation, and so on. You acknowledge, you realise; many times you realise that even when they acknowledge, it is a verbal acknowledgement, and even with the risk of ending up in prison—if they have been*

> *preventively arrested, it has not led them to see their mistake. Declaratively they tell you: 'Yes, I regret the act,' but their attitude tells you the complete opposite (IRO08).*

2.4.3. The Moral Dimension of Probation Practice

Respondents draw a distinction between the dimension of professional ethics, viewed as having a strong normative component, and the moral dimension, which represents the personal and humanised side of the probation officer's intervention. Morality is related to the person of the professional, to their own visions of correctness. The moral sense should not necessarily derive from legal obligation or from different forms of social control, but from one's own moral judgement. The construction of the individual's moral judgement constitutes a component of probation practice, which aims at the internalisation of correct social conduct by the supervised person and the replacement of antisocial behaviour with socially accepted behaviour on the basis of the subject's own moral needs and convictions. For the construction of moral behaviour, the development of empathy is important—the offender's capacity to put themselves in the victim's position and to understand the consequences of their act from the victim's perspective.

> *Ethics is morality stripped of any element of spirituality. It is something raw, severe. Ethics means rule. You must keep the correct rule. Morality also presupposes a human attachment, a responsibility. Yes, I see it as a moral matter. Because I see morality first and foremost in relation to myself, to my own person. Not what it means to be correct. I must be correct. Not because the law tells me so, or my friends, or my mother. Because I feel that, being correct, I am happy, content, and those around me are equally content. I must not make excuses for myself. I violated because others violated—no; I complied because that is right, because it is correct towards others to comply. I have a young man under supervision who was complaining that, oh, a room of his caught fire. What happened? 'Well, from a candle the curtain caught fire, the room burned, and the fence burned too, and the neighbour is demanding compensation. But I have no money.' Well, talk to the neighbour, at least work to offset the damage. Because he could take you to court. 'Oh, but I*

> *have no money...' But if your house had burned, what would have happened? How would you have seen things? 'Oh, yes, you are right.' We must teach people to put themselves in others' place; perhaps then something will change. And so, yes, I give it a moral dimension (IRO08).*

The moral approach to probation practice is tangential to the humanist vision: beyond the act committed lies the person of the offender. The emphasis falls on the person, on motivating them to change their conduct, on leading them to understand the significance and consequences of their act, the reason for which they were punished, on persuading them to change a series of antisocial habituses, to leave the criminogenic peer group, and so forth.

> *First of all, we respect the legislation in force, the deadlines, the documents in the file, but this is only a formal part of things. Beyond the file, which is visible and is something material and tangible, there is also the person behind the file, who is very important in successfully completing the supervision period, and whom we must motivate; we must lead them to understand why they are with us, what the ways of overcoming all the obstacles are—obstacles that would constitute grounds for recidivism, so to speak. And the moment when the supervision period is successfully completed, the moment when they have reintegrated, found employment, changed their conduct in a desirable way—in the sense of leaving the peer group. This depends on the case. If it is a minor, we also intervene with the parents, and when we see that the conduct has changed and recidivism disappears, we consider that a case brought to a successful conclusion (IRO09).*

The Role of the Probation Officer in the Social Construction of the Supervised Person's Autonomy

The term autonomy is understood in a moral key as defining a social commitment. This moral commitment should be made in the sense of assuming responsibility for compliance with social norms, and especially with laws, and avoiding the commission of new offences.

> *The moral significance of the term autonomy I would define as a social commitment. Or, in the capacity of a beneficiary, I should say that I commit myself with responsibility to conform to social norms and to avoid committing new offences (IRO01).*

The process of (re)constructing the moral and social autonomy of supervised persons involves the formation of social skills in communication, relationships, and organisation. Probation must (re)create the structure upon which the subject will subsequently build their own autonomy, through the acquisition of information, knowledge, and skills.

> *The social role—the development of social skills in communication, relationships, organisation—that is the social role. Knowledge is added as to a tree. You come along nicely, you have a green tree, and you just keep adding an ornament. It is somewhat the same here: the social role of probation practice is to create the skeleton upon which you will in the future add information, knowledge, and especially skills (IRO08).*

The construction of social autonomy and moral agency is carried out simultaneously with the responsibilisation of individuals to do what they need to do. Supervised persons must find their own inner resources to go to the various institutions where they must report, whether to fulfil the measures imposed by the court or to achieve the best possible social integration. The probation officer may carry out institutional advocacy activities, but only within the limits of the individual's assumption of task-oriented behaviour. The respondent's discourse is centred on the imperative *must*; the assumption of one's own moral and social duty is the key to the person's anticipatory socialisation on the basis of socially accepted values.

> *We try to make them responsible, to show them that it is within their power to do certain things. I can remedy a certain relationship with a certain institution, I can put in a good word, so to speak, but it is within their power to go there, to speak for themselves, to show up, to do these things. I can show them the direction, but I cannot go and speak for them; I cannot go and explain what the person should do (IRO11).*

The construction of autonomy—both relational and functional autonomy, as well as one's own moral agency [200]—enables the offender to build a management of self-care and self-transformation. Probation practice centred on the supervised person's strengths—appreciative probation [172]—will mobilise and motivate the person to use their own inner resources in the process of social reintegration. We note that the respondent includes probation practice within the sphere of professions allied to social work, with which it shares precisely the process of helping the vulnerable person in the (re)construction of their autonomy.

> *The autonomy of the beneficiary is very important, because they will learn on their own those methods of self-help. It is as in any assistance process—as in social work or in other situations in which a person is dependent on help—and here self-determination or autonomy are very important, because the convicted person, through the helping process directed by the probation officer, will acquire those self-help abilities; that is, they will focus on their strengths, on what will lead them to use their inner resources in the process of social reintegration (IRO01).*

Unfortunately, persons under supervision were unable to formulate a clear definition of autonomy or responsibility, could not explain what autonomy means, and did not manage to describe their own progress towards autonomous and responsible behaviour. Nevertheless, in describing the activity of the probation officer, beneficiaries indicate that the officer: *"teaches us, gives us advice so that we do not offend again, so that we are careful not to offend again. That is, in a good sense, so that we do good" (IBM02).*

Probation is seen as entailing the unconditional support of the officer towards the client in the process of implementing the decision for change taken by the supervised person themselves. The officer's support and assistance should not substitute the supervised person's individual efforts.

> *First of all, you have to work so that they (the supervised persons) see that they can benefit from our help. That is, I always offer them help, but somehow the decisions should be made by them, because there is a trap here: if they always wait for me to make the decision, they*

will never be able to make a decision on their own. That is, I somehow show them that they benefit from my support, from my guidance, but the steps and activities they undertake to achieve an objective must be done by them, not by me (IRO04).

There is a reluctance among respondents towards a problem-centred approach to probation, termed by the respondent the *Norwegian model*. The problem-centred approach is considered ineffective, leading to a negative psychological burden on the supervised person, which is not conducive to discouraging recidivism. On the contrary, focusing on solutions, and especially on the subject's prior successful experiences, allows them to identify cognitive-behavioural strategies capable of generating and sustaining the process of social reintegration.

Here in Romania, and I speak from the perspective of my seventeen years of work experience, we are centred on the problem, but I believe that worldwide as well, we highlight the problem and bring it back into discussion. I do not see this as the most appropriate approach. I did not say I do not see it as an approach—as I said about the Norwegians—but telling a person that they were wrong, wrong, wrong means burdening them negatively. Come, tell the person: 'You were wrong. OK. Let us see what can be done. Let us do this, let us do that...' so that the person becomes emotionally charged in a positive way, so that they have positive thinking (...). That should be the practical purpose of any initiative, whether it is an educational or a professional one. You do not tell the employee: 'You are stupid, you are an idiot'; you tell them: 'Look, you do have some gaps, let us overcome them. You are good at that thing—let us make use of it.' Then you encourage them like a child, little by little, and then the person, gaining courage, becomes autonomous, especially mentally. Mental autonomy determines personal autonomy, financial autonomy, and so on. With our convicted persons, if we talk about them, they lack this type of positive thinking, and I believe that is what we should focus on—on changing the type of thinking (IRO08).

From the perspective of supervised persons, the social reintegration of the offender is a priority function of the probation system, since *everyone makes mistakes, that is, so that everyone can set themselves right (IBM02).* The operational definition of responsibility with which probation officers work is the assumption of consequences for the acts committed.

> *In the criminal framework, responsibility means that each person bears the consequences of the act committed (IRO09).*

Probation officers engage in remodelling the supervised person's behaviour and restoring their motivation for social integration.

> *We help people remodel their behaviour or maintain it, because there are also cases that have a high motivation from the beginning. More recently, they come for sentence re-evaluation; they do not have the status of convicted persons; they are integrated people and have no problems (IRO04).*

The officers' trust in the capacity of supervised persons to take responsibility for their own conduct is a component of their discourse about practice. Responsibilisation is a gradual process, simultaneously a social development and a sociotherapy (IRO04; IMD03). The process of responsibilisation is constructive, being dependent on a series of personality factors of the subject as well as on a series of factors from the socio-economic environment in which they operate.

> *(The responsibilisation of persons who have committed criminal acts) It is possible. The level of responsibilisation differs depending on the person, their personality, their development, their life experience, their level of education, the conditions in their family, and their social, economic, and financial situation. But it is possible gradually. I know there are cases that have a low level and you cannot reach beyond that—all these factors impede you. There are persons who reach a responsibilisation almost approaching totality (IRO07).*

The construction of responsibility is correlated with the officer's attitude of suspending moral judgement regarding both the supervised person and the act they have committed.

> *We work with a behaviour that you do not know. You have to give yourself time to get to know it, but I am not in a position to judge them for what they have done (IRO08).*

The essential characteristic of the probation officer should be the guidance of practice by norms. In order to be able to assist in the construction of the autonomy and responsibility of supervised persons, officers must carry out their professional activity with impartiality and with respect for norms, but also with the imposition of moral principles—derived from professional values—to which officers adhere mentally and even affectively.

> *First of all, I believe that a professional is someone who is guided by principles and norms. Even though we work with people, we must never forget that we must first of all be impartial and hold very firmly to our principles, those that guide our activity. And this gives us a certain weight but also a certain responsibility, and if we do not hold to those moral, legal, and ethical principles that guide our activity, we can easily fall into less pleasant situations (IRO11).*

Responsibility for the consequences of one's own actions is constructed starting from the honest assumption of the act. This is considered one of the most important objectives of the probation officer in working with the supervised person.

> *I believe that the assumption of the act would be one of the problems, and we work a great deal with this aspect. The assumption of the act is one of the most important facets we work with. To become a responsible person, you must understand that there are norms you must not cross. If others do not cross them, then neither should you (IRO11).*

The supervision process is seen as a process of responsibilising the offender. This responsibilisation is the objective of the counselling, supportive, and also restrictive actions carried out by the officer. The respondent emphasises the necessity of congruence between the individual actions of the offender and those of the community aimed at the offender's social integration.

> *The supervision process itself is a process of responsibilisation. Through everything the probation officer does, they responsibilise the convicted person to assume and to comply as optimally as possible with the measures and obligations imposed upon them by the judge, and to bring their full contribution so that all their actions are congruent towards as successful an integration into the community as possible (IRO01).*

The probation officer employs a symbolic coercion in the process of responsibilising the offender towards their own future actions, by invoking the possibility of revoking the non-custodial measures and reverting to imprisonment.

> *Well, of course it is possible, because you also have certain levers—that is, you bring it to their attention and ask them: 'Do you value your freedom? If you do not respect the measures, I will file a self-referral report and you will end up in prison. You will not see your family, you will no longer contribute to their support, and you will have lost your job and your image in the community.' And so that is how I responsibilise them. That is how I see it (IRO04).*

Respondents indicate that the process of responsibilising supervised persons can start from the identification of situations in which they have demonstrated responsibility previously—for example, parental responsibility—and the transfer of that successful experience to the assumption of responsibility in their own process of social reintegration.

> *There are persons who are on the record of the probation service but who are responsible parents, for example (IRO05).*

The respondent analyses the dynamics of the responsibilisation process within probation. In the first part of the officer–supervised person interaction, responsibility is constructed as the assumption of accountability for one's acts. In the absence of this assumption, the communication between the supervised person and the officer is inauthentic. The assumption of accountability for the consequences of one's own acts is complemented by the assumption of accountability for initiating the process of social reintegration. Ultimately, the success of the counselling process represents the attainment of the subject's capacity to be responsible for all facets of their existence.

> *Well, (responsibility) has a very important significance. One of the objectives of our activity, at least at the beginning of the supervision period, is their responsibilisation—that is, it is very important. In practice, even communication without their responsibilisation is almost not established and is not authentic communication. Because at the moment when the person is not responsible for assuming the acts committed, the consequences of the acts—but also for assuming their social reintegration, their readaptation to the correct, natural, positive social environment—then responsibilisation is one of our objectives throughout the entire period. In the end, the satisfaction and the success of the case would be for the person to be responsible regarding every aspect of their life, as much as possible (IRO07).*

Responsibility is correlated with care for the other, placing probation within the sphere of the ethics of care [164, pp. 28–47] and not merely within that of justice-based ethics, as might be expected of a profession situated within the criminal enforcement system. The paradigm of restorative justice, which underpins Romanian probation practice, despite its dual normative discourse, is ultimately tributary to a postmodern societal model. The postmodern elements targeted by the Romanian restorative probation model are principally represented by the dissolution of duty [36] and its interpretive drift towards social responsibility. The duty model is convergent with the idea of retributive justice, while social responsibility implies a model of restorative justice.

> *Something rare in our days. We speak very easily about responsibility. As I have said before, it means caring about yourself and about others. That is how I would see responsibility. The moment you care about yourself, you also adopt that behaviour so as not to harm those around you. And it also means assuming your failures. Being responsible presupposes acknowledging, confronting, and finding solutions—as much as it is in your power to repair something, with the risk of being blamed, with the risk of being judged by others. For me, it matters not only to*

> *acknowledge the thing; if you can also repair a little, that always counts much more (IRO08).*

The importance of the communication dimension in the officer–supervised person relationship is also underlined by respondents from among the supervised persons: *To help me through the conversations we have (IBM01).*

2.4.4. Why Are Offenders Punished

The sanction represents the individual's accountability for their act. The mere sanction represents only half the road towards rehabilitation. The assumption of accountability for the act for which the individual was sanctioned, the awareness of the antisocial character of the act, represents the true educative function of punishment. The sanction is considered incomplete in the absence of rehabilitation. The offence should not be automatically associated with the sanction, but with the rehabilitation of the offender. The role of the justice system—and of the probation system, author's note—is social therapeutics.

> *(The purpose of applying a sentence is the retribution/sanctioning of a wrong committed) That is only half the problem. Sanctioning is merely accountability. Just as the doctor would say: 'Because you did not have an adequate lifestyle, you fell ill; I am giving you some medication.' The medication does not solve the whole problem, because in addition to the sanction, the person must follow that path of behavioural change. Yes, in addition to the medical treatment, one says to oneself: 'You must follow a diet. You must eat less, you must get less upset.' Things that the medication does not do, but are solely your own actions in order to continue in good health. That is how I see the justice side as well. One thing is to sanction, and another is to rehabilitate the person. I give you a slap, but I explain why, and I lead you to find a solution so that you do not end up in that situation again. So for me, the offence is not just about the sanction (IRO08).*

One of the respondents considers that the pronouncement of the sentence is important for the nature of the sanction. The retributive discourse is evident. The imperative of punishment is incontestable; only its repressive force must be graduated according to the degree of culpability. The judge is expected to exercise a just deliberation that allows for the appropriate sentence. The respondent's discourse places them within a modern, objectivist understanding of the sanction, with justice understood somewhat immanently, as an *in itself* that exists outside the process of the social construction of justice.

> *The sentence must be pronounced in the sense that the person must be sanctioned. The court must take into account the degree, the intention, the premeditation, in order to pass an appropriate sentence (IRO02).*

The same retributive perspective, according to which offenders are punished because an antisocial act once committed must be sanctioned, and possibly also to set an example, is evident in the responses of the supervised persons (IBM 1, 2, 4, 5, 6, 7, IBRO 1, 3, 5, 6). Some respondents nuance the idea, introducing a distinction based on whether the offence was committed intentionally or through negligence, as well as on its gravity and social danger: *There are offenders who committed by mistake, but there are offenders who want to commit, and they must be punished according to the act (...) If the offence is very, very serious, they should be imprisoned, but if the offence is not serious, they should be given a fine or something else (IBM06).*

A series of opinions expressed by respondents emphasise the preventive role of the sanction rather than the retributive one, the role of punishment being the deterrence of the commission of new offences.

> *There exists since antiquity the proverb according to which a person is not punished because they have erred—because the wrong that was done is done—but is punished so that in the future they do not reiterate the behaviour (IRO05).*

From this perspective, custodial punishment is less effective than non-custodial measures. The prison environment constitutes a source of alternative deviant socialisation; therefore, incarceration may lead to an accentuation of the deviant career, through the acquisition of criminal experience via close communication with other offenders.

> *Indeed, persons who enter a closed environment come into contact with other persons where they can become much more experienced than they are at present (IRO05).*

Another opinion regarding the purpose of punishment places it within the sphere of the protection of society. This protective role is closely correlated with the preventive one, only raised to the rank of social justice. Retribution is delegated by the individual to society, thus invoking the perspective of the social contract as the foundation of justice. The sanction as public retribution replaces the individual's right to apply retribution, the latter being—on the basis of the social contract—the monopoly of the state.

> *Well, the reason is a natural one. Society punishes offenders in order to protect itself, because offenders, regardless of what acts they commit, cause harm to persons—well, directly or indirectly; some perhaps directly, others perhaps indirectly. And so society must react, because through the justice system each person affected reacts—or rather, each person who bears the consequences of a criminal act. If offences were unsanctioned, they would probably perpetuate themselves more and more, and then chaos would ensue (IRO07).*

The sanctioning of offenders has, beyond the formal aspect—the violation of the law automatically attracting the sanction—also a communitarian dimension. The offence is viewed as a handicap, taking the form of the individual's incapacity to see their own life clearly. By placing criminality within the perspective of social handicap, the respondent effectively invokes society's responsibility towards it, on the same model by which persons suffering from other forms of handicap require social protection.

> *(why offenders are punished) Well, it depends on how you take it. If you take it from a legal point of view, it is effectively the violation of the law. If you take it from a communitarian point of view, it is a handicap of the person in seeing their own life. The first variant is simple: you have the law, you do not respect it, and so on (IRO08).*

Punishment serves as a kind of example, because any punishment entails a limitation of certain rights. As such, by limiting some rights, the person feels that they have been punished. However, community sanctions are far more effective because the supervised person in the community has more possibilities and opportunities for reintegration than in the custodial environment, respectively in the penitentiary. Once there, the person internalises more criminal patterns than they assimilate educational programmes. For this reason, I consider that the opportunity of non-custodial sanctions is a trend that we, probation officers, support, and we hope that the probation system will open itself to these opportunities (IRO01).

> *(the implementation of counselling and offender–victim mediation programmes) I do not think so, and I think it would greatly complicate the situation for the victim. Beyond being a victim, you are a person, and you expect society to recognise this, while society merely smooths the situation over (IRO02).*

The exemplary nature of punishment is correlated with awareness of it. In the absence of awareness, the harshness of the sanction is not sufficient to reduce the risk of recidivism. The respondent indicates that there is no necessary correlation between punishment and recidivism. Opposed to the retributive paradigm, probation practice is seen as centred on the value of humanism, on the discovery of the positive elements inherent in every person, and on the development of these positive elements towards the social reintegration of the supervised person. The practice of appreciative probation [172, pp. 37–52]—centred on the elements of inherent positivity of each individual—constitutes precisely the motivation for practice for some of the respondents.

> *As long as they are not aware, the punishment does not set an example. So if they are not aware and have no motivation for change regarding their acts, you can give them a prison sentence and they will serve another sentence. I consider that if you work with a person, every person has something good in them; if you discover it and dig into it, you can help them. That is why I have stayed in this field. But not all who are punished will refrain from committing again. They will continue to commit offences (IRO04).*

Respondents draw a distinction between two forms of suspended sentence specific to Romanian legislation: the deferral of the application of the sentence and the suspension of execution under supervision. In the case of the deferral of the application of the sentence, the respondent indicates that this concerns convicted persons for whom the court, at the proposal of the probation service, determines that there is a minor risk of recidivism. The deferral of the application of the sentence is also considered a punishment, which is, however, replaced by conditional suspension. Regarding the suspension under supervision as a sanctioning measure, the respondent reports the difficulty of working with this category of convicted persons, as there are numerous conditions of the suspension that must be monitored. Probation practice also includes a particular form—the deferral of the pronouncement of the sentence for a probation period—in which, in the absence of a pronounced sentence, the presumption of innocence remains operative. If the alleged offender does not commit any further act during the probation period and possibly follows a series of measures—educational ones, for example—the judge may pronounce the closure of the case without ruling on the offender's guilt, who thus does not have the act recorded in their criminal record and is not exposed to the risk of stigmatisation and social exclusion. This deferral of pronouncement, although existing in the Romanian criminal code, does not appear as such in the respondents' discourses, probably because there is no systematic court practice in this direction. It is interesting that respondents consider this practice of deferral of pronouncement for a probation period more effective and believe it should have been the sole form of deferral under supervision.

> *The deferral of the application of the sentence is also a punishment replaced by conditional suspension. There, in general, are persons who do not have such a great risk of committing offences, and they are the persons we work with most easily. Suspension under supervision—there it is very difficult to work. There are convictions that also have very many obligations, which again we have to monitor, and again we take steps—a great many steps. Nowadays we also collaborate with hospitals and doctors. There are also very many specialised terms, and you have to be very careful about how you communicate, because nobody understands those terms. So it is quite difficult, what I can say; they should leave us only with the suspension under supervision and the deferral of the application of the sentence. Not to commit further. As it was before: they had a probation period, and if they did not commit another offence, they would no longer be convicted; and then to have kept only the suspension under supervision—that is how I see it (IRO04).*

The respondent nuances the point, explaining that the probation period cannot be indeterminate, as difficulties arise in knowing who determines and under what conditions the supervision is lifted. The respondent also indicates that the deferral of pronouncement and/or of the application of the sentence, which would result in the act not being entered in the criminal record, may be debatable from the perspective that certain criminal acts should be publicly known, especially in the case of serious offences.

> *At this moment, we have the suspension under supervision and the deferral of the application of the sentence. What you mention, about the deferral for an indeterminate period—here we leave room for interpretation: indeterminate until when, and who decides when it ends? I believe that certain limits must be set in both cases, each with its advantage and disadvantage. The suspension normally remains in the criminal record for a certain period after the person has finished supervision—a period of three years. With the deferral, it should not appear in the criminal record. It depends on a case-by-case basis. There are offences that should draw attention to the fact that the person has committed a certain type of offence in the past, or certain serious offences. These are case-by-case discussions. I cannot say that I would opt for one or the other (IRO05).*

Other respondents consider that the deferral of the pronouncement of the sentence and/or of the ruling on guilt is too risky, with the suspension of execution under supervision being preferred.

> *(The sentence to be pronounced, with suspension conditional on following a probation programme, or the pronouncement of the sentence to be deferred by the judge for an indeterminate period and, in the event of the success of social reintegration programmes, the sentence not to be pronounced at all.) I would go with the first option, the one with supervision for a determinate period; the other option seems to me a little too permissive (IRO06).*

Retributivity is called into question from the perspective of the possibility of resocialisation and social reintegration of offenders. The educative dimension of punishment—the fostering of the process of understanding the social significance of the act—should underpin the pronouncement of sentences, and not the mere punishment/retribution for the act committed. The elimination of the talionic mentality and the replacement of retribution in the signification of punishment can be considered a postmodern element in the discourse of probation practitioners. Punishment is no longer an exercise of power [22], but rather one of the reconstruction of social cohesion through communicative actions. Punishment is a consequence of the act in the sense of the inevitability of the assumption of accountability, but once responsibility has been assumed, it exhausts the power charge of the punishment. Punishment is no longer a mere consequence of the social contract, when it served the role of collective vengeance by society and the victim for the harm caused, but rather an active contribution of the (co-)responsible community to the resocialisation of the individual.

> *I do not agree with this view (Offenders deserve to be punished because they have committed a bad/antisocial act), because if we pursue retributivity, I do not know whether we will manage to reintegrate them into society afterwards. There are cases at present—there have always been persons who do not necessarily commit acts, but must be punished so that they come to understand why they erred, not necessarily because of the act itself (IRO07).*

The educative role of punishment is seen as differing according to the subjective perception that the individual has of the punishment, of the act, and even of the system of criminal sanctions itself. A possible perverse effect of probation practice is mentioned—namely, that some offenders, knowing the specifics of the intervention, are encouraged to commit criminal acts, considering the non-custodial sanction acceptable.

> *The role of punishment cannot be entirely eliminated, because I would not deny this statement entirely. I do not know to what extent it sets an example, because it depends on how this example reaches the other members of society. Members who are closer to the punished person understand it in one way, because they are closer and talk with them. There are members of society who learn about the effects, let us say, of our very intervention from the press. The press is more or less*

> *informed, in the sense that there are also people in the press who do not necessarily have direct and very accurate knowledge of the practice of the probation system, of the concrete intervention. And so that is why I say the exemplary role differs. There are persons who have agreed to commit acts based on the idea that they will surely come to probation and that they know what happens here. About thirty per cent—I agree with it (IRO07).*

There must exist—the social equilibrium prejudiced by the criminal act between offender, victim, and society must be re-established. The purpose of probation is simultaneously the social reintegration of the offender and the increase of public safety.

> *Yes, it is one of the purposes of our intervention until the end of the supervision period. Of course, once the equilibrium is established, this in fact means a reintegration of the person, a protection of society against the commission of new acts, and so yes, I believe that is correctly stated (IRO07).*

The exemplary nature of punishment should lead to the deterrence of criminogenic behaviour. The offender should know the advantages and disadvantages of the (future) commission of an offence. The respondent even mentions the existence of a specific technique in probation work, which is based on the offender's understanding of the strengths and weaknesses entailed by a certain behaviour, of the gains and losses that may arise from the reiteration of the respective criminogenic behaviour. This approach appears to be grounded in certain theories concerning the rationality of the social actor and the rational character of social action. Criminogenic behaviour, however, is not entirely rational. The appeal to illegitimate opportunities may be an example of the rationality of the deviant social actor, but this cost-benefit analysis is not always implicated. Often, momentary impulses lacking any cost-benefit calculation are involved. On the contrary, the cost-benefit type of calculation seems more logically correlated with premeditated behaviour than, for example, with the commission of an antisocial act through negligence. The risk-benefit awareness technique may nevertheless be particularly useful in forming habits of rationalising social behaviour and of cost-benefit calculation regarding any illegitimate opportunities that arise.

> *Yes, punishment must set an example; punishment must discourage the behaviour. Punishment must lead the person to think about what is to their advantage and disadvantage. We have in probation, and not only, the technique of highlighting the strengths and weaknesses of committing an offence, of a behaviour. We try to work with gains and losses. We tell the person: 'Hey, what did you gain? OK, prestige among the friends with whom you committed the offence, fine; some money, fine. What did you lose? Prison, because you go to prison; your entire future is destroyed.' So one can continue to work with this approach. For us, it is highly recommended, because people usually think in dual terms (IRO08).*

The mere sanction is considered insufficient for correcting criminogenic behaviour. Resocialisation should be based on education—through explanation and understanding, including experiential understanding, and through involvement in positive, prosocial actions.

> *What more could I say here. It is not enough; it is not enough to view everything as a sanction; it is not enough for the community. If you have a child and they have erred and you give them one slap, then a second, and a third time when they err, but without telling them, explaining, involving them in something, letting them see the positive side of things—their behaviour will not change (IRO08).*

The social role of probation is represented by the recovery of desirable behaviour. Behavioural changes are considered to be correlated with the will for change of the supervised persons.

> *For us, probation must recover human behaviour; it must help in the recovery of positive human behaviour, and to do this you need time. We work with people's will. We cannot be held accountable for the mistakes made by people.*

Restorative justice is seen in the form of the reparation that the offender makes to the victim and to society for the harm caused by the commission of the criminal act. The respondent considers it absolutely necessary, especially towards the victim. This reparation leads to awareness of the harm, ultimately resulting in the re-establishment of the equilibrium in the community disrupted in the offender–victim relationship by the commission of the criminal act. The purpose of probation is the protection of the community through the reduction of the risk of new offences, both as recidivism on the part of the offender and on the part of other community members, through processes of social learning of criminal behaviour, through retributive acts assumed personally by the victim or members of their social network, and so forth.

> *I will say more about another aspect. It concerns restorative justice—that is, the reparation that the offender brings to the community. My opinion is that this form of reparation towards the victim, whether a natural person, a legal person, or an institution, must exist. It raises awareness of the harm produced. Most of the time, the harm caused to others is not perceived unless it also rebounds upon oneself. Yes, my opinion is that this equilibrium must be re-established. The ultimate purpose of probation is the protection of the community through the reduction of the risk of committing new offences, in collaboration with community institutions (IRO08).*

One of the answers to the question of why offenders are punished is also the tendency to label (IRO10), evident at the level of Romanian society. The exemplary nature of punishment as an instrument for deterring criminal behaviour is rejected by the respondent on the basis of pragmatic arguments, related to the lack of significant experiences demonstrating a correlation between the severity of sentences applied to other offenders and the reduction of criminal risk. On the contrary, the respondent emphasises the individualisation of the sentence to the concrete situation of the offender, correlated with accountability for one's own acts. Accountability, however, in order to be effective, must not have an anticipatory character.

> *I do not believe that punishment should be an example for others. I have not seen anyone to date. I have not seen a single beneficiary who says: 'Yes, I saw that the court gave that person four years of imprisonment, and that is why I did not do that.' I believe that the individualisation of the sentence should be strongly pursued. I believe very much in this. And I believe that each person should answer for their own act and not for future acts (IRO11).*

Some respondents call into question the reality of the reconstruction of the victim–offender–society equilibrium as the foundation of restorative probation. It is difficult to achieve adequate compensation; thus, in practice, either the offender pays a greater compensation than the harm produced, or the victim and society remain at a loss even after the payment of the established compensations. Retribution through custodial punishment is futile, since the restriction of the offender's freedom does not produce compensation for the victim or for society. Moreover, custodial punishment consumes additional societal resources for its administration. The retributive paradigm is thus rejected from two perspectives: that of the equity of retribution—that is, from the very perspective of the realisation of justice, its constitutive value—and from the utilitarian perspective of the futility of the costs of retribution and the lack of its justification for society.

> *It would be good if it were so, but most of the time this equilibrium is not achieved, and there are all manner of situations. There are situations in which the offender pays more than the harm caused to the victim, or sometimes the victim and society are left with such a great loss that not in three lifetimes could the offender pay. So enormous sums of money remain uncovered. And even if the person serves time in prison for the respective fraud—OK, what do we end up with? Since during those five years, it is still we who pay for their food (IRO11).*

2.5. Thematic Axis V. Victim–Offender Mediation

2.5.1. Victim–Offender Mediation as a Constitutive Element of the Restorative Justice Paradigm

Regarding victim–offender mediation, some respondents express extreme reservations, considering separate intervention with the victim and the offender to be more effective.

> *The situation is a little more delicate. I would envision at least initially separate interventions, and I do not know—I would not see them as equally combined even at the end. That is, it seems to me quite delicate. And even on a case-by-case basis, at least at the beginning, I would work separately (IRO06).*

The respondent rejects the utility of reconciliation programmes through mediation between the victim and the offender. Although this practice is seen as being customary within probation services in various countries, its success is strictly conditional upon both persons' willingness to change.

> *(the implementation of counselling and offender–victim mediation programmes would lead to the responsibilisation of offenders) No. This is a strictly personal answer. Many probation systems—and not only the probation system but also the child protection system in the family domain—address that mediation relationship between the victim and the offender or with the person with whom they were in conflict. The essential thing is not this type of approach; it is the willingness of both persons to change something (IRO08).*

The respondent indicates that the mere obligation upon the offender to contact the victim and possibly express regret may be carried out formally, without leading to a genuine transformation. Such solutions pronounced by judges belonging to various legal systems are considered insufficient for ensuring the reconstruction of social equilibrium.

> *If there is only a single obligation upon the offender, the convicted person, to contact the victim, they might do so in a strictly formal manner. So there are judges in this world who impose this type of mediation and counselling obligation with the victim (IRO08).*

The rejection of this restorative practice—based on offender–victim mediation—is considered unsuitable for the Romanian probation system, owing to the psychological particularities of the Romanian offender, who is reticent towards such an approach, and the heightened risks of re-victimisation of the victim. In the respondent's experience, such a practice is very difficult to carry out on the basis of freely expressed consent to participate by both parties and involving a genuine dialogue between them.

> *My opinion is that, at least for the Romanian system, victim–offender mediation is not effective from two standpoints. First, the psychology of the Romanian offender is very closed to such an approach. Second, the*

> *reliving of the trauma by the victim will not lead to an improvement of the situation but will further accentuate negative feelings. To see yourself face to face with the person who raped you or beat you—I do not think that the Romanian offender, or the typology of offender I have worked with for fifteen years, would be willing to do so voluntarily (IRO08).*

The respondent indicates that, in their capacity as head of a probation service, they left it to the discretion of the officers within the service they coordinate to carry out or not such victim–offender reconciliation programmes, although personally, the respondent declares themselves opposed. This permission granted to subordinate officers is rather debatable, since the Romanian legislative framework does not include such practices among the responsibilities of probation officers. Of course, nor does it expressly prohibit them, and their application constitutes a particular practice at the level of a specific service. This is difficult to accept given the case overload—over 230 in the case of some respondents—the extremely limited time resources, and the excessive bureaucratisation of practice (IRO06).

> *I told my colleagues: do as you see fit, but from my point of view as head of the service, it is not exactly effective, because the victim will never say a good thing about the offender and, on the contrary, will accentuate the negative information, which you will have to record and which will cause harm. But perhaps that person had a single incident, after which they never had another. The reliving of the event does not do good in many cases. Perhaps for the English, perhaps for the Americans, but I honestly, at least at this moment, do not believe so (IRO08).*

The rejection of victim–offender mediation programmes, nearly unanimous among respondents, is motivated by the respondent by the pressures of the family environment as well as the psychological pressures weighing upon both the offender and the victim, raised by the prospect of the two parties seeing each other again. The respondent acknowledges the utility of such programmes, but they require an extraordinary effort and mediation competencies that exceed those of the probation officer.

(Would the implementation of counselling and offender–victim mediation programmes lead to the responsibilisation of offenders?) I think it could, but such an undertaking is very difficult, because most of the time there are certain external pressures, family pressures. It is hard for me to accept that I was wrong; it is hard for the person opposite to accept that they have to see me again. It would require a very great human effort on the part of the probation officer to mediate, to bring the persons to that equilibrium that would allow such a face-to-face undertaking. And I think such an undertaking could only be done by resorting to specialised counselling and mediation services—aspects that do not necessarily pertain to the specifics of our profession (IRO11).

2.5.2. The Functional Paradigm of the Profession: Restorative Justice, Human Rights-Centred Justice, Retributive Justice

The principle of the universality of negative retribution in the event of norm violation is viewed axiomatically by the majority of respondents. Respondents indicate that probation practitioners consider themselves very pleased when courts grant convicted persons the chance to benefit from adequate counselling support and even social assistance services from the probation service. In our view, this approach is relatively deficient, since in their capacity as probation officers, it would be desirable for them to advocate for the reduction of the level of retributivity and for the humanisation of punishments. Custodial sanctions should come to constitute an exception rather than a rule, especially if we correlate this information with the respondents' assertion that the recidivism rate for persons in probation is as much as ten times lower than that of persons who have served a custodial sentence. Even though in principle non-custodial sanctions are applied to first-time offenders, who usually regret the act committed—circumstances that tend to diminish the risk of recidivism—the role of the probation officer in reducing this risk should not be ignored, just as the role of the prison period in constructing a deviant career for inmates, extensively discussed by the respondents, should not be overlooked. Accordingly, we consider that the expression of gratification at the judge's understanding of the benefit of supervision is somewhat the result of a lack of confidence in the social acceptability of the profession of probation officer, given its relative novelty.

> *Of course, any violation of a social norm attracts a sanction. However, we probation officers are open and very pleased when the judge gives the supervised person the chance to benefit from the adequate support of the probation officer through counselling and assistance. We are very pleased when the judge understands the benefit of supervision and social assistance, and we come with great willingness to meet their criminogenic needs (IRO01).*

We observe a discursive specificity tributary to the retributive paradigm with utilitarian-restorative elements, rather than a discourse specific to the restorative justice paradigm. Punishment is considered an example, through the very limitation of certain rights that constitutes the essence of punishment. The respondent draws attention to the fact that this limitation of rights should be felt as such by the punished person in order for this coercive function to be fulfilled. Community sanctions are accordingly seen as effective, precisely because of the high degree of social reintegration of persons who serve such non-custodial sanctions. The prison environment, on the contrary, allows the person to internalise illegitimate behavioural patterns, to the detriment of the desirable habituses transmitted by the re-education programmes in penitentiaries. The respondent is aware of the importance of actively promoting the significance of non-custodial sanctions and of the role of probation services in this promotional activity. Discriminatory mentalities existing within certain communities may lead to an exaggerated affinity towards retributivity. The idea of systematic retributivity is seen as a substitution of the legal system by society in a situation of systemic anomie.

> *Perhaps the lack of justice—somehow society tries to substitute itself for the system and to deliver justice. It is possible that in some communities there is also a discriminatory, labelling mentality (IRO09).*

The respondent indicates that a series of constructive actions fall within the responsibility of the probation officer—establishing and following the rehabilitative course, consisting in the order and the effective manner of executing non-custodial measures, as the officer considers useful for enhancing the offender's social reintegration.

> *But once the judge has thought in this way, it means it is the most suitable for the person. We enforce, and here we can choose the obligations—that is, they are*

established by the judge, but we have the role of somehow introducing the person to obligations or removing them from obligations, and not necessarily at the period that the person must comply with. That is, the probation officer also has their own method of individualisation and of working with the person (IRO09).

Conclusions of the Research: Axes of the Social Construction of the Probation Officer Profession. Qualitative Research in the North-Eastern Region of Romania and in the Republic of Moldova

Probation developed on the basis of a series of experimental models aimed at introducing restorative justice as the foundation for non-custodial sentences. In this context, professionals whose initial training is multidisciplinary operate within the probation system, particularly from the helping professions—social work, psychology, special psychopedagogy, and so forth. Alongside them, there are professionals in the system whose initial training is in the field of law. Probation officers regard continuing professional development as a constitutive element of professional success. The desire for professional improvement is present among all respondents and, from their observations, among the majority of officers in the system. Inter-institutional cooperation is deficient in certain situations, a fact attributed to low institutional respect, partially due to the novelty of the field and partially to the accentuated retributive mentality existing at the level of Romanian society. The Romanian model represents a combination of the four paradigms—retributive justice, restorative justice, utilitarian justice, and justice based on humanist values and human rights partly due to the model of probation development in Romania and Moldova on the basis of private initiatives (the NGO sector), the introduction of restorative justice, and the predominance of the helping-profession character of the practice. The dominant discourse is a predominantly retributive one, the majority of respondents indicating that punishment is necessary because the antisocial act must attract a sanctioning response from society. The restorative and human rights-based elements substitute retributivity when the question arises of the manner of application and the type of applicable sanctions. The social value of responsibility is particularly important, intervening in three situations: the responsibility of the probation officer, the responsibility of society, and the construction of the offender's responsibility as a key element of their social reintegration. The Romanian model represents a combination of the four paradigms—retributive justice, restorative justice, utilitarian justice, and justice based on humanist values and human rights—partly due to the model of probation development in Romania and Moldova on the basis of private initiatives (the NGO sector), the introduction of restorative justice, and the predominance of the helping-profession character of the practice. The dominant discourse is a predominantly retributive one, the majority of respondents indicating that punishment is necessary because the antisocial act must attract a sanctioning response from society. The restorative and human rights-based elements substitute retributivity when the question arises of the manner of application and the type of applicable sanctions. The social value of responsibility is particularly important, intervening in three situations: the responsibility of the probation officer, the responsibility of society, and the construction of the offender's responsibility as a key element of their social reintegration.

2.6. Elements of Model Validation. The Micro-Research: Probation Officers' Perspectives on Professional Practice

2.6.1. Clarifications of the Problem Context

Within the complex research project *The Social Construction of the Probation Officer Profession*, carried out between April 2016 and January 2017 in the North-Eastern Region of Romania and in the Republic of Moldova, a first dimension had among its objectives the identification of the main discursive axes through which the process of social construction of the probation officer profession is carried out [211]. These objectives were fulfilled through the research *Axes of the Social Construction of the Probation Officer Profession*, conducted on the basis of a qualitative, inductive methodology entitled Grounded Theory. The specificity of this methodology is the reversal of the classical research path, which starts from working hypotheses drawn from the literature and tested through various quantitative and/or qualitative methods. In Grounded Theory, the research starts effectively from the data collected through qualitative instruments—interviews, focus groups—and through successive inductions arrives at an increasingly complex theory with the power to explain the phenomenon. What are traditionally viewed as hypotheses are, for Grounded Theory, a final product, representing constituent parts of the proposed theoretical model. As such, the research does not aim to obtain a validation of hypotheses; consequently, the resulting theoretical model cannot be analysed as valid or invalid, but rather as plausible and generalisable or not. Nevertheless, the resulting theoretical constructs may have the value of hypotheses that could be statistically verifiable through subsequent research.

2.6.2. Hypotheses Generated from the Study: Axes of the Social Construction of the Probation Officer Profession

Within the aforementioned research, a series of results with the value of hypotheses for the present micro-research were constructed: **H1.** The Romanian and Moldavian model of probation is a multi- and transdisciplinary one, with strong helping-profession and social-therapeutic emphases. **H2.** The helping-profession perspective is fundamental to the professional practice of the probation officer. **H3.** There is no clear specialisation of probation officers in one or another activity, each officer being able to carry out any of the specific professional activities. **H4.** The success of probation practice is defined in terms of the number of persons reintegrated and the absence of recidivism. **H5.** The functioning of probation services is based on good communication, both at the personal and institutional levels, with the representatives of the other institutions with which they collaborate: courts, police, prosecution offices, public administration, civil society, penitentiaries, and so forth. **H6.** Probation officers in Romania place greater emphasis on interpersonal, informal communication strategies, while their counterparts in the Republic of Moldova are more interested in formal, institutionalised communication, in both cases with full and strict compliance with the law.

2.6.3. Research Questions

The research questions are subsumed under the central question: Can the model of the social construction of the probation officer profession, obtained inductively within the research *Axes of the Social Construction of the Probation Officer Profession* [124, 173], be considered valid, or at least plausible? Do probation officers in Romania and the Republic of Moldova adhere to the specificity of practice presupposed by the aforementioned model?

Purpose

The purpose of the micro-research *Probation Officers' Perspectives on Professional Practice* is to verify the plausibility and generalisability of the main results of the research *Axes of the Social Construction of the Probation Officer Profession* [124, 173] and to clarify the adherence of probation officers in both countries to the model constructed within it.

2.6.4. Methodology

Based on the results obtained, a questionnaire addressed to probation officers in both countries was constructed and administered online, using the Google platform. An invitation to respond to the questionnaire was sent by email to all probation services/offices in Romania and the Republic of Moldova. The questionnaire comprises 18 closed-ended questions concerning: the specificity and importance of professional training in the capacity of probation officer, the specificity of professional activity and the type of activities carried out, the institutional relationships between probation services/the probation officer and other professionals involved in the sphere of justice administration, the relationship of the probation services/offices with civil society, the constitutive and operational ethical values of the probation officer profession, and the professionals' adherence to the retributive/restorative model of functioning of probation services/offices. Twenty-four probation officers from Romania (14 female and 10 male) and 34 from the Republic of Moldova (25 female and 9 male) responded to the online questionnaire.

2.6.5. Discussion

The small size of the sample—the low number of probation officers who agreed to complete the online form—means that this micro-research cannot be credited with statistical validity. The online mode of administration and the small number of probation officers existing in the system—350 in Romania—resulted in a low number of respondents, thus not permitting a genuine statistical analysis of the data. Nevertheless, we note that the respondents represent approximately 7% of the number of probation officers existing in the system at the time of administration.

2.6.6. Results

57% of respondents from Romania and 9% from Moldova have more than 10 years of experience in the system; 30% of respondents from Romania and 48% from Moldova have been in the system for a period between 5 and 10 years; and the remaining 13% from Romania and 41% from Moldova have less than 5 years of experience; 2% of respondents from the Republic of Moldova declined to answer this question. Regarding professional training: 36% of respondents from Romania and 48% of respondents from the Republic of Moldova stated that they are graduates of a Faculty of Law; 29% of respondents from Romania and

5% of respondents from the Republic of Moldova stated that they are graduates of a Faculty of Social Work; 16% of respondents from Romania and 11% of respondents from the Republic of Moldova stated that they are graduates of a Faculty of Psychology; 13% of respondents from Romania and 21% of respondents from the Republic of Moldova stated that they are graduates of a Master's programme in Probation; 6% of respondents from Romania and 7% of respondents from the Republic of Moldova stated that they are graduates of short-duration courses in the field of probation. We note a significant difference between practitioners in Romania and the Republic of Moldova regarding initial training. Although in both countries the initial training of respondents is predominantly legal, in Moldova the prevalence of those with legal training approaches 50%. In Romania, the proportion of those who declare training in the helping-profession sphere is greater than in Moldova, which may partially explain the different emphasis placed on the importance of communication—non-formal and interpersonal among respondents from Romania, and formal, institutional, and institutionalised among respondents from Moldova. The number of respondents who declare that they have completed a master's programme in the field is quite low in both countries, which may support the idea of the necessity of such training programmes within the universities of both countries, preferably even programmes based on inter-institutional cooperation between higher education institutions in both countries, such as dual-degree master's programmes.

Regarding how they evaluate the importance of knowledge from the field of "social work" for the professional activity of the probation officer, 52% of respondents from Romania and 69% of respondents from the Republic of Moldova stated that this is important or very important; 30% of respondents from Romania and 27% of respondents from the Republic of Moldova stated that it is neither important nor unimportant; 9% of respondents from Romania and 4% of respondents from the Republic of Moldova stated that initial training in the helping-profession sphere is of little or very little importance. The responses received to these questionnaires support the hypothesis—resulting from the study *Axes of the Social Construction of the Probation Officer Profession*—according to which the helping-profession perspective is fundamental to professional practice. This interpretive coherence with the results obtained in the qualitative stage of the research constitutes an element of model validation, and the result can be partially attributed to the autonomisation of the probation profession, both in terms of its specific intervention methodology and its social function. Moreover, possible differences of opinion may arise due to the understanding—increasingly frequent—of social work exclusively in its dimension as a system for administering social benefits, a dimension that intersects the least with probation practice, where the helping dimension is realised from the perspective of an ethos of care and systemic theories, centred on the reconstruction of the moral agency of the supervised person.

Regarding the importance accorded to knowledge from the legal field for the professional activity of the probation officer, 91% of respondents from Romania and 89% of those from the Republic of Moldova stated that these are important or very important; 9% of respondents from Romania and 2% of respondents from the Republic of Moldova stated that they are neither important nor unimportant; none of the respondents from Romania and 9% of respondents from the Republic of Moldova stated that they are of little or very little importance. The importance of legal knowledge is considered even greater than that of the helping-profession domain, the vast majority of respondents agreeing on this point.

Regarding the perceived importance of knowledge from the field of "psychology" for the professional activity of the probation officer, none of the respondents from Romania and only 2% of those from the Republic of Moldova stated that these are of little or very little importance; 22% of respondents from Romania and 5% of those from the Republic of Moldova stated that these are neither important nor unimportant; while 65% of respondents from Romania and 93% of respondents from the Republic of Moldova stated that this knowledge is important or very important. A significant difference is noted in the direction of Moldavian respondents regarding the preference for the field of psychology, which, for our respondents from Moldova, even exceeds in perceived importance the knowledge from the fields of law and social work. The results obtained regarding the perceived importance of knowledge in the different professional areas allow us to consider plausible the hypothesis—generated by the study *Axes of the Social Construction of the Probation Officer Profession*—according to which the Romanian and Moldavian model of probation is a multi- and transdisciplinary one, with strong helping-profession and social-therapeutic emphases. The results for the three questions support the constructed model regarding the transdisciplinarity of probation and its autonomisation.

In response to the question regarding which specific activities of the probation officer the respondents are or have been involved in, they indicate the following: 19% (RO) and 18% (MD) stated involvement in the elaboration of pre-sentence evaluation reports; 19% (RO) and 27% (MD) stated involvement in the supervision of persons convicted with a suspended sentence; 8% (RO) and 15% (MD) stated involvement in the supervision of conditionally released persons; 16% (RO) and 9% (MD) stated involvement in the supervision of minors serving an educational measure; 14% (RO) and 9% (MD) stated involvement in social reintegration programmes; 13% (RO) and 6% (MD) stated involvement in participation in the conditional release commission; 2% (RO) and 1% (MD) stated involvement in victim–offender mediation; 9% (RO) and 7% (MD) stated involvement in working with persons in the penitentiary; 8% (MD) did not express an opinion at all. Although the dispersion of responses may be considered significant, it should be borne in mind that the question received multiple-choice answers and that, in practice, by relating to the number of respondents rather than valid responses, we obtain a high degree of uniformity, confirming the hypothesis that there is no clear specialisation of probation officers in one or another activity, each officer being able to carry out any of the specific professional activities. Certain responsibilities, such as participation in the conditional release commission, have a lower degree of representation in the overall proportion of officers' activity, precisely because they are not carried out at the level of all Probation Directorates/Offices—in our example, because in a given county there is no penitentiary, and therefore there is no participation in conditional release commissions. Nevertheless, a greater degree of specialisation is observed among officers in Moldova, where at the level of Probation Offices there exists such a distribution of tasks. Activities such as victim–offender mediation are not represented precisely because this responsibility, although specific to probation in other countries, is not assigned to probation officers in the two countries.

In response to the question *How do you evaluate the relationship between yourself, as a probation officer, and the persons under supervision?*—none of the respondents from Romania and only 4% of respondents from Moldova stated that the relationship is a slightly or very slightly good one; 9% (RO) and 9% (MD) stated that the relationship is an acceptably good one; 91% (RO) and 87% (MD) stated that the relationship is a good or very good one. The fact that nearly all respondents—probation officers—characterise their relationships with beneficiaries as good or very good may signify a valuation of the officer–

supervised person communication models and allows us to consider that the number of failure situations in probation practice in both countries is limited.

Respondents evaluate their relationships with the courts in appreciative terms, with 87% (RO) and 87% (MD) considering them good or very good, no respondent from Romania and only 2% (MD) considering them slightly or very slightly good, and the remaining 13% (RO) and 11% (MD) considering them neither good nor slightly good. Regarding the question concerning the relationship between the probation officer and representatives of public authorities—4% (RO) of respondents stated that the relationship is a slightly good one; none of the Moldavian respondents declared that their relationship with representatives of other public institutions with which they have service relations is slightly or very slightly good; 35% (RO) and 27% (MD) stated that the relationship is acceptably good; 48% (RO) and 43% (MD) stated that the relationship is a good one; 13% (RO) and 30% (MD) stated that the relationship is a very good one.

When asked to evaluate the relationship they have, as a probation officer, with representatives of civil society (NGOs)—78% (RO) and 63% (MD) rated it as good or very good; only 4% (RO) and 14% (MD) declared it slightly or very slightly good; while 18% (RO) and 18% (MD) were undecided, choosing the median value, coded by us as acceptably good. Regarding the relationship with representatives of the police—77% (RO) and 24% (MD) of respondents stated that the relationship is a good or very good one; 0% (RO) and 71% (MD) rate it as slightly or very slightly good; and 23% (RO) and 1% (MD) chose the middle position, acceptably good. We note differences that may be considered significant between respondents in the two countries regarding the relationship of probation officers with the police, with respondents from Romania being reserved at 23% but not expressing negative opinions about this collaboration, while Moldavian respondents criticise it in a significant proportion.

The relationship with representatives of the penitentiary is seen as good or very good by 83% (RO) and 54% (MD), while no respondent from Romania and 54% (MD) consider it slightly or very slightly good; 14% (RO) and 24% (MD) are undecided. Again, we note significant differences between respondents in the two countries, with Moldavian probation officers being less satisfied with communication with penitentiary representatives. Analysing the responses to the questions regarding the relationship between probation officers and the representatives of the other state institutions with which they collaborate in a unitary manner, these confirm the presupposition generated within the study *Axes of the Social Construction of the Probation Officer Profession*—namely, that the functioning of probation services is based on good communication, both at the personal and institutional levels, with the representatives of the other institutions with which they collaborate: courts, police, prosecution offices, public administration, civil society, penitentiaries, and so forth. The few differences between the results obtained from officers in Romania and those in Moldova also confirm the slight differences regarding the emphasis on institutional/interpersonal communication highlighted in the qualitative data analysis. Good relations with the representatives of the other institutions ensure the framework for the efficient functioning of probation services.

In response to the question *Which of the following statements do you consider most applicable to your relationships with the other institutions with which you collaborate?*—13% (RO) and 22% (MD) consider that the most important form of communication is written, formalised, and standardised communication; 83% (RO) and 73% (MD) consider that beyond written institutional communication, the interpersonal relationship with other professionals within the limits of legal compliance is important; and 4% (RO) and 5% (MD) did not express an opinion. Although Moldavian respondents pronounce themselves in a greater proportion in favour of institutional communication, the results only partially confirm the hypothesis according to which probation officers in Romania place more emphasis on the interpersonal dimension of communication, while their Moldavian counterparts place it on the institutional and formalised dimension. In fact, in both countries, the surveyed respondents appreciated the importance of interpersonal communication. Although significant in incidence, we cannot however consider that the emphasis on the written and formalised dimension is characteristic of Moldavian probation as opposed to Romanian probation, since Moldavian officers also express the exceptional importance of the interpersonal and non-formal dimension of communication in probation practice.

When asked to specify which ethical value they consider the most important for the professional practice of the probation officer—4% (RO) and 13% (MD) of respondents consider that the most important value is the respect for and encouragement of beneficiaries' autonomy (the capacity to make and assume one's own decisions); 8% (RO) consider that the most important value is respect for beneficiaries' dignity; 25%

(RO) and 29% (MD) consider that the most important value is the responsibility and responsibilisation of beneficiaries; 21% (RO) and 38% (MD) consider that the most important value is effective communication between the officer and the beneficiary; 20% (RO) and 4% (MD) consider that the most important value is trust in the officer–beneficiary relationship; and 4% (RO) did not express an opinion at all. The most important value for officers in Romania is the respect for and encouragement of beneficiaries' autonomy, at 38% (RO), followed by the responsibility and responsibilisation of beneficiaries at 25% (RO), and effective communication between the officer and the beneficiary, which, although not an ethical value per se, represents a value of practice. Trust is less valued by respondents, with only 4% (RO) choosing it as the most important. Among respondents from the Republic of Moldova, 38% (MD) situate communication, 29% (MD) situate responsibility and the responsibilisation of beneficiaries, 20% (MD) situate trust and respect, and 13% (MD) situate beneficiaries' autonomy as the most important value.

In response to the question that aims to evaluate the respondents' adherence to the retributive model of the sanction—*How do you evaluate the statement: "Offenders deserve to be punished because they have committed a bad/antisocial act"?*—4% (RO) and 7% (MD) of respondents state that they are in total disagreement with this statement; 31% (RO) and 7% (MD) state that they partially disagree; 31% (RO) and 22% (MD) state that they neither agree nor disagree; 17% (RO) and 32% (MD) state that they partially agree; and 17% (RO) and 32% (MD) state that they totally agree. These responses confirm our hypothesis according to which the probation model developed in the two countries is one centred on the retributive dimension of punishment, with the level of adherence to the retributive model of justice being higher in Moldova. Nevertheless, respondents partially understand the need to ground probation in an alternative model of justice, whether restorative, utilitarian, or centred on human rights. The sanctioning function of punishment remains significant, with professionals accepting it as a perspective on practice.

In response to the question *How do you evaluate the statement: "Offenders are punished in order to set an example for society"?*—9% (RO) and 16% (MD) of respondents state that they are in total disagreement; 31% (RO) and 12% (MD) state that they partially disagree; 30% (RO) and 21% (MD) state that they neither agree nor disagree; 17% (RO) and 21% (MD) state that they partially agree; and 30% (RO) and 13% (MD) state that they totally agree. The exemplary function of punishment is also important for respondents, with the ideology of the exemplary nature of punishment also being accepted as an axiological foundation of probation practice. The re-education and social reintegration function is also a component of the ideology that theoretically underpins probation practice, forming part of the practice-centred values to which officers in both countries adhere. 43% (RO) and 64% (MD) of respondents declare themselves in total or partial agreement with the fact that the re-education of offenders is a particularly important, if not the principal, function of punishment. 31% (RO) and 18% (MD) consider that this function is not among the most important functions of punishment, while 26% (RO) and 55% (MD) chose a neutral opinion, interpreted by us as neither agreement nor disagreement. We note that adherence to the educative and resocialisation function of probation is more significant among probation officers in Moldova. Analysing the responses to the questions concerning the functions of punishment, we support the hypothesis according to which the Romanian/ Moldavian model of probation is one based on a theoretical métissage, being a convergence between the retributive and the restorative model, with an almost equal emphasis on the social reintegration function and on the retributive function among professionals in Romania, and with a slight emphasis on the reintegrative function among those in Moldova.

When asked to select the statement that best defines the professional success of the probation officer, 9% (RO) and 7% (MD) of respondents state that this is best defined by the supervised person having finished serving the measures and obligations imposed without any incident; 11% (RO) and 12% (MD) state that professional success is best defined by the supervised person not having reoffended; 72% (RO) and 62% (MD) state that professional success is best defined by the supervised person having reintegrated into the community; 4% (RO) and 9% (MD) state that professional success is best defined by compliance with all legal provisions in the work with the beneficiary.

2.6.7. Conclusions of the Micro-Research

Considering the purpose of the micro-research, although the small number of respondents cannot lead to statistical validation, it can be said that the results obtained within this micro-research may be significant for supporting the plausibility of the model. The hypotheses of the micro-research are confirmed at the level of the studied sample. **H1.** The hypothesis that the Romanian and Moldavian model of probation is a multi- and transdisciplinary one, with strong helping-profession and social-therapeutic emphases, is verified for both countries, the differences consisting especially in the different weight of the legal component. **H2.** The hypothesis that the helping-profession perspective is fundamental to the professional practice of the probation officer is verified for respondents in both countries, with a greater preponderance among respondents from the Republic of Moldova. **H3.** The hypothesis according to which there is no clear specialisation of probation officers in one or another activity, each officer being able to carry out any of the specific professional activities, is verified for probation officers in Romania and only partially for those in Moldova, where the responses show a greater degree of practice specialisation. **H4.** The success of probation practice is defined in terms of the number of persons reintegrated and the absence of recidivism. The hypothesis is verified for respondents in both countries. **H5.** The functioning of probation services is based on good communication, both at the personal and institutional levels, with the representatives of the other institutions with which they collaborate: courts, police, prosecution offices, public administration, civil society, penitentiaries, and so forth. The hypothesis is partially verified for respondents in both countries, with the particularity that those from the Republic of Moldova highlighted a series of dissatisfactions concerning collaboration with certain institutions, principally with the police. The degree of dissatisfaction suggested is, however, minor and does not visibly influence the institutional collaboration between probation offices and the police. **H6.** Probation officers in Romania place greater emphasis on interpersonal, informal communication strategies, while their counterparts in the Republic of Moldova are more interested in formal, institutionalised communication, in both cases with full and strict compliance with the law. The hypothesis is partially verified for respondents in both countries, with the note that the preponderance of one or the other form of non-formal/formal communication represents a tendency, not an absolute particularity.

3. Retributiveness and Public Perception of Non-Custodial Sanctions.

A Study in the North-Eastern Region of Romania and in the Republic of Moldova

The research on *Retributiveness and Public Perception of Non-Custodial Sanctions in the North-East of Romania and in the Republic of Moldova* was based on a quantitative methodological design, grounded in the questionnaire-based survey method.

3.1. Research Hypotheses

1. Both in Romania and in the Republic of Moldova, a strong retributive tendency prevails, accompanied by a low degree of social tolerance toward individuals who commit criminal offences. The formulation of this hypothesis originates in the presupposition that general living conditions influence the degree of social tolerance. **2.** Non-custodial alternatives are socially acceptable punishments, particularly for sanctioning offenders whose acts do not pose a very high level of social danger. **3.** Both in Romania and in the Republic of Moldova, the activity of probation services is insufficiently known, a circumstance that may lead to a lower acceptance of non-custodial sanctions.

3.2. Methodology

The questionnaire comprised 20 items to which the respondents from the North-Eastern region of Romania and from the Republic of Moldova were asked to respond. The questionnaire addressed two thematic areas, namely: highlighting the degree of retributiveness versus openness toward non-custodial sanctions among the investigated population, and the level of awareness regarding the existence and functioning of probation services. The questionnaire-based survey was administered with the assistance of field operators, who received instructions regarding the type of persons to be surveyed – see the sampling procedure of the study – and the mode of questionnaire administration: direct, face-to-face, preceded by the reading of a statement informing respondents of their right to withdraw from the study at any time, to refrain from answering uncomfortable questions or questions to which their answers were uncertain, and of the fact that all data obtained are strictly confidential, their processing being carried out through exclusively statistical methods. This statement also served as the participants' informed consent to participate in the research.

The sample is a convenience sample, non-random and non-probabilistic. Sampling was conducted using the snowball method, whereby the field operators were asked to select 10 respondents each from among members of their own social network. Participants in the questionnaire-based study originated from the North-Eastern region of Romania, totalling 1,056 respondents (484 male and 572 female), while from the Republic of Moldova, 432 respondents participated – 202 male and 230 female.

The age distribution of Romanian respondents is as follows: 49% under 35 years of age, 31% between 35 and 45 years of age, and 20% over 45 years of age. The age distribution of Moldavian respondents is: 63% under 35 years of age, 18% between 35 and 45 years of age, and 19% over 45 years of age.

The educational level of Romanian respondents is: 4% with no formal education, 44% with secondary education, 47% with university education, and 5% with postgraduate education. The educational level of Moldavian respondents is: 5% with no formal education, 32% with secondary education, 53% with university education, and 10% with postgraduate education.

The income level of Romanian respondents is: 32% up to 1,000 lei (Romanian lei), 34% between 1,000 and 2,000 lei, 11% between 2,000 and 3,000 lei, 5% over 3,000 lei, and 18% non-responses. The income level of Moldavian respondents is: 23% up to 1,000 lei (Moldavian lei), 38% between 1,000 and 2,000 lei, 24% between 2,000 and 3,000 lei, 17% over 3,000 lei, and 8% non-responses. The Romanian leu/Moldavian leu exchange rate during the period of questionnaire administration was 1:4.6.

The high rate of non-responses indicates, in our view, a high degree of frustration with the standard of living, expressed through income levels – a frustration that may amplify attitudes toward individuals who have committed criminal offences, particularly offences (especially corruption-related ones) that are perceived as contributing to the dramatic decline in the standard of living in both countries.

3.3. Results

Regarding the reason for which offenders are punished, 35% of Romanian respondents favour a retributive option (they deserve to be punished because they have committed a wrongful, antisocial act), whereas 32% of Moldavian respondents choose the same option. The results partially confirm our hypothesis that a strong retributive tendency exists in both countries.

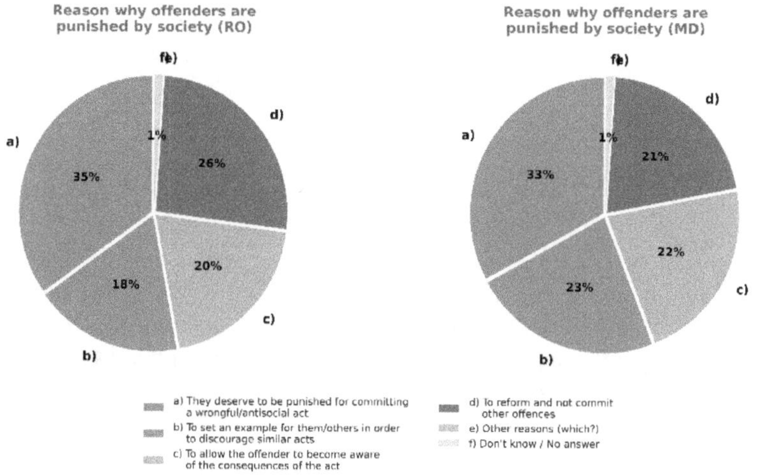

The correlation between the retributive option and income level is positive: 65% of Romanian respondents who opted for the retributive alternative have an income level below 2,000 lei per month. A similar score – 67% – was obtained among Moldavian respondents as well. No significant correlation could be established between the respondents' educational level and the retributive option. Regarding the other response options, these were directed toward the deterrence of recidivism (26% RO, 21% MD), the affirmation of the educative role of punishment (20% RO, 22% MD), and setting an example for other members of society (18% RO, 23% MD).

Regarding the severity of sentences in Romania, 40% of respondents considered them lenient or very lenient; 36% considered them neither harsh nor lenient; and only 20% considered them harsh or very harsh.

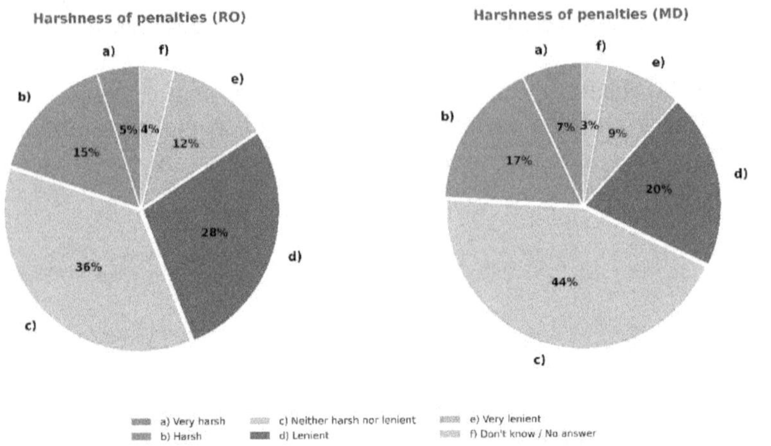

Moldavian respondents leaned even more toward the moderate option, according to which sentences are neither harsh nor lenient (44%); 29% consider sentences lenient or very lenient, while only 24% consider them harsh or very harsh.

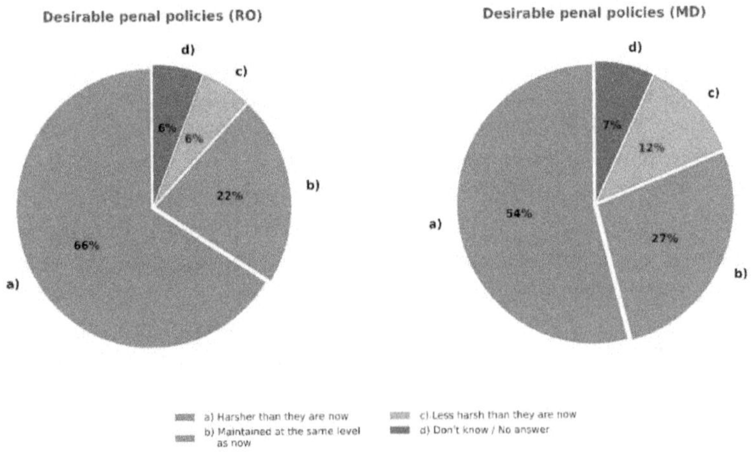

With regard to our hypothesis that both societies exhibit a high level of intransigence toward the commission of criminal offences, the large number of responses from Romania characterising sentences as lenient and very lenient partially confirms it. In the Republic of Moldova, the majority of respondents chose the moderate option. In neither country was there a preponderance of opinions suggesting that sentences are harsh or too harsh, which continues to indicate a retributive tendency.

Regarding desirable penal policies, 66% of respondents in Romania consider a toughening of sentences necessary, 22% believe they should be maintained at the current level, and only 6% consider that their severity should be reduced. In the Republic of Moldova, the desirable penal policy also envisions an increase in the severity of sentences, favoured by 54% of respondents, while 27% believe that the severity of sentences should be maintained at the same level, and only 12% believe that their harshness should be diminished.

The retributive orientation is once again evident in the large number of responses that consider an increase in the level of punishment for offenders necessary. The responses are consistent with those obtained for the previous question. If the current level of punishment is perceived as low or moderate, the retributive attitude of respondents manifests as a preference for tougher sentences. The small number of respondents who consider that sentences should be reduced also appears to confirm our hypothesis that the degree of tolerance toward individuals who have committed criminal offences – even those of low social danger – is very low.

Regarding the respondents' positioning toward punishment, those from Romania adopt an objectivist retributive position (if they have committed an antisocial act, they must be imprisoned, 25%); a social, non-prison-centric position, open to social alternatives (prison is a school for offenders, 22%); and a humanistic stance (even though they have committed an offence, offenders also have a set of rights, 17%). When explicitly asked about offences whose social danger is limited, 32% of respondents indicated that imprisonment does not constitute a solution for this type of offence.

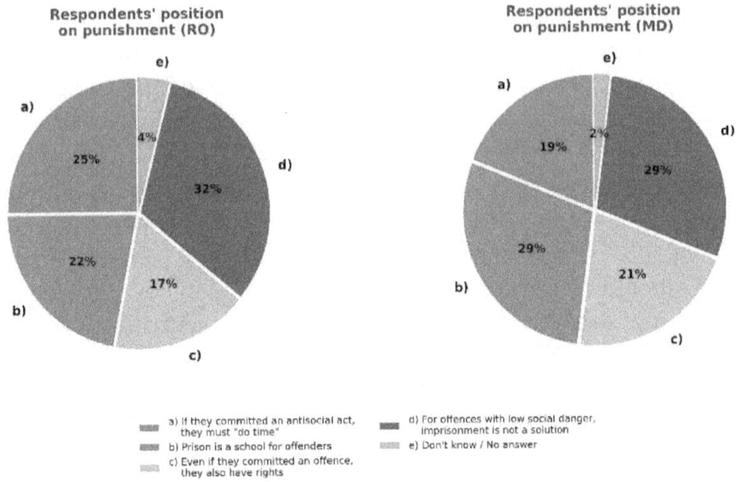

The position of Moldavian respondents is similar: 29% consider that imprisonment is not an option for punishing offenders whose acts pose a low social danger, and 29% are convinced that prison is a school for offenders. Only 19% of respondents are convinced that imprisonment has universal applicability. In practical terms, 52% of Romanian respondents and 58% of Moldavian respondents declare themselves, in one form or another, favourable to alternatives to imprisonment.

Correlated with the preference for tougher sanctions, we believe that what is actually desired is a differentiation of sanctions according to social danger: increasing sanctions where social danger is high and progressively transitioning toward non-custodial sanctions where social danger is minor and the social costs of incarceration are high. The general attitude remains, in our view, a retributive one, with alternative punishments to imprisonment still being viewed in a retributive manner. Evidence that this opinion can be supported by the responses received is the rate of 25% and 19%, respectively, of respondents who choose the prison-centric option, even when confronted with alternatives that point to social options and with options that evoke the social costs of incarceration.

With regard to a human rights-centred justice, 17% of Romanian respondents and 21% of Moldavian respondents consider it a priority.

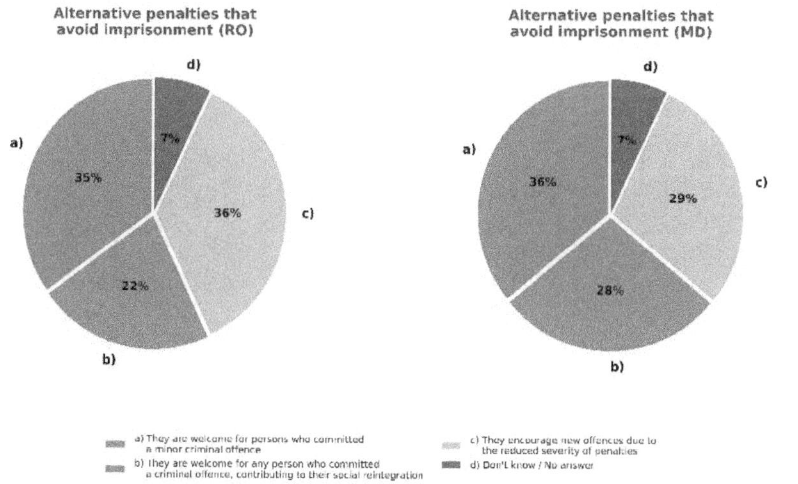

Regarding non-custodial alternatives as a whole, 35% of Romanian respondents are in favour of their use in punishing offenders whose criminal acts do not pose a major social danger, and 22% are in favour of their use in punishing any type of offender, while 36% of respondents oppose their use, considering them to be generators of new offences precisely because of their reduced severity. Moldavian respondents are in favour in a considerably higher proportion – 36% – of using these alternative sanctions to imprisonment only in the case of offences with low social danger, with only 28% of Moldavian respondents agreeing with the use of this type of sanction for any type of offence. Twenty-nine percent of respondents from the Republic of Moldova consider this type of sanction as leading to an increased risk of recidivism and to the encouragement of criminality in general.

When explicitly asked about the usefulness of imprisonment in the social reintegration of offenders who have committed offences of low social danger, the majority of Romanian respondents agreed (59%) that it is partially useful or very useful, and only 21% expressed opposition to the usefulness of this form of punishment for offenders whose acts carry a low degree of social danger. Fifteen percent of respondents consider that imprisonment can be regarded as neither useful nor useless.

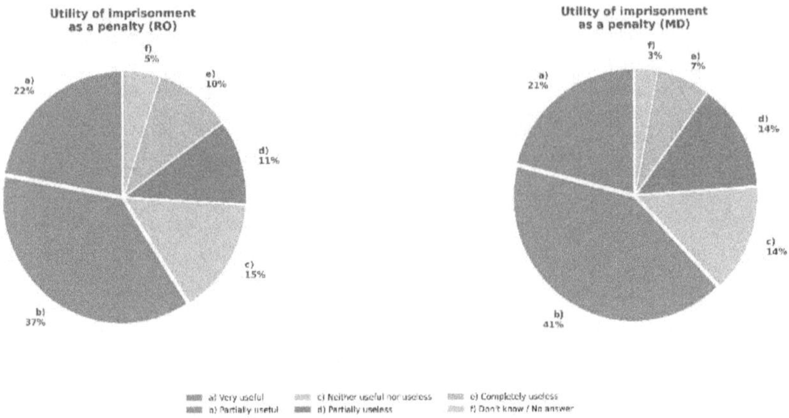

In the case of respondents from the Republic of Moldova, imprisonment for offenders whose acts present a low antisocial danger is viewed as partially useful and very useful by 62% of respondents, and as partially useless and completely useless by 21% of respondents, while 14% consider it neither useful nor useless. In practical terms, respondents from both countries perceive imprisonment as useful in a proportion exceeding half of the total number of respondents, without, however, a significant difference between the opinions expressed by respondents from the Republic of Moldova and those from Romania. The retributive tendency is evident, with the prison-centric perspective being preferred by the majority of respondents. The following item concerns the assessment of the usefulness of suspended sentences and of the measure of sentence suspension under the supervision of a specialised professional (probation counsellor). Regarding the suspended sentence – in the form in which it was applied under the former Criminal Code of Romania – 61% of respondents considered it partially useful and very useful, while only 18% considered it partially useless or completely useless, and 16% regarded it as neither useful nor useless.

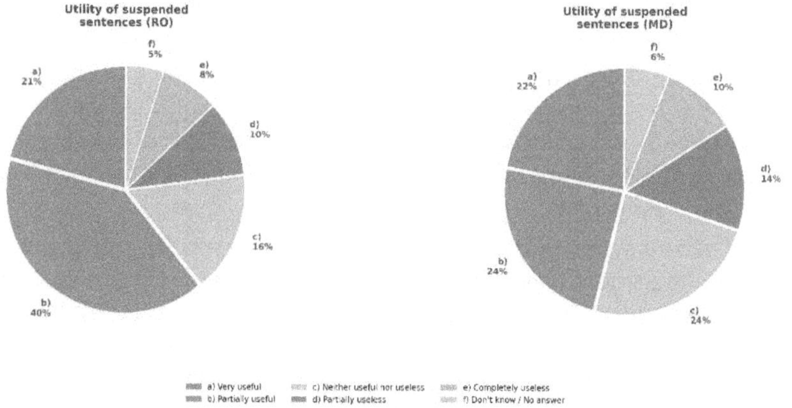

In turn, respondents from the Republic of Moldova assessed the suspended sentence as follows: 46% consider it partially useful or very useful, and 24% consider it partially useless or even completely useless, while 24% view it as neither useful nor useless. Regarding the suspension of the sentence under the supervision of a specialist – a probation counsellor – this measure is viewed as partially useful and very useful by 69% of respondents, while only 13% consider it partially useless or completely useless.

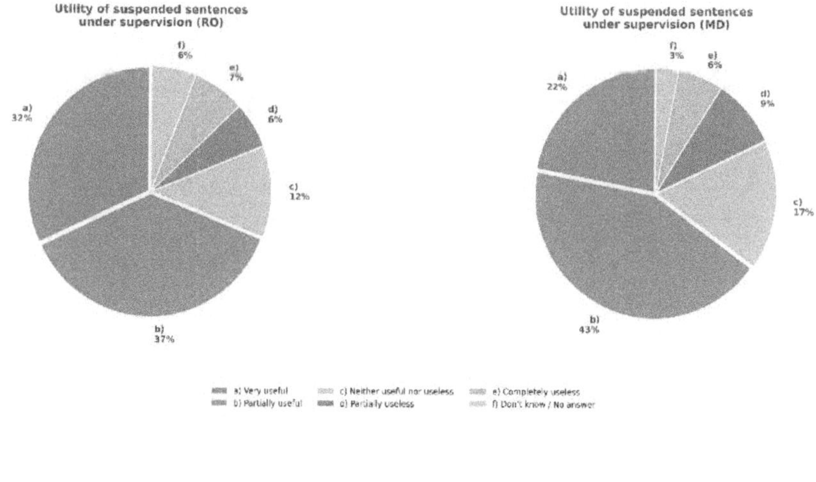

In the Republic of Moldova, 67% of respondents considered the suspension of sentence execution under the supervision of a specialised professional – a probation counsellor – to be partially useful or very useful, while the partial or total uselessness of this form of punishing offenders is mentioned by only 15% of respondents. Seventeen percent of respondents do not consider this measure to be either useful or useless for the social reintegration of offenders who have committed antisocial acts of minor social danger.

The responses to the two questions concerning the suspension of sentence execution and the suspension of sentence execution under supervision, together with the subsequent questions regarding unpaid community service work, as well as the execution of the sentence at the workplace – a form of sanction that no longer exists in the current version of the criminal code in either country, but which existed as such during the communist period – were intended to test public attitudes toward non-custodial sanctions.

Another category of non-custodial sanctions concerns community service work. Seventy-four percent of Romanian respondents express themselves in favour of its usefulness in the punishment and social reintegration of offenders who have committed criminal acts of low social danger, while only 14% express opposition to its usefulness, and 10% consider it neither useful nor useless.

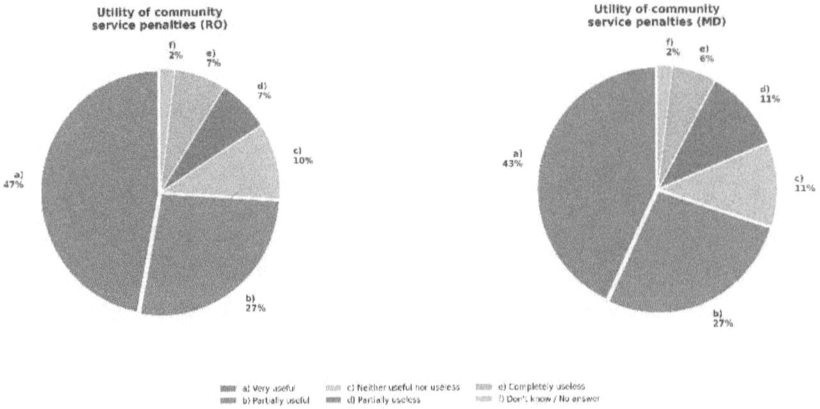

In turn, 70% of respondents from the Republic of Moldova expressed themselves in favour of community service work as a form of non-custodial sanction, 22% consider it useless, and only 6% consider it neither useful nor useless. Regarding the sanction of imprisonment at the workplace, which existed in the Criminal Code during the communist period, it is viewed positively by 50% of Romanian respondents and 67% of Moldovan respondents. The lower percentage of respondents who express themselves in favour of this form of sentence execution indicates that the public in both countries regards modern forms of sanctioning with greater confidence than those of communist origin.

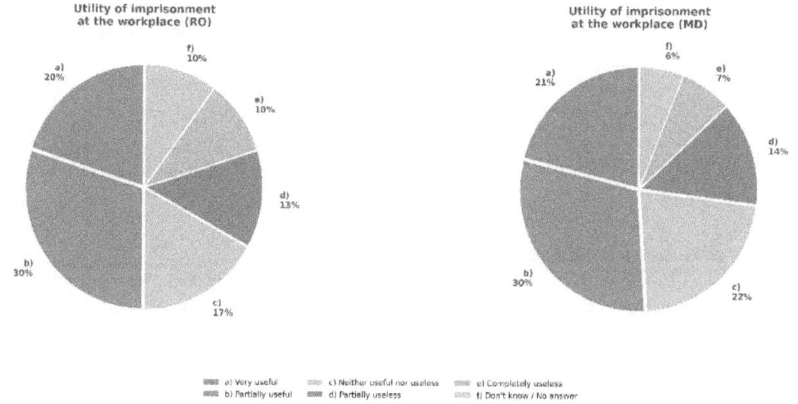

Regarding the obligation for the offender to attend a series of reintegration programmes, this measure is viewed favourably by 69% of Romanian respondents and 69% of Moldovan respondents, while only 12% of respondents from Romania and 12% of those from the Republic of Moldova express opposition to the usefulness of this type of sanction, and 12% (RO) and 12% (MD), respectively, consider it neither useful nor useless.

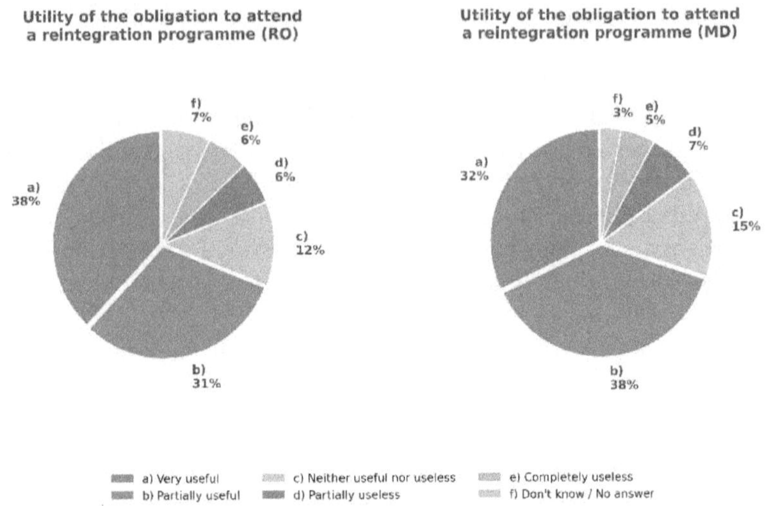

The respondents' attitude is supportive toward the suspension of sentence execution, particularly when the execution of sanctioning measures is supervised by specialised professionals – probation counsellors. We chose to formulate the question by including both the term "specialised professional" and "probation counsellor," proceeding from the premise that at least some respondents are not familiar with the designation of probation counsellor, as this is a relatively new profession in both countries.

The degree of acceptability of non-custodial measures such as the suspension of sentence execution is higher than that which respondents exhibit toward custodial measures, especially when non-custodial measures are accompanied by qualified supervision, which leads the general public to recognise their sanctioning character. The fact that the public values the importance of non-custodial sanctions more highly than the carceral sanction allows us to affirm that the implementation of policies promoting the social importance of probation services and their effectiveness in the social rehabilitation of offenders – particularly in the case of acts of low social danger – would lead to an increase in social tolerance toward this category of offenders.

The two sets of questions pertained to the perceived importance of the carceral sanction and of the non-custodial alternative, respectively, and were not intended to measure retributive attitudes per se (which were partially assessed in the preceding sets of questions). We may consider that, despite a predominantly retributive attitude that demands a relative severity of sentences and an increase thereof, when the perspective of the offender's social reintegration is brought into discussion, although custodial methods remain important, non-custodial ones are perceived as more effective.

The following set of questions concerns the degree of public awareness regarding the existence and specific activities of probation services/probation offices. Fifty-nine percent of Romanian respondents and 53% of Moldovan respondents declare that they have no knowledge of the existence of probation services. To these results, we consider it necessary to add the 11% (RO)/12% (MD) non-responses, which can be partially attributed to the lack of information regarding the existence and functioning of these services.

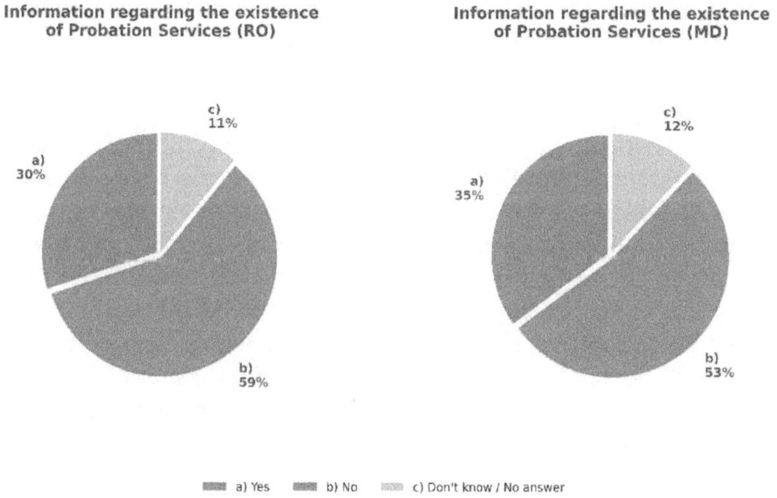

In the following question in this series, respondents were presented with a range of activities specific to probation services and asked to select the activity or activities they consider important for the social rehabilitation of offenders. The question was subsequently repeated as a control question, with slightly modified items, in order to determine whether significant variations exist, which could raise concerns regarding the validity and reliability of the results.

In the first formulation of the question, 38% (RO) and 21% (MD) of respondents, respectively, considered that the supervision of measures imposed by the court constitutes the object of activity of probation services; 17% (RO) and 23% (MD), respectively, identified the supervision of unpaid community service work; and 19% (RO) and 14% (MD), respectively, identified counselling activities for persons under supervision.

In the second formulation of the question (the control question), respondents assessed the role of the probation counsellor as follows: 20% (RO) and 20% (MD), respectively, indicated the supervision of the application of measures imposed by the judge in the case of non-custodial sanctions; 23% (RO) and 21% (MD), respectively, indicated counselling activities with persons under supervision; 11% (RO) and 15% (MD), respectively, indicated the supervision of unpaid community service work; and 27% (RO) and 24% (MD), respectively, indicated social assistance activities in favour of persons under supervision (an option absent from the first formulation of the question).

The differences in response options between the first and second formulations are generally minor; the only difference we consider significant pertains to the option regarding the supervision of the execution of non-custodial measures, where the discrepancies do not exceed 10% between the first and second questions. In our view, these differences are explicable through the differences in question formulation: in the first instance, there were in fact two options – the supervision of the execution of measures imposed by the judge upon conditional release, and the supervision of the execution of measures imposed by the judge upon the pronouncement of a suspended sentence – whereas in the control question, the two options were merged under the form: supervision of the execution of measures imposed by the judge. Both questions allowed for multiple responses, with respondents being able to select one or more options. Respondents who answered the first question in the sense of supervision of the execution of measures imposed by the judge simultaneously selected both forms of this option in a proportion of 11% (RO) and 15% (MD), respectively, which renders the responses compatible across both questions. In our view, the convergent responses to the two questions (in both the original formulation and the control question) for both Romania and the Republic of Moldova allow us to affirm the validity and reliability of the data obtained.

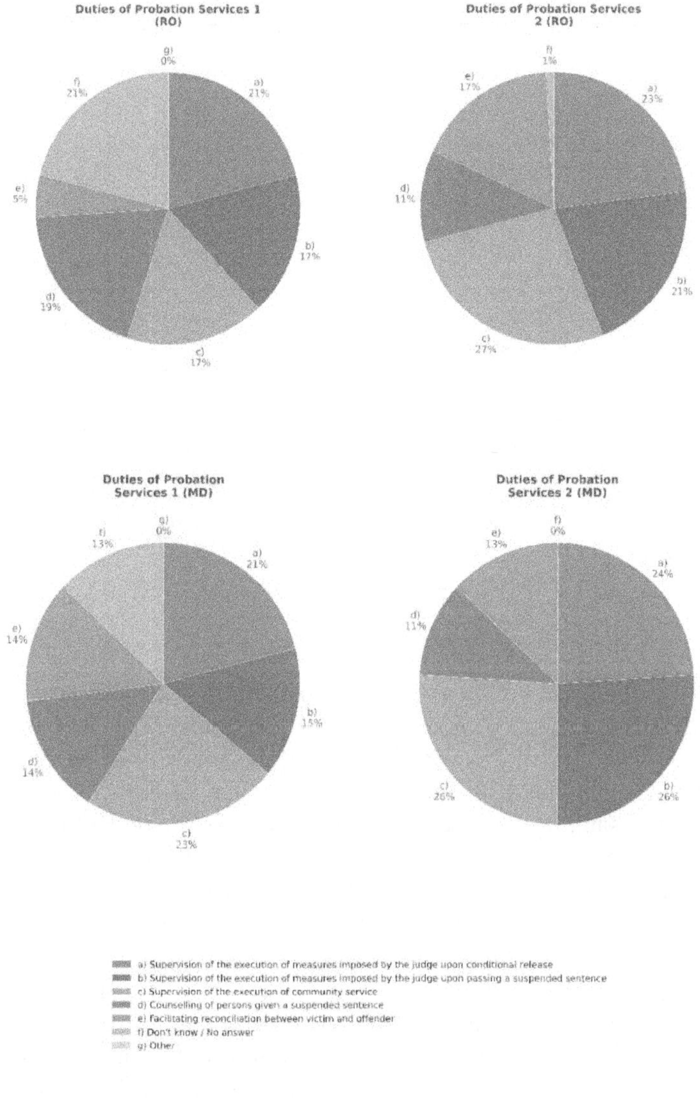

Again with a view to gauging the level of public awareness of the work of the probation services, respondents were asked to indicate whether their acquaintances included any individuals currently under the supervision of the probation services. 69% of respondents in Romania and 68% of those in the Republic of Moldova reported that they had no such persons among their acquaintances. These responses are consistent with those given to the preceding questions, including the one in which approximately 59% of respondents in both countries stated that they were unaware of the existence and activity of the probation services.

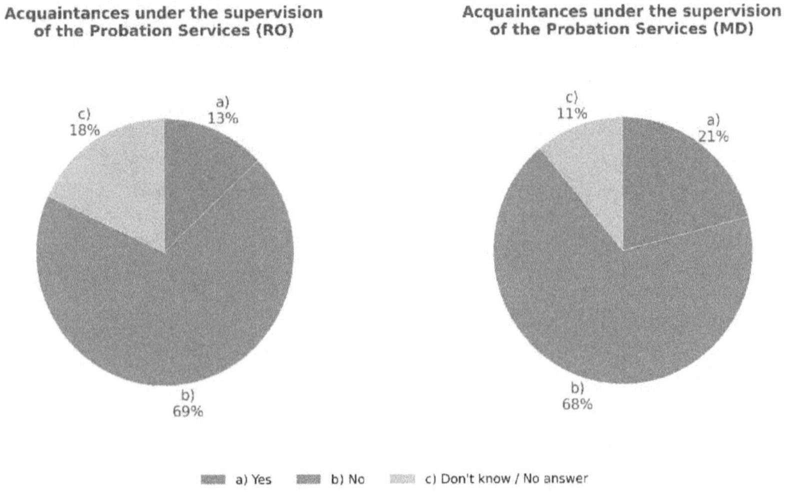

Regarding the social acceptance of persons who have committed criminal offences and who are serving a non-custodial sanction, this acceptance is high in both countries: 29% of respondents in Romania and 33% of those in the Republic of Moldova indicated that they would maintain the same type of relationship with such persons. Only 15% of respondents in Romania and 14% of those in the Republic of Moldova would attempt to avoid contact with these persons, whereas 35% and 39% respectively would seek to support them in the process of social reintegration. The attitude of social acceptance towards persons serving a non-custodial sentence partially contradicts our initial hypothesis, according to which Romanian society, and likewise Moldovan society, both undergoing a prolonged transition, exhibit a low tolerance towards persons who commit criminal offences; however, it confirms the second hypothesis concerning the social acceptability of non-custodial penalties. The high rate of non-responses—21% and 14% respectively—we interpret as reflecting a lack of knowledge regarding the functioning and duties of the probation services, which translates into an uncertainty projected onto the beneficiaries of these services, an uncertainty that cannot be resolved either in the direction of social trust or in the creation of social distance.

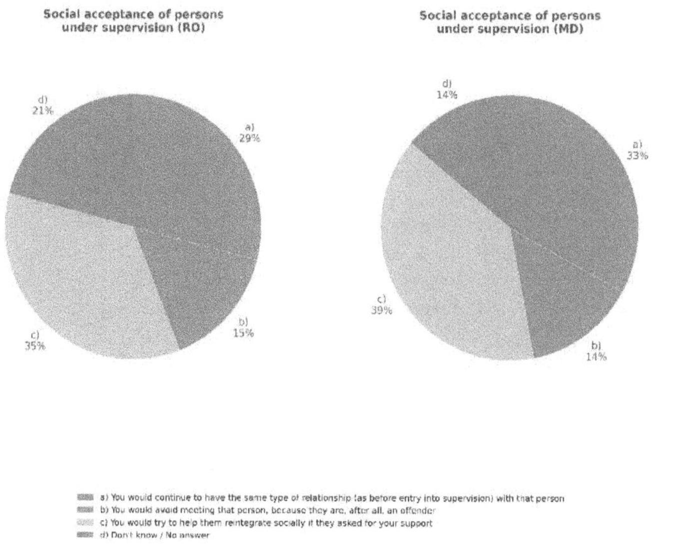

Regarding the categories of offenders for whom respondents consider it useful to apply non-custodial sanctions under the supervision of the probation services, these are: minors who have committed a criminal offence (27% RO and 31% MD); persons who have committed a criminal offence for the first time and who regret it (28% RO and 29% MD); persons who sincerely regret the offence committed, even if they have previously committed other criminal offences (11% RO and 14% MD); persons who have committed criminal offences of reduced gravity, even if they have previously committed other criminal offences (7% RO and 11% MD); and persons who have committed criminal offences whose damage has been recovered and where reconciliation with the victim has taken place (12% RO and 7% MD). It can be observed that recidivism is regarded as an impediment to the execution of non-custodial measures, even where the social danger posed by the offence is low. Likewise, the recovery of the damage and reconciliation with the victim do not constitute grounds for supporting the non-custodial option, which is nonetheless widely endorsed in the case of sanctioning minors or first-time offenders who regret the offence committed.

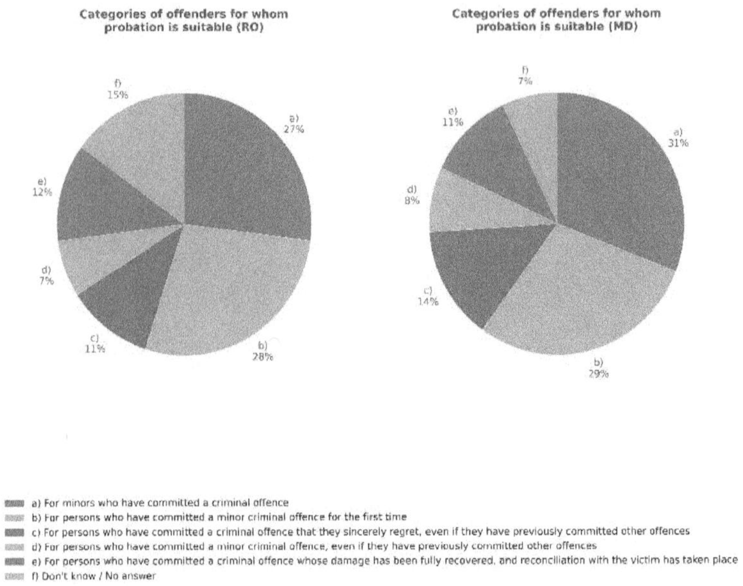

Regarding the professional training that probation counsellors should, in the respondents' opinion, possess, this should be in the field of social work (17% RO, 16% MD), law (16% RO, 21% MD), psychology (23% RO, 21% MD), pedagogy (7% RO, 8% MD), probation (15% RO, 17% MD), policing (8% RO, 11% MD), or any kind of initial education (4% RO, 3% MD). A predominance of preferences for training in the psycho-social sphere is evident (47% RO, 45% MD), followed by that of law and other professions within the sphere of public safety and the administration of justice. The preference for psycho-social training indicates that, in the respondents' opinion, counselling and support activities should take priority over the strictly supervisory function.

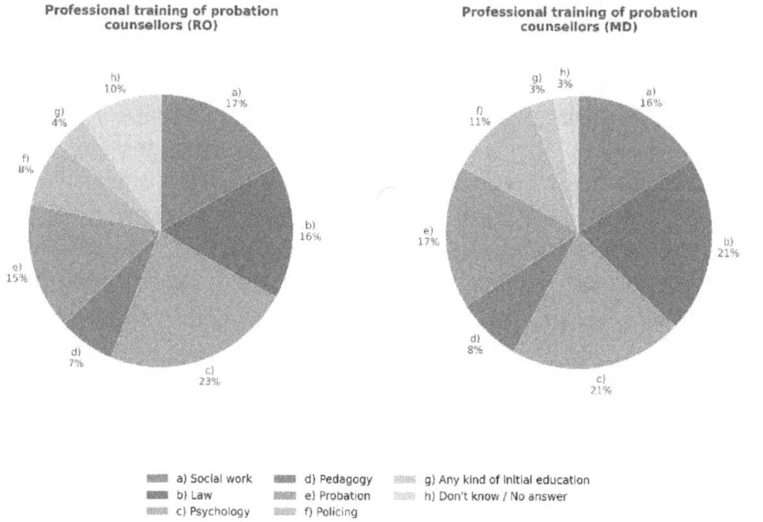

3.4. Conclusions of the study Retributiveness and Public Perception of Non-custodial Sanctions. Research in the North-Eastern Region of Romania

Based on the responses received, there emerges, in our view, a *humanist–utilitarian* model of probation, with retributive accents. Hypothesis 1, concerning the existence of a strong retributive current in Romanian society, is confirmed, in the sense that, although there is a fairly strong opinion that offenders should be punished in an exemplary manner, and that the level of punishment ought to be increased in the two societies. Respondents indicated that non-custodial penalties may be viewed pragmatically, being more effective than custodial ones for the social reintegration of offenders, especially in the case of minors and first-time offenders whose consequences and level of social danger are not particularly serious and who regret the offence committed. The elevated level of retributiveness present within society does not negatively influence the perception of non-custodial sanctions; rather, it is the lack of information regarding the major reforms undertaken in both societies that does so. The hypothesis according to which the work of the probation services is little known in the two societies, which may lead to a lower degree of acceptance of non-custodial penalties, is only partially supported, in the sense that, although the majority of respondents have no knowledge regarding the existence, duties, and functioning of the probation services, they are generally open to sanctions alternative to imprisonment in the case of offences posing a minor social danger. In general, public perception of non-custodial sanctions is positive, both in Romanian and in Moldovan society, but sustained promotion of probation work may further increase public support for the efforts of probation counsellors.

4. A Theoretical Model of the Social Construction of Probation and Its Implications for the Design of Public Policies Concerning the Implementation of Non-custodial Sanctions in North-Eastern Romania and the Republic of Moldova

The models underlying the formation of the restorative paradigm are heterogeneous, but all are grounded in the return of justice to the hands of those directly concerned: the victim, the offender, and the community [178]. We understand the term *social construction* from a social-constructionist perspective [77], that is, from the perspective of the contexts in which individuals apprehend and represent social reality. Social constructs—such as those of *institution*, *punishment*, and also that of *probation*—are internalised by subjects following processes of (re)interpretation of reality, according to the context in which the construct is formed. The process of social construction of a concept follows a series of constructive axes that define the contexts in which individuals arrive at the definition of that context. As regards probation, such axes may be: the normative and institutional dimension, the interpersonal dimension, the dimension of the counsellor–supervised person relationship, the human-resources dimension, and so forth. In the analysis of probation as a social practice, several theoretical models have been identified, of which the most appropriate is considered to be that of restorative justice [4]. *Retributive justice* [92] represents a classical paradigm for understanding punishment, being based on reciprocity. The purpose of punishment is the retribution of the offender for the act committed, and it remains a paradigm still dominant at the level of public perception regarding the aims of punishment. This hypothesis is empirically supported by research highlighting public perception of the aims of punishment [137, pp. 77–89; 141, pp. 317–335; 155, pp. 255–267]. The reform of penal enforcement systems in Europe, and indeed throughout the world, over the past 20 years, is grounded in a progressive de-penalisation of punishment and the transfer to the community of responsibility for the social reintegration of offenders [233]. In general, a simultaneous increase in both custodial and non-custodial sentences is recorded, but, for example in the case of Scotland, the capacity of the probation services to offer an alternative to the custodial penalty has been demonstrated. *Restorative justice*—holds that the role of punishment is to facilitate the rehabilitation of the offender, introducing the idea of the co-responsibility of the state in the rehabilitation process. Whereas the reparation proposed by the retributive model is unilateral—through the incarceration of the offender—restorative justice is grounded in the reaffirmation of the consensus of values shared at the community level through a process that is at least bilateral—offender–victim—if not trilateral—offender–victim–community [178, pp. 375–389]. The restorative-justice model is based on active reparatory activities and on the offender's awareness of the impact of the offence upon the victim. This model partially eliminates the risk of recidivism generated by the penitentiary career and by the discrimination to which former inmates are subjected. The implementation of restorative justice is achieved by emphasising the social dimension of criminal liability [205, pp. 33–54], which in fact presupposes a social (re)construction of responsibility. The aim of restorative justice is the de-penalisation of the sanction [82]. In the given context of a constructionist approach to probation, we view restorative justice as representing, first and foremost, an interpretive agreement regarding the object of the conflict and the relationship between victim and offender, its sources and causes, the consequences of one or another of the possible resolutions, and, not least, the most favourable solution for all parties [49, p. 34]. The role of punishment, viewed from the perspective of restorative justice, is to facilitate rehabilitation, the state being co-responsible for rehabilitation. The specialist literature highlights a current of opinion favourable to the transfer of responsibility for the social reintegration of the offender to the community [145, pp. 235–256], a space conducive to rehabilitative and re-socialising social interactions. The restorative-justice model is based on active reparatory activities and on the offender's awareness of the impact of the offence upon the victim [30, pp. 58–70; 205, pp. 33–54]. This model partially eliminates the risk of recidivism generated by the penitentiary career and by the discrimination to which former inmates are subjected. In this way, the educational role of the sanction is maximised to the detriment of its punitive role [49, p. 207]. The restorative emphasis is placed on the offender's understanding of the harm produced and on the acceptance of responsibility for repairing the damage [126, pp. 1–4]. The implementation of restorative justice is achieved by emphasising the social dimension of criminal liability [205, pp. 33–54; 207], which in fact presupposes a social (re)construction of responsibility. The data analysed have highlighted that the changes to the normative frameworks governing the functioning of probation have brought about a series of dysfunctions, related in particular to inconsistencies between the various normative frameworks applied, the case overload of professionals, and the partial inadequacy of practice models—based on the experience of other states (especially Great Britain and Norway)—to the Romanian reality. Both the Romanian and the Moldovan probation systems are relatively new, dating officially back 15 and 12 years respectively, even though elements specific to restorative justice and non-custodial sanctions existed both in the interwar period and under communism. The construction of probation in Romania was carried out principally by adopting successful elements from the models of other states, especially Great Britain and Norway, which are, however, only partially adaptable to the Romanian situation, from the perspective of the legal system and the dominant penal philosophy, the mentalities of the population, the criminogenic profile, and the particularities of communication. The Moldovan probation system is to a greater extent a creation of local professionals, more adapted to the local socio-cultural specificity, as evidenced by the heightened welfare emphasis, which is to be expected for a country with a lower standard of living than the European average. An essential characteristic of the Romanian system is the strongly personalised dimension of communication, both at the institutional and the inter-institutional level, which contrasts with the orientation towards formalism of the Moldovan system. This emphasis on communication orients the system towards the counselling aspect, with therapeutic accents, to the detriment of the punitive one, whereas the preference for the formalisation of institutional communication has led to the emergence of a welfare aspect based on the identification of, and the facilitation of access to, resources on behalf of the beneficiary. This welfare dimension converges with the European perspective on probation practice. Supervised persons appreciate the assumption by the probation counsellor of duties specific to the social worker, with a view to obtaining concrete results intended to diminish the risk of recidivism [107]. The results of our own interviews with supervised persons confirm this opinion. The restorative mentality is evident in the discourse of respondents, but it is ambivalent. On the one hand, emphasis is placed on strict compliance with the law and on the educational function of punishment, when respondents discuss the role of punishment expressly; on the other hand, the aspects highlighted as the principal elements of success are those that position Romanian probation as a socio-therapy of social reinsertion. By contrast, Moldovan probation is closer to the model of the probation officer—a person of authority who strictly oversees the execution of non-custodial measures. It is the welfare aspect that ensures the success of the practice, the social reintegration of supervised persons being particularly important for avoiding recidivism. The complementarity between the welfare aspect and the supervisory one shows that the model is in fact closer to the counselling model than respondents wish to convey, the excess of formalisation being a result of institutional pressure. Personnel within the system are aware that the orientation of Romanian probation is more towards the spirit of the law—aiming in fact at the social recovery of offenders—than towards the letter of the law, as in the systems of the Nordic countries, which place emphasis on the exemplary rigour of punishment, even of the non-custodial kind. This emphasis on the spirit of the law is somewhat problematic, since the definition of the educational role of punishment has been removed from the criminal law, which no longer defines the role of punishment in any way. Previous legislation defined the role of punishment as both a measure of constraint and a means of re-educating the convicted person. Nonetheless, Romanian doctrine and judicial practice continue to affirm—even after the penal reform of 2014—that the educational role is placed axiologically ahead of the retributive one. The same emphasis on interpersonal communication is identified—according to what respondents stated—in the relations between the probation services and other institutions, such as the trial and enforcement courts, the penitentiary, the town halls, and the police. Direct communication, from professional to professional, is preferred to official, institutionalised communication. The latter is seen as difficult, bureaucratic, and yielding fewer results. The personalisation of relations between professionals is beneficial for the institutions, up until the moment when the departure of a professional from the system limits institutional communication with the representatives of other public institutions. Excessive personalisation may lead to a fluidisation of the limits of institutional communication, with situations of inter-institutional collaboration being reported in some cases even in the absence of formal agreement on the part of the management of the partner institution. By contrast, the Moldovan professional places emphasis on limiting the personal element to the maximum extent, in favour of the formalised one, as far as possible in accordance with precise normative frameworks that leave a minimal possibility of error. The formalism mentioned is a form of perfectionism that defines the respondents' idea of professionalism. Professionalism is defined in accordance with the norm, in a legitimist type of approach. In opposition, respondents from Romania define professionalism in terms of efficiency, though of course without neglecting the normative orientation. The excess of normativity, we consider, may be the result of a collective mentality based on objectivism, which may have its origins in the Soviet era. We argue this on the grounds that the Soviet mentality was totalitarian, a single truth being admitted—the official one. This ideological monism is justified through the modern ideal of objectivity. The objectivist epistemic orientation, of a modern character, was transmitted through Marxist ideology in the form of a rigid realism that has, in essence, a connotation of epistemic non-dualism. Two valid truths cannot exist simultaneously; the guilty person is guilty and must be punished, and so forth. Epistemic objectivism may generate, at the level of mentalities, a normative rigidity: *"where there is law, there is no bargaining"*. The contrary attitude is grounded in a mentality that places emphasis on the interpersonal, on normative minimalism. The communist experience generated in Romania a contraction of the normative, a mentality of the double standard. This may, for example, explain why institutional communication is effective despite the opposition of certain decision-makers within the organisation. Normativity is viewed minimally, as a minimum threshold of the acceptability of a given conduct. The relation to the norm is a key to understanding the probation system as a penal enforcement system. In Foucauldian terms [22], the execution of punishment and the types of punishment are forms of the codification of power. Any enforcement system is an expression of the power of society over the individual. In this sense, respondents' answers regarding the professional prestige generated in the relationship with the other professional categories involved in the execution of non-custodial penalties could be interpreted in consonance with the Foucauldian approach to power games on the symbolic plane, in the sense that probation, being part of the penal enforcement system, is the bearer of a symbolic power transferred to it from the penal system in general, which invests probation counsellors with professional prestige, even despite the low visibility of the profession in the public sphere. Professional prestige is, however, ambivalent, since it is partially overshadowed by the transfer of negative notoriety from beneficiaries to professionals. If a maximalist relation to the norm codifies a system laden with the responsibility of the individual, then the minimalist approach unburdens the individual of responsibility. The system's centring on communication could codify an attitude of the fluidisation of normativity, present at the level of Romanian society. The fluidity of normativity may generate social creativity, whereas normative maximalism may generate identity construction, through common adherence to a set of normatively codified values. From the perspective of probation, both approaches—both normative fluidity and normative maximalism—are key dimensions, being, we consider, present simultaneously in probation practice in both countries, but discursively codified in different ways, according to the differing appreciation of the constitutive values within the community. One limitation of the probation system is the lack of visibility and public recognition of its role within the penal enforcement system. The remarkable effects of non-custodial practices, where the risk of recidivism is at the national level around 5% as against 45% for persons who have undergone a custodial sentence, ought to be made known to the public and to decision-makers in matters of penal policy. The data are almost identical for the probation systems of both countries. The low human and material costs, both for the offender and for society, ought to be more intensely promoted, starting for example from the argument that an extremely small number of probation counsellors (350 counsellors in Romania) manage the execution of the non-custodial penalties of 40,000 persons, as against 15,000 officials of the Penitentiary System who manage 12,000 inmates. A better understanding of the social importance of probation would be afforded by an education of the public towards understanding the real risks to which the community is exposed owing to the execution of non-custodial measures—risks that are extremely low, provided that in the pre-sentence evaluation carried out, likewise by probation counsellors, these risks have been correctly assessed for each individual situation. A far more active role in changing public mentality regarding the execution of sanctions in the community, and in general in eliminating the prejudices of the public and the labelling of persons who have committed criminal offences—especially circumstantially and whose social danger is minimal—ought to fall to the National Probation Directorate. In particularising the specificity of probation within a given socio-cultural space, its adequacy to the profile of criminality in the respective region is demonstrated. We note a tone of optimism in the discourse of the Moldovan respondents, who highlighted the increasing visibility of the profession and its degree of social acceptance. This increase holds for Romania as well, but the tone of optimism is avoided in the discursive strategies of the respondents. The predominant discursive strategy of the respondents from Romania is constituted around the idea of communication and its importance at all levels. The narrative approach is generally enthusiastic, professional belonging being a strong source of professional identity. The high degree of task overload of probation counsellors is the most serious problem existing within the system, threatening its correct functioning. The counselling practices specific to Romanian probation require time, whereas an overload of more than 250 cases, as against 30 in other countries, makes the correct and complete application of the working instruments—built up over time on the basis of experience and collaboration with specialists from other countries—impossible. There is an increased risk of the bureaucratisation of probation, of the transformation of the counsellor into a mere evaluator of the exact execution of the measures imposed by the court, who no longer has the capacity to help the convicted person to transform, in the very process of executing the non-custodial measures.

4.1. The Epistemic and Axiological Dimension of the Constitution of the Probation Services in Romania and the Republic of Moldova

The constitutive values of probation practice recognised by the Romanian legislator are: fundamental human rights and freedoms; the dignity of the person and the right to private life. The operational values of the Romanian and Moldovan probation systems concern: non-discrimination and equal treatment; respect for the law and for judicial decisions as an expression of the rule of law; confidentiality; and the protection of personal data. The constitutive and operational values of probation practice are operationalised in the principle of the individualisation of the intervention according to the needs of the person, the risk of committing new offences, and the particular circumstances of each case, thereby transposing into practice the theoretical-methodological perspective on the uniqueness of each case, and on the individual as a value in itself, of case management within the probation system. The development of a positive relationship and the individual's involvement in their own rehabilitation process places emphasis on the individual and on their resources for self-management of recovery [49, p. 247]. The beneficiary of the probation system is society, while the principal resource is the person of the offender, as central to the process of their own recovery, carried out on the basis of the agreement and with the full cooperation of the person within the probation system, if they give their consent. The probation counsellor is bound (Art. 10, Law 252/2013) to pursue the development of a positive relationship with the person under supervision, which requires a person-centred approach, trust, and respect for their potential for social reintegration. The interdisciplinary approach to each case and the coordination of the activities undertaken with those of community institutions ensure the balance between the needs of the supervised person and those of the community. Informing the supervised person about the nature and content of the principal acts carried out (Art. 11, Law 252/2013) within probation work, and their informed consent, is absolutely necessary; otherwise, reintegration strategies through community-service work would contravene fundamental human rights and Recommendation (92)16 concerning the European rules on community sanctions and measures. The Recommendation of the Committee of Ministers of the Council of Europe of 19 October 1992 expressly provides for the necessity of the consent of the person concerned for the imposition of any measure applied in the community before trial, or in lieu of a decision on the sanction [49, p. 247; 181, pp. 69–105]. Even if the supervised person has given their consent in principle regarding the execution of the supervision measures imposed by the court at the moment of the suspension of the execution of the custodial penalty, a separate agreement on each measure included in the supervision activity—especially those concerning unpaid community-service work—is considered necessary. Informed consent is an instrument considered necessary upon the institution of each intervention measure comprised within case management, precisely in order to respect the dignity of the person, the positive relationship with them, and the right to information from which they benefit. Information is provided in a language, or form of language, that the supervised person understands (Art. 11, Law 252/2013) [49, p. 248].

The probation counsellor between profession and vocation | The career of the probation counsellor is relatively new in Romania and the Republic of Moldova. This makes the human resource involved in probation absolutely insufficient, which leads to an increased task overload for each individual counsellor, in practice lowering professional motivation while also affecting the efficiency of the practice. The welfare nature of the profession was imprinted from the beginnings of the organisation of probation work, in particular through non-governmental organisations offering principally social services. The training in social work of those who initiated the first probation programmes somewhat imprinted this welfare directive upon the evolution of the profession, those professionals being among those who devised the first methodologies and working instruments, and being also among the first employed in the system at the moment when probation-counsellor positions were opened to competition. The organisation of probation master's programmes within social-work specialisations contributed to imprinting a welfare specificity upon the profession. At present, the profession of probation counsellor is considered a profession distinct from social work, as evidenced by the entry into the profession of specialists with a different initial professional training. The accumulation of work tasks limits the capacity of probation counsellors to offer effective support to persons under supervision. The choice of probation as a career opportunity is grounded in a series of subjective criteria, among which its accessibility at a given moment, the absence of requirements of prior professional experience, and the accessibility of the profession to graduates from several fields of initial training: social work, psychology, pedagogy, and law. Vocation and interest in working with people, but also with the specific legal instruments, were likewise motivations for orientation towards the probation career. Continuing professional training is seen as absolutely necessary for the acquisition of the competences specific to the profession, which are not fully assimilated within initial training. The supplementary training whose need professionals feel is generally complementary to the initial one, leading to the improvement of the level of competences in fields such as social work, psychology, sociology, and law, but also in those specific to probation as a self-standing social practice, such as the social-reintegration programmes for persons under supervision. The most recent research shows that the practice of supervising offenders by probation counsellors specially trained for this activity yields distinctly relevant results, as against the situation in which supervision officers do not have specialist training [139, pp. 977–989]. Reflection on the nature of the practice leads a significant proportion of probation counsellors to identify the necessity of continuing professionalisation and of permanent adaptation to changing professional standards. A study carried out in Great Britain following the implementation of the reform of the Probation Services [161, pp. 5–18] shows that experienced practitioners, trained in the clinical model of practice, find themselves in the situation of having to reconsider their practice by identifying the *'punitive managerial'* mode of practice. The transformation of the interpretive paradigm regarding the practice also modifies the discourse of professionals, orienting it, in the case of the study mentioned, towards a model based on the ethics of care and the social construction of responsibility, convergent with the restorative paradigm. The same directive of the orientation of practice towards the values specific to the operational paradigm is found in a study from New Zealand, which positions probation as part of social work, precisely because the respondents, probation counsellors, highlighted as fundamental values precisely those specific to social work: client orientation, supportive practices, and so forth [231, pp. 4–11]. Professional training in the welfare sphere represents an element of the social construction of the profession, since it defines for the professional the discursive frameworks within the limits of which they operate at the professional level. Moreover, the article cited raises the question of the construction of professional identity starting from a status based on ethical values, knowledge, and skills, which contrasts with the mere application, without prior reflection, of an administratively imposed practice manual.

The professional duties of probation counsellors | The professional duties incumbent upon probation counsellors are: the drawing up of (pre-sentence) evaluation reports; activities with minors executing non-custodial educational measures; the supervision of persons sentenced with suspension under supervision; the supervision of persons conditionally released from the penitentiary; participation in the conditional-release commissions of penitentiaries; and the implementation of reintegration programmes. In synthesis, we may consider that Romanian and Moldovan probation practice comprises the following types of probation, with the particularities deriving from the normative framework specific to each country:

- *pre-sentence*—involves the psycho-social evaluation of the accused (indicted) person;
- *sentential in the community*—the supervision and social reintegration of persons sentenced with suspension under supervision, including social-reintegration programmes, assistance, control, and supervision of the behaviour of the supervised person;
- *penitentiary probation*—reduced, after 2014, to participation in the conditional-release commissions, in accordance with Romanian legislation, which excludes probation counsellors from the implementation of socio-educational programmes within the penitentiary and from preparation for conditional release; and, respectively, with the intervention of probation counsellors in the release-preparation programmes conducted in the penitentiaries of the Republic of Moldova;

- *post-penitentiary*—the community supervision of conditionally released persons;
- *juvenile probation*—the supervision of the implementation of non-custodial educational measures.

The professional identity of probation counsellors | The persons interviewed remarked upon the social importance of the profession, it being one of the few welfare professions whose social value is recognised both by the public and by professionals. One of the possible explanations is the association of probation with the professions of the judicial system—probation being part of the penal enforcement system. The prestige enjoyed by the legal professions is transferred to probation counsellors. An interesting discussion concerning professional status is the fact that there is as yet no officially, legally regulated status of the probation counsellor, but only an informal status of probation counsellors (FG). The positive self-perception of counsellors in Romania regarding the prestige of the probation-counsellor profession is also contributed to by the high salary level, compared with that of other professionals in welfare fields (FG). This element of salary motivation is absent in the case of Moldovan colleagues. An interesting discussion was the one that arose (FG) concerning the change of the name of the profession from probation counsellor to supervision officer. From the respondents' point of view, the change of name would afford an additional prestige to professionals in the field. The term *officer* in Romanian has a strong military connotation, heavily laden as regards professional prestige. Respondents suggest the existence of an additional authority deriving from the association with the military dimension of the term *officer*. From the constructionist perspective, we consider that the change of name to probation officer will detach the profession from among the welfare ones, significantly shifting the emphasis onto the supervision dimension to the detriment of the counselling and reintegrative one. This shift is coherent with the retributive perspective dominant in the discourse of probation counsellors. The majority of respondents indicate the existence of a balance between the counselling-reintegrative aspect and the supervisory one, with an emphasis on supervision, motivated by the task overload of counsellors, who thus carry out with greater difficulty the counselling activities that require a greater expenditure of time. It should be noted that the specialist literature [145, pp. 235–256] draws a distinction between the *social reintegration* and the *rehabilitation* of the offender, the former being included within the sphere of welfare (social) measures, while the latter is included within the sphere of psychological action. The fact that the probation model evidenced in the two countries is grounded in the social reintegration of the offender—an aim highlighted both in the interviews with the majority of respondents and in the normative frameworks in force—positions the probation of the two countries within the sphere of the social professions, with a strong welfare specificity. Professional optimism and attachment to the values of the profession are apparent from all the interviews conducted, professional identity being strong, and belonging to the profession of probation counsellor being regarded as a personal achievement. The prestige of the profession is transferred to the person of the probation counsellor, who sees themselves as professionally fulfilled, while being aware of the necessity of continuous training and improvement. The sense of belonging to a prestigious profession is motivating in itself, even though respondents draw attention to task overload and the possibility of the appearance of a burnout syndrome and demotivation.

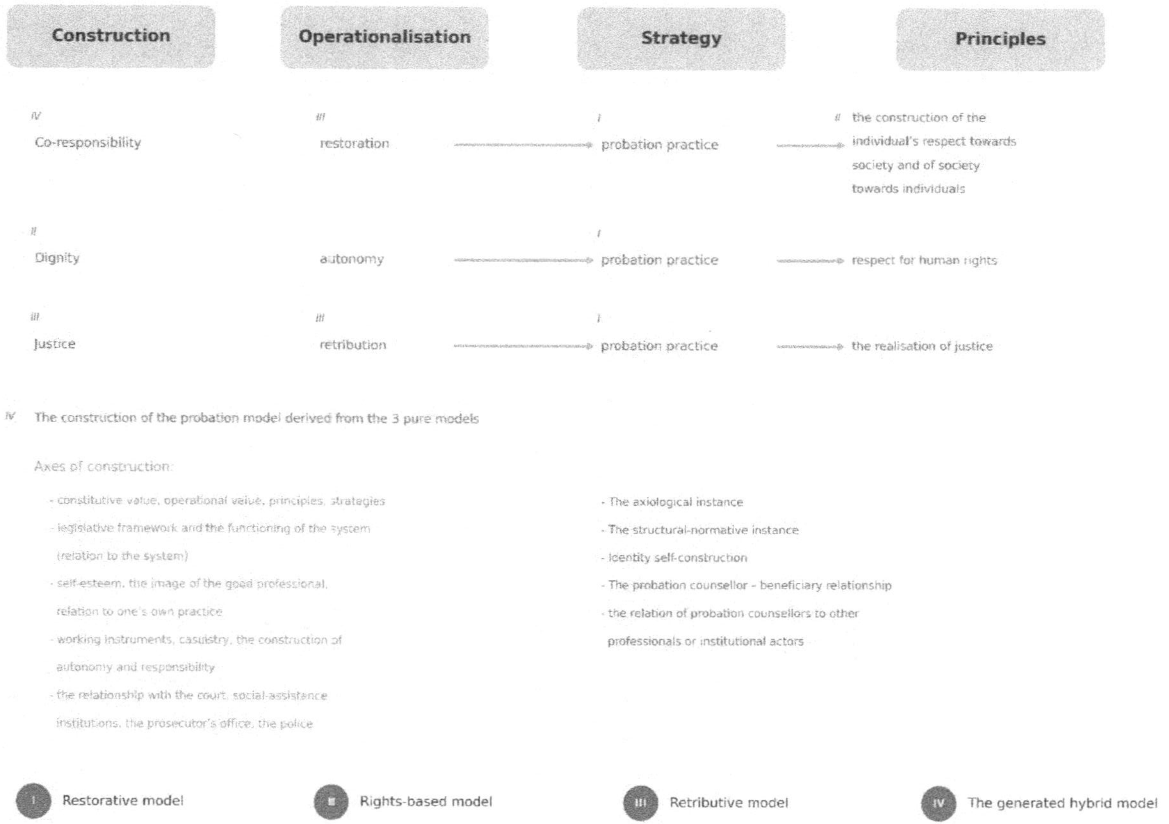
Construction
Operationalisation
Strategy
Principles
IV
Co-responsibility
III
restoration
I
probation practice
II
the construction of the individual's respect towards society and of society towards individuals
II
Dignity
autonomy
I
probation practice
respect for human rights
III
Justice
III
retribution
I
probation practice
the realisation of justice
IV
The construction of the probation model derived from the 3 pure models
Axes of construction:
- constitutive value, operational value, principles, strategies
- legislative framework and the functioning of the system (relation to the system)
- self-esteem, the image of the good professional, relation to one's own practice
- working instruments, casuistry, the construction of autonomy and responsibility
- the relationship with the court, social-assistance institutions, the prosecutor's office, the police
- The axiological instance
- The structural-normative instance
- Identity self-construction
- The probation counsellor – beneficiary relationship
- the relation of probation counsellors to other professionals or institutional actors
I
Restorative model
II
Rights-based model
III
Retributive model
IV
The generated hybrid model

Probation Practice Centred on Ethical Values

The model of values-centred probation in Romania and the Republic of Moldova rests on a process of theoretical hybridisation among the paradigm of retributive justice – in its non-prison-centred form – the paradigm of restorative justice, and the paradigm of human-rights-centred justice. The constitutive values of the Romanian model of probation are justice – understood as retribution – responsibility, and dignity as a universal human value. Each of these values derives from a distinct ethical construction. Justice as retribution, whose origins lie in the law of talion, aims at the subjective equalisation of the relations among social actors on the basis of the universality of retribution and of its personalisation according to the harm caused and the circumstances in which the offence was committed. The central expression of the model is the certainty of retribution, which guarantees equity among individuals and their equality before the law. The prison-centred paradigm is regarded as an excessive and costly form of retribution; probation introduces social models of retribution: community service, the restriction of certain rights, and supervised liberty.

Responsibility towards the individual arises from an awareness of society's co-responsibility towards the offender and the victim alike. It is society that has failed to secure sociability, that is, the legitimate framework for interactions among individuals. Society's responsibility gives rise to a model of the transmission of responsibility, of responsibilisation. Retribution is no longer paramount; rather, it is the social integration of offenders. In these contexts, the prison-centred paradigm is rejected as failing to generate responsibility in the offender. Moreover, incarceration eliminates society's assumption of responsibility towards the individual, whom it isolates from the rest of society. On the contrary, society's responsibility is made manifest through the effort to rehabilitate and reintegrate offenders and to reduce the risk of reoffending. Within this model, responsibility is substituted for equality, and rehabilitation takes the place of retribution. A particular definition of responsibility derives from the Ethics of Care [26, 27, 43, 44, 45, 115, pp. 143–183, 235, pp. 36–39], where it is understood as a caring, welfare-oriented practice. An interesting connection between the Ethics of Care and the practice of probation through restorative justice is established by Marilyn J. Gregory [117, pp. 60–77], who situates restorative justice within the sphere of the ethics of care. This view is consistent with our own findings: the elements of restorative justice present in the discourse of the probation counsellors interviewed are most often contextualised by the idea of responsibility – the community's co-responsibility for the offender's social reintegration – and by the responsibilisation of the offender. The counselling process is itself a caring, welfare-oriented process, and thus contains a series of elements related to the Ethics of Care. Other research likewise situates caring practice as a central element of probation work, for instance when conducted with offenders who have mental health problems [232].

The human-rights-centred model has as its central value the dignity of the individual, in his or her capacity as a human being, beyond his or her actions. This value appears in the respondents' discourse in the form of concern for respecting offenders' rights. The humanist paradigm of probation emphasises social reintegration, correlated with retribution, yet always within a context of constant concern for the observance of offenders' rights. Neither retribution nor reintegration, however, constitutes the most important value; that value is trust, as a component of the probation process. The human-rights-centred model comprises an important dimension relating to the humanisation of penalties, through their individualisation and their correlation with the offender's personality and with the circumstances in which the offence was committed. The human-rights-centred model rejects the prison-centred paradigm above all on the ground that it represents the most severe restriction of individual rights and entails the greatest departure from respect for the dignity of the individual. Punishment must be humanised and exercised strictly within the limits of the law, which protects a series of fundamental rights of the convicted person.

We regard restorative justice as the foundation of probation services and, more generally, professional practice in the field of probation as grounded in a series of constitutive values of an ethical nature, among which is the dignity of the individual – that of the offender as well as that of the victim – understood as respect for the autonomy of the individual within the context of the social reconstruction of the responsibility of the person who has committed criminal acts. The perspective on the autonomy and moral responsibility of offenders as significant constructs within the culture of probation is little addressed in the specialist literature, an exception being the work of Robinson [110], who analyses this issue from the standpoint of the discourse on practice in the United States. Findings obtained in 2014 in the USA emphasise the importance of the counsellor's professional autonomy for the effectiveness of his or her work. We identify a twofold perspective on autonomy: as an intrinsic foundation of practice, in the form of the counsellor's professional autonomy, and as an outcome of that practice, in the form of a moral competence acquired by the offender.

Restorative justice aims at restoring the social equilibrium disrupted by the commission of the offence. This equilibrium can best be re-established through the assumption of responsibility by all the parties involved, and not solely by the offender. The assumption of responsibility cannot be an imposed practice; on the contrary, it should be grounded in an autonomous decision on the part of the subjects involved – offenders, victim, and community. The institutions empowered to implement restorative justice – the probation services – are responsible for the process of the social construction of autonomy and responsibility, a construction that we regard as a strategy based on communicative action, and not merely on social action as is presently the case [23, 52, 118, pp. 57–60]. Responsibility denotes the characteristic of the agent (individual or collective) of acting in full knowledge of the facts, possessing competence, maturity, and preparation, together with conditions [213, pp. 661–666] of freedom, such that the agent recognises himself or herself in the acts performed and assumes their consequences [184]. The symbolic forms specific to restorative justice emphasise the development of the offender's autonomy and responsibility within educational contexts [52, pp. 63–92]. Answerability, as a form of responsibility, undergoes transformations in the structure of the meaning ascribed to it, from a historical perspective, according to the entity that is subrogated as the recipient of responsibility. The holder of the infringed right is the passive subject of responsibility and the holder of the right to reparation. Levinas's ethics [34, 35, 84, 208, pp. 75–87, 209, pp. 345–359], as the philosophical paradigm of the ethics of care, is grounded on this same model of responsibility towards a passive subject. The modern senses of responsibility represent a semantic drift of the concept of duty under the influence of the reception of alterity as complementary rather than as opposed.

The model of deliberative and restorative justice is grounded in communicative action, which generates consensus, in place of traditional adjudication, which generates obligations [213, pp. 661–666]. The resulting model represents a combination of four paradigms – retributive justice, restorative justice, utilitarian justice, and justice based on humanist values and human rights – partly owing to the model by which probation developed in Romania and Moldova, on the basis of private (non-governmental) initiatives to introduce restorative justice, and to the predominance of the caring, welfare-oriented character of practice. The dominant discourse is predominantly retributive, the majority of respondents indicating that punishment is necessary because an antisocial act must elicit a sanctioning response from society. Restorative and human-rights-based elements are substituted for retributivity when the question arises of the manner of application and the type of sanctions to be imposed. The social value of responsibility is particularly important; it intervenes in three situations: the responsibility of the probation counsellor, the responsibility of society, and the construction of the offender's responsibility as a key element of his or her social reintegration.

We have identified a series of constitutive and operational values of practice, constructing a specific model for the two countries, with the corresponding similarities and differences, and demonstrating how the particular model thus created converges with those already in existence while nonetheless attaining autonomy in relation to them. Starting from this model, we advance the idea that the process of the social construction of an institution – probation – is grounded in a series of prior interpretative agreements concerning certain dominant values – the constitutive values – which generate the normative ideological framework within which that institution functions, the social construction proper unfolding on the basis of operational values that generate the constructive context, that is, the discourse on practice. The existence of these quasi-universals – quasi-transcendentals – which we identify as the constitutive values – themselves once the object of processes of social construction – effectively bridges the social-constructionist paradigm and the realist-objectivist paradigm in the understanding of social institutions: the constructive frames are essential elements that appear, in a sense, a priori in the discourse on practice, being taken as given. In our case, retributivity – offenders are punished because they have committed an antisocial act – appears as a factual datum with regard to which respondents see no need for post-paradigmatic reflection.

Strengths-Based Probation and the Appreciative Model of Probation

A pragmatic perspective emerging from the in-depth analysis of the interviews concerns the respondents' focus on what works – the strengths-based approach to practice [93, 154, pp. 91–107]. This approach, grounded in the subject's strengths, may be regarded as part of the appreciative paradigm of probation [172, pp. 37–52]. Appreciative inquiry is a form of the progressive discovery of what works in organisations, communities, and individual experiences, and of the gradual development of the potentialities of individuals, communities, and organisations towards the attainment of objectives that they set for themselves [172, pp. 37–52]. The strengths-based (appreciative) approach complements the problem-centred approach, which is often considered less effective in the process of the rehabilitation and social reintegration of offenders [145, pp. 235–256].

The principles of appreciative inquiry are set out by Cooperrider and Whitney [70]. **The constructionist principle**: social reality is a construction that emerges as the result of the negotiation of mental and interpretative models of reality. **The principle of simultaneity**: individuals, organisations, and communities will develop in the direction towards which their attention is focused within the research-intervention process. **The poetic principle**: social reality, socially constructed as a permanent negotiation of interpretations, possesses a creative and self-transformative capacity, such that individuals, groups, communities, and organisations define and create themselves within the process of social interaction by questioning their own experiences, aspirations, and interpretations. **The principle of anticipation**: the evolution of individuals, groups, communities, and organisations is constructed through the subjective projections of a desirable future that individuals make for themselves or in their capacity as members of groups, organisations, communities, and so forth. **The affirmative principle**: appreciative inquiry focuses on the successful experiences of individuals, groups, communities, and so forth, abandoning the paradigm of deficiency [11]. Interrogating failure, problems, and deficiencies and focusing exclusively on their resolution will generate new sources of problems, deficiencies, and failures to perform.

Judy Larkins [239] and Alison Liebling, Charles Elliot, and Helen Arnold [140], for example, analyse the implementation of elements of appreciative probation in British prisons, as a possible connection between appreciative practices (Appreciative Inquiry [11, 90]) and Restorative Justice, regarding appreciative inquiry as a solid theoretical basis for reforming the practice of the social integration of persons who have committed criminal acts [172, pp. 35–52]. As regards the application of the appreciative model of restorative justice within the Romanian space, it has been analysed in the context of juvenile justice practice, as a particular dimension of probation practice [114, pp. 142–161]. The practice of the appreciative methodology begins with the identification of the strengths of supervised persons – those strengths that, in various situations, have enabled their optimal integration into society – and with the transfer of their individual resources from different areas of their social lives towards the dimension of their own social integration.

Affirmative action (the term used in American research, or positive discrimination, the term used in research of European, and especially British, origin) consists of a series of actions undertaken in support of various minority categories: ethnic and cultural, religious, sexual, and conscience-based minorities, minorities defined according to state of health or disability, gender minorities, and so forth. Affirmative actions usually take the form of granting minority categories preferential access to education, health and social protection services, employment integration, and so on [172, pp. 35–52]. Affirmative measures are an integral part of diversity management as understood in postmodern society. The vision underlying the institution of affirmative measures is that of the insufficiency of the protection afforded to certain categories by the mere prohibition of discrimination, and the need for concrete actions directed at vulnerable categories so as to enable them genuinely to accede to the exercise of their own rights. This philosophy is congruent with the appreciative ideology in the sense of identifying what is positive and successful in communication with the various disadvantaged categories and of extrapolating successful strategies into strategies of affirmative protection. In this respect, we observe a shift in the discourse on human rights, from one centred on the paradigm of deficiency – of the lack or violation of rights – to an affirmative one, of the concrete construction of frameworks for the exercise of rights. In this regard, there is a tendency within the European Union towards the generalisation of the most favourable practices [14].

The Relationship Between the Probation Counsellor and the Supervised Person

Probation is based on a counsellor–supervised-person relationship established along two fundamental dimensions: supervision, and support, assistance, and counselling. The need for support – on the part of the counsellors as well as of the social and institutional environment of offenders – is not only reflected in the discourse of the beneficiaries interviewed but is also consistent with the international literature [145, pp. 235–256], which draws attention to the need for psychological [230] and social support both for the rehabilitation and, above all, for the social reintegration of offenders. The two dimensions are complementary, both being present in any probation relationship. Effective supervision entails establishing certain limits to the counsellor–supervised-person relationship and an awareness that the probation relationship constitutes the execution of a penalty. Accordingly, the supervisory dimension emphasises monitoring the execution of the measures and obligations imposed by the court, whereas the counselling dimension emphasises communication with the beneficiary and interview strategies deriving from cognitive-behavioural therapy. Effective communication presupposes first establishing the limits of communication and, at the same time, constructing a relationship based on sincerity, trust, and mutual empathy. The effectiveness of the construction of trust is all the greater where the counsellor also seeks, from other sources, to validate the accuracy of the offender's statements.

In the literature, an interesting synthesis of the models of probation, delineated through the perspective of its practice in the United States, concerns the participation-process model of probation formulated by Craig S. Schwalbe [175, pp. 185–201]. This model emphasises participation and communication, combined with supportive practices. The aims of probation in the sphere of protecting public safety are achieved through counselling practices. This model is consistent with our own findings. In contrast to the model highlighted by Schwalbe [175, pp. 185–201], the model that emerges from our own research foregrounds the centrality of communication in both the Republic of Moldova and Romania, with particularities regarding the type of counsellor–supervised-person relationship: counselling-supportive in Romania and caring, welfare-oriented – with an emphasis on mediating access to the resources necessary for reintegration – in the Republic of Moldova.

The Competent Professional, Professional Recognition and Professional Success

The professionalism of the probation counsellor is seen to be closely linked with effectiveness in the social reintegration of supervised persons. Professional values, including ethical ones such as dignity – both the dignified attitude of the professional and respect for the dignity of the supervised person – are cited as sources of the professionals' credibility. The dignified attitude displayed by professionals legitimises the practice of probation and enables the establishment of a relationship of trust with supervised persons, as well as guiding the latter in making durable changes at the behavioural level, in the direction of social integration. An important coordinate of professional success is the small number of instances of reoffending, which many respondents regard as evidence of the effectiveness of probation as a social practice and of the professionals as practitioners. Professional optimism and a high level of motivation for work in the field are characteristics apparent from all the interviews conducted. The social status and professional prestige afforded translate into motivation for good practice. This professional optimism is transposed into the relationship with supervised persons, moving beyond mere supervision, in the sense of humanising the relationship and transforming it into one of support specific to probation carried out from within a restorative paradigm. A genuine involvement in professional activity is evident among the respondents, a fact that brings them satisfaction. For them, the practice of the probation counsellor becomes a source for the construction of their own identity, in the form of a successful career. This occurs despite the fact that respondents are aware of the overload of tasks, of the discrepancy between the professional workload of counsellors in Romania and the Republic of Moldova and that of their colleagues in the EU, and of the fact that this overload of tasks may lead to a diminution in the quality of practice.

Uncertainties, Problems and Dilemmas in Professional Practice

A series of uncertainties were signalled with regard to the future of the profession, given an excessive bureaucratisation of practice and the shift from a specifically caring, welfare-oriented practice to a formal one, excessively oriented towards supervision. The large number of cases falling to each counsellor (between 105 and 400 supervision cases, to which are added pre-sentence reports, reports concerning conditional early release from prison, and so forth) leads to a decline in the quality of practice. This problem is common to the two probation systems analysed. Respondents point to deficiencies in communication with certain state institutions, such as those which ought to make possible the performance of community service by persons on whom this obligation has been imposed by the court. There are also a number of discrepancies among the various normative frameworks in operation, an example being the impossibility of enforcing the obligation, imposed on certain supervised persons, to attend vocational training courses where they have not previously completed eight grades of schooling, since the legislation governing vocational training prohibits the attendance of such courses by persons who have not completed eight grades.

4.2. Public Policy Proposals in the Field of Probation and Restorative Justice

Starting from the two studies – The Social Construction of the Probation Counsellor Profession: A Comparative Qualitative Analysis in Romania and the Republic of Moldova, and Retributivity and Public

Perception of Non-Custodial Sanctions. A Micro-Study in North-Eastern Romania and in the Republic of Moldova – we consider warranted a series of measures aimed at the implementation of restorative justice and of non-custodial alternatives. A first measure concerns the elaboration of a national strategy, specific to each of the two countries, for public information regarding the advantages of probation from the standpoint of reducing the costs of incarceration and lowering the risk of reoffending. The campaign should aim at a modification of the external stereotypes held within public opinion concerning persons who have committed various offences, especially those of low social danger. The findings obtained, as well as recent appearances in the Romanian media, show that within public opinion a number of criminal acts with particularly serious consequences for society – such as acts of corruption and, respectively, violent acts, including sexual ones – are identified as generically coextensive with the very idea of a criminal act. Consequently, a distinction should be drawn, within public opinion, between those criminal acts that have particularly serious consequences, are committed intentionally and in full knowledge of the facts, and those that have minor social consequences and/or are committed through negligence, without clear and manifest intent, and which the offender sincerely regrets. The latter should be viewed from a social-humanist but also pragmatic perspective, bearing in mind that non-custodial community sanctions are better able to bring about the offender's social reintegration, to avert the victimisation of the offender and of his or her family, and to reduce the risk of reoffending. The social and financial costs of applying non-custodial measures are low, while at the same time reducing prison overcrowding, which would help to avoid ECtHR convictions on this matter.

The information campaign should be conducted primarily through the mass media, in the form of advertising spots, but above all through campaigns within formal and non-formal education environments, by means of programmes similar to those of legal education in secondary schools [16]. Raising public awareness with regard to tolerance and, above all, to the rights of prisoners as human beings must be grounded in the distinction between the individual as a human being and the act committed. Modern legal systems are called upon to punish acts, deterring the offender's antisocial behaviour, but only with observance of the offender's dignity as a human being. This idea of the dignity of the human being should be placed at the centre of public policies concerning the punishment of offenders.

Another public policy that ought to be implemented concerns, in our view, the clarification of the function of punishment in national legislation. Among the traditional functions of punishment, the most important are: the retributive function – the effective punishment of acts on grounds of the necessity of retribution, as a logical and legal consequence of the act; the restorative function – punishment in order to re-establish the offender–victim–society equilibrium; and the ecological function – deterring reoffending and the commission of the criminal act by the same or another offender. In our view, emphasis should be placed on the restorative function, which permits a heightened social homeostasis and minimal costs of implementing penal policy. This entails the implementation of appreciative probation through the running of social reintegration programmes for offenders, grounded in their strengths and in the strategies they have pursued over time in order to gain legitimate access to resources, and the implementation of these strategies of offenders' social functioning in place of those aimed at illegitimate access to resources. For the purpose of implementing appreciative probation, training programmes should be run for persons executing non-custodial sanctions, incorporating elements of the management of sociability. The encouragement of a professionally active life and of the employment of offenders must be counterbalanced by making the non-custodial measure conditional upon the offender's involvement in active social life, whether within the education and vocational training system or in employment. The offender's failure to become actively involved and his or her refusal to participate in reintegration programmes, including the refusal to take up a position, should be capable of constituting grounds for the revocation of the non-custodial measure.

Given that the population surveyed considers penalties to be rather insufficiently severe, while at the same time showing itself partly favourable to non-custodial measures in the case of offences of reduced social danger, a public policy for deterring reoffending might be based on extending the use of non-custodial sanctions in the case of a first offence – especially where the social danger is not particularly serious and the offender regrets the acts committed – and on the toughening of sanctions in the event of reoffending and, respectively, of breaching the conditions and measures imposed by the court for the suspension of the execution of the penalty. In this respect, it would be desirable to introduce the possibility for the court to hand down solutions suspending the pronouncement of the sentence for a probationary period; and, where the offender fully complies with the measures imposed and does not commit a new offence within a given interval, for the judge to pronounce an acquittal on the ground of the non-existence of social danger. Under these conditions, the act would not be entered on the offender's criminal record, thereby avoiding his or her stigmatisation. In a context in which a possible public policy concerning the pardon and amnesty of certain categories of offence is under discussion, we believe it would be useful for such a decriminalisation policy to be conducted through the emergence of the institution of a judicial decision commuting the penalty for a particular category of offence, on the basis of the evaluation report of the probation service, which would estimate the risk of reoffending and the offender's prospects for reintegration. In this respect, we commend the model existing in the Republic of Moldova of conditional release, granted only after partial recovery of the harm caused and, where appropriate, after soliciting the position of the injured party.

We regard as useful an increase in the competences of probation counsellors with regard to mediating the offender–victim relationship, thereby better implementing the principles of restorative justice. Victim–offender reconciliation can be more readily mediated by a service concerned with the offender's social reintegration than by mere authorised mediators. We consider it necessary to establish, within the National Probation Directorate, a victim-assistance service that would evaluate the possibility and the risks of such mediation, from the perspective of the victim and also of the enhanced prospects for the offender's reintegration. Where the risks are deemed acceptable, there may be restorative justice programmes aimed at genuine compensation of the harm by the offender – not merely financial, but also through the offering of apologies and other means of recovering the material and moral harm, aiming, so far as possible, at the principle of restitutio in integrum. We consider it necessary to develop probation services institutionally by dividing them into functional departments: pre-sentence probation and relations with the courts; post-sentence probation and the supervision of the execution of non-custodial penalties; cooperation with the prison and conditional release; counselling and post-prison probation; and so forth. We consider it necessary to strengthen the social dimension of probation practice, with the emphasis placed on social reintegration and/or rehabilitation programmes. The Romanian and Moldovan models of probation are oriented rather towards caring, welfare-oriented practices than towards the effective supervision of offenders, this latter function being subordinated to that of the social reinsertion of the supervised person. In this respect, it would be desirable to strengthen the methodological basis of practice and to professionalise it in a unified manner, as well as to provide unified professional training for practitioners. To this end we propose a curriculum model for a possible master's programme in the field of Probation and Public Policy in the Sphere of Restorative Justice.

4.3. Assessment of Training Needs in Probation and Restorative Justice

Starting from the two studies – The Social Construction of the Probation Counsellor Profession: A Comparative Qualitative Analysis in Romania and the Republic of Moldova, and Retributivity and Public Perception of Non-Custodial Sanctions. A Study in North-Eastern Romania and in the Republic of Moldova – we sought to highlight a series of training needs of the future probation counsellors of the two countries, in order to address the need to finalise a national model of probation aligned with European and global standards in the sphere of probation and restorative justice. Respondents from both countries emphasised that the profession of probation counsellor requires continuous professional development, one that would place at the professional's disposal a body of transdisciplinary knowledge centred on the caring, welfare-oriented professions – social work, psychology – while also possessing a sound legal grounding. Respondents highlighted the need for knowledge concerning the specific working methodology of probation, the social context in which probation and restorative justice are implemented, and the institutional normative framework governing its operation. The research data likewise revealed the importance of familiarising probation counsellors with the principal techniques of communication, both institutional and interpersonal.

A further need of the probation services is that of increasing their visibility within the public sphere, given the necessity of changing opinion regarding the roles of punishment and of forming a conviction among the public as to the beneficial role of non-custodial alternatives in the management of criminality – through the reduction of the costs of incarceration, both material and social, the reduction of prison overpopulation, a more effective social reintegration of offenders, and a responsibilisation of society towards them. The profession of probation counsellor has today attained autonomy, having emerged from the sphere of social work, and as such the need for training in the field of probation is evident, so that training programmes at the academic level, carried out in partnership with the National Probation Directorate / Central Probation Office, would set a positive course for the professionalisation of probation counsellors in the two countries. In what follows, we present a draft curriculum and a brief description of the proposed disciplines, in strict correlation with the training needs identified. We note that the proposal was submitted for evaluation to the Academic Council of the Faculty of Law and Administrative Sciences of Ștefan cel Mare University of Suceava, the university to which the author of the study belongs.

Field: Social Work

Study programme: Probation and Public Policy in the Sphere of Restorative Justice

Form of study: full-time, Master's degree

Duration of studies: 2 years

Valid from the academic year: 2017–2018

YEAR I

No.	Compulsory disciplines	Discipline code	Sem. 1							Sem. 2						
			C	S	L	P	I*	Form of assessment	No. of credits	C	S	L	P	I*	Form of assessment	No. of credits
1	History of Probation and of Social Alternatives to Incarceration		1	1				E	6							
2	Contemporary Penal Philosophies. Retributive, Human-Rights-Centred, and Restorative Justice		1	1				E	6							
3	Penal Enforcement Law		2	2				E	6							
4	Probation Centred on Ethical Values		2	1				E	6							
5	Organisation of the National Probation System		2	1				E	6							
6	The Regime for the Execution of Custodial/Non-Custodial Penalties									1	1				E	6
7	Legal Communication. Institutional and Interpersonal Communication within the Justice System									1	1				E	6
8	Prison Social Work and Post-Custodial Social Services									1	1				E	6
9	Human Resource Management in the National Justice System									2	1				E	6
Total compulsory hours per week			8	6				5E	30	5	4				4E	24
			14							9						

Nr. crt.	Compulsory disciplines	Discipline code	Sem. 1							Sem. 2						
			C	S	L	P	I*	Form of assessment	No. of credits	C	S	L	P	I*	Form of assessment	No. of credits
10	Communication in English															
11	Counselling Techniques in Probation									1	2				E	6
12	Evaluation of Social Programmes															
Total compulsory hours per week										1	2				1E	6
										3						

C	S	L	P	I*	Form of assessment	No. of credits	C	S	L	P	I*	Form of assessment	No. of credits
8	6				5E	30	6	6				5E	30
14							12						

Recapitulation

I. **History of Probation and of Social Alternatives to Incarceration.** In studying this discipline, students will become familiar with the evolution of probation systems throughout the world, being provided with a series of theories on practice in their diachronic order. Graduates will possess: the capacity to analyse a probation system and its advantages relative to custodial sanctions; the capacity to use the concepts and terminology specific to probation and, more generally, to any forms of restorative justice.

II. **Contemporary Penal Philosophies. Retributive, Human-Rights-Centred, and Restorative Justice.** In studying this discipline, students will acquire the capacity to operate with the concepts specific to the principal paradigms upon which modern probation is constituted, understanding the dynamics of the evolution of probation systems in correlation with the development of theory concerning the role of the sanction.

III. **Penal Enforcement Law.** Graduates will be able to apply the norms of penal enforcement law in various professional settings, both custodial and non-custodial, including within probation services.

IV. **Probation Centred on Ethical Values.** In studying this discipline, students will acquire the capacity to operate with the principal ethical concepts involved in the development of probation services: responsibility; autonomy; trust; the assumption of answerability; and so forth. They will be capable of proposing and implementing specific programmes and techniques of individual and group counselling designed to develop, in supervised persons, conduct centred on ethical values. Graduates will likewise be capable of carrying out their work as probation counsellors in observance of all the ethical standards specific to the profession contained in the codes of conduct that regulate it.

V. **Organisation of the National Probation System.** Graduates will be acquainted with the organisation of the national probation system, as well as with the legal norms that regulate the activity of the probation counsellor and the supervision of the execution of non-custodial measures.

VI. **The Regime for the Execution of Custodial/Non-Custodial Penalties.** Graduates will be acquainted with the regulations in force concerning the execution of penalties, both custodial and non-custodial, being able to carry out specific activities in working with detainees and/or with persons sentenced to non-custodial sanctions.

VII. **Legal Communication. Institutional and Interpersonal Communication within the Justice System.** Graduates will possess the capacity to communicate effectively, both formally and informally, with professionals from other institutions involved in the sphere of the justice system as well as with their own beneficiaries.

VIII. **Prison Social Work and Post-Custodial Social Services.** Graduates will be acquainted with the social work needs and, more generally, the social service needs of incarcerated persons and of those recently released from prison, as well as with the work of prison social work services, and will be acquainted with the system of services available to persons who have executed a custodial sanction.

IX. **Human Resource Management in the National Justice System.** Graduates will possess knowledge concerning the evolution of human resources in the various sectors of the national justice system, the need for human resource development within the justice system \u2014 particularly at the level of the enforcement system \u2014 and will be acquainted with the career development opportunities available to the various legal professions.

X. **Communication in English.** Graduates will possess knowledge of English for special purposes in the legal field.

XI. **Counselling Techniques in Probation.** Graduates will possess knowledge concerning the principal socio-psychological counselling techniques applicable in the practice of probation work: the non-directive approach; the client-centred approach; and the rational-emotive approach. Graduates will be able to implement appreciative probation.

XII. **Evaluation of Social Programmes.** Graduates will possess competences in the analysis and evaluation of programmes and public policies in the sphere of justice, with an emphasis on those aimed at the implementation of restorative justice.

YEAR II

No.	Compulsory disciplines	Discipline code	Sem. 3							Sem. 4						
			C	S	L	P	I*	Form of assessment	No. of credits	C	S	L	P	I*	Form of assessment	No. of credits
1	Specific Methodology in Probation Practice		1	2				E	6							
2	Legal Protection of Human Rights		2	1				E	6							
3	Supervision of Social Services		1	2				E	6							
4	Human Ecology		2	1				E	7							
5	Marketing of Public Services. Campaigns for the Promotion of Restorative Justice and Probation		1	1				E	5							
6	Research Methodology in the Social Sciences												1		C	10
7	Practicum — 3 hours/day × 4 days/week, 14 weeks												12		C	10
8	Preparation of the Dissertation Thesis												1		C	10
Total compulsory hours per week			7	7				**5E**	**30**	0	0		14		**3C**	**30**
			14							**14**						

I. **Specific Methodology in Probation Practice.** Graduates will be familiarised with the principal working techniques in probation, both pre-sentence and post-sentence. Among the techniques included will be the psycho-social evaluation report, as well as supervision reports, and so forth. They will be able to apply the specific methodology in strict conformity with the normative framework in force.

II. **Legal Protection of Human Rights.** Graduates will be acquainted with the principal means of the legal protection of human rights, within the United Nations system as well as those of the Council of Europe and the European Union.

III. **Supervision of Social Services.** Graduates will be acquainted with the principal means of supervising the social services provided to persons on the records of the probation services or of other penal enforcement services, including within the National Prison Administration.

IV. **Human Ecology.** Graduates will be familiarised with the principal norms relating to human ecology, including the national and international regulations in force for the functioning of total and closed institutions, with a predominant focus on the prison environment. Emphasis will be placed on the importance of respecting the dignity of persons executing custodial/non-custodial penalties, including through elements of human ecology: the elimination of prison overcrowding; detainee–guard relations grounded in respect for human dignity and human rights; and so forth.

V. **Marketing of Public Services. Campaigns for the Promotion of Restorative Justice and Probation.** Graduates will be acquainted with means of promoting public services in the sphere of restorative justice, possessing the capacity to conduct communication with the media and civil society that responds both to the general interest in public information and to the right to confidentiality of convicted persons.

VI. **Research Methodology in the Social Sciences.** Graduates will be acquainted with the principal methods and techniques of research in the social sciences, being capable of carrying out micro-studies within their own sphere of activity.

VII. **Practicum — 3 hours/day × 4 days/week, 14 weeks.** Graduates will be capable of implementing in practice the various methodologies of intervention within the sphere of the penal enforcement system, particularly within the probation services.

VIII. **Preparation of the Dissertation Thesis.**

4.4. Preliminary Conclusions on the Model of the Social Construction of Probation in Romania and the Republic of Moldova

The conclusions of our research relate, in general terms, to a marked impact of the probation services from the standpoint of the social reintegration of persons who have committed criminal acts. The conclusions likewise foreground a high degree of adherence on the part of probation counsellors to professional values and a heightened work satisfaction. The professional values indicated by the respondents were, in particular, responsibility, the dignity of the human being, and, most notably, communication both with the "beneficiaries" and with the other institutions with which the probation services collaborate. Openness to communication constitutes, in general, the central element of the Romanian specificity of probation practice, as emerged from the interviews conducted. An increased volume of work was also mentioned, especially following the amendment of the Law on Probation in 2013 and of the New Code of Criminal Procedure in 2014.

General Conclusions and Recommendations

Following the analysis and synthesis of the results obtained within the two studies — *Axes of the Social Construction of the Probation*

Counsellor Profession and *Retributivity and Public Perception of Non-Custodial Sanctions* — and of the micro-study *Probation Counsellors' Perspectives on Professional Practice*, which constitute the data sources of the present work, as well as of the model constructed, we consider that we have attained our research objectives as follows:

Objective 1 consists of the identification of the principal discursive axes through which the process of the social construction of the counsellor profession is realised. The principal axes of the social construction of the probation counsellor profession are: *Thematic Axis I. The Instrumental and Institutional Framework*; *Thematic Axis II. Human Resource Development*; *Thematic Axis III. The Relationship Between the Probation Counsellor and Supervised Persons*; *Thematic Axis IV. Values-Centred Probation. The Theoretical-Ideological Dimension of the Social Construction of the Probation Counsellor Profession*; *Thematic Axis V. Victim–Offender Mediation.* Within each axis, a series of conceptual categories were brought to light that describe the particular directions of the process of social construction along each of the axes. The categories we identified were: the normative framework of functioning; the institutional framework of functioning; the evolution of probation practice in Romania and Moldova; the attributions of the probation counsellor in relation to the types of beneficiaries; professional socialisation; the professional identity of probation counsellors; professional dilemmas and problems in probation practice; the specificity of the probation counsellor–supervised-person relationship; case management between supervision and counselling; the probation counsellor–supervised-person relationship as a therapeutic relationship; stories about practice; strategies for balancing power; working instruments; the change of attitude towards society and towards normativity; constitutive values; operational values of practice; the moral dimension of probation practice; why offenders are punished; victim–offender mediation as a constitutive element of the restorative justice paradigm; and the functional paradigm of the profession (restorative justice / human-rights-centred justice / retributive justice). Some of the broader categories were divided into subcategories that are more readily operationalisable at the conceptual level.

Objective 2 consists of highlighting the perspective of probation counsellors from the north-eastern region of Romania regarding their own professional development and their strategies of career construction, as a dimension of the social construction of the probation counsellor profession. The principal perspectives brought to light in the discourse of probation counsellors regarding their own professional training are the following: to their initial training in the field of social work, psychology, pedagogy, or law was necessarily added a specific training in probation, carried out at the level of the National Probation Directorate / Central Probation Office. The need for continuous transdisciplinary training was noted, most respondents emphasising the need for knowledge of caring and counselling techniques and procedures. Starting from these results, a curriculum model was formulated for the master's-level professional training of specialists in probation. A heightened level of professional motivation and optimism was observed, most often attributed to the increased professional prestige of this occupation relative to the other professions within the caring sphere, precisely on account of its integration into the sphere of the penal enforcement system. A number of aspects with demotivating potential are also signalled, in particular the overload of cases (Romania) and the low level of remuneration (Moldova).

Objective 3 consists of the identification of the constitutive and operational values of probation practice and of the manner in which the representation of these values is reflected in the discourse on practice. The constitutive values that gave rise to the necessity of professional practice belong, in general, to the sphere of the values that constitute a humanist ethos: tolerance, respect for human dignity, and society's co-responsibility for the disequilibrium generated by the commission of the offence. The model proposed rests principally on values specific to a restorative ethics — the value of co-responsibility — but also on retributive values: the need for an awareness of the offence, of the social danger of the act, and of the sanction that follows logically (in a manner somewhat akin to talionic logic). Nonetheless, the central human value of the person of the offender, beyond the act committed, leads to a discourse on practice centred on social reintegration. The operational values of practice are, in general, subsumed under an ethics of discourse, communicative practices being considered the most important elements of probation practice in Romania, whereas effective assistance in identifying and implementing legitimate strategies of access to resources, including public support, appears to dominate the discourse on probation of the Moldovan respondents. Respect for the autonomy of beneficiaries is correlated with the strategy of forming their responsibility.

Objective 4 consists of the identification of the model of good practice and of the operational definition of professional success, which may serve as the basis for the construction of a model of appreciative probation. At the level of models of good practice, two constructive models are identified: one that emphasises the interpersonal and the non-formal within the limits of the letter and spirit of the law (Romania), and a second that emphasises formalised communication within the letter of the law (Moldova).

Objective 5 consists of measuring public perception of non-custodial sanctions and of the role of the probation services. Public opinion, both in Romania and in the Republic of Moldova, is little acquainted with the role and activity of the probation services. In this respect, we have formulated policy proposals aimed at increasing the social acceptance of non-custodial penalties. In general, the mentality of the respondents is retributive, tending rather to hold that penalties ought to be made more severe. The custodial penalty of imprisonment is considered appropriate even for offences of minor social danger. Nonetheless, respondents are partly open to accepting alternatives to incarceration when placed in a position to reflect upon them. In this respect, we have formulated a series of proposals aimed at the application of a model of appreciative probation. We cannot speak of the verification of hypotheses through the Grounded Theory methodology, but rather of the credibility of certain presuppositions underlying the interpretative model. Hypotheses H1–H3 are generated a posteriori, through the specific inductive procedures, and are not pre-formulated on the basis of the support of the specialist literature. Hypotheses H1–H3 are, in effect, the result of the process of theoretical generation.

Research Hypotheses. *H1.* The institutional perspective and the professional socialisation of probation counsellors leave their imprint on the construction of their professional identity and, respectively, on the quality of practice, directly influencing the outcomes of probation activity. This hypothesis represents the constructive result of the study *Axes of the Social Construction of the Probation Counsellor Profession.* The hypothesis is plausible in accordance with the results. The discourse on probation is infused with the institutional perspective, with the models in which the professionals were trained, beginning with the British model and, subsequently, that of the Nordic countries. *H2.* The constitutive values — those that render necessary the emergence of a profession, and more generally of a social institution — of probation practice, in the two countries, are centred on social reintegration, the model of probation being caring/welfare-oriented and counselling-based. The constitutive values of probation practice derive from the sphere of humanism, the emphasis being on the (moral) value of the individual in himself or herself, beyond that of his or her actions. The constitutive values brought to light were society's co-responsibility for the disruption of the equilibrium, human dignity, and — as a consequence of respect for the autonomy and dignity of the person — the practice of a restorative probation centred on human rights. Nonetheless, retributive values relating to justice and to the accomplishment of justice through just retribution are also identified in the respondents' answers. *H3.* The operational values — those that guide practice — derive from the three principal models of probation: retributive, restorative, and human-rights-based, the resulting model being the product of a theoretical hybridisation as the outcome of the process of the social construction of reality. The principal operational values are constituted by respect for human dignity, the construction of trust between counsellor and supervised person, the construction of the autonomy and responsibility of supervised persons, the importance of communication as the foundation of counselling practice, the therapeutic alliance, and respect for the law and for judicial decisions. Hypotheses H4–H5 were verified through quantitative methodology, by means of a questionnaire-based survey.

H4. In both Romania and the Republic of Moldova, a strong retributive current predominates, with a low degree of social tolerance towards persons who commit criminal acts. The formulation of this hypothesis originates in the presupposition according to which general living conditions influence the degree of social tolerance. The hypothesis was partially verified. *H5.* Non-custodial alternatives are socially acceptable penalties, especially for punishing offenders whose acts do not present a very high social danger. The hypothesis was partially verified. *H6.* In both Romania and the Republic of Moldova, the activity of the probation services is little known, a fact that may lead to a lower acceptance of non-custodial penalties. The hypothesis was partially verified.

Bibliography

Books

In Romanian

Abraham P., Nicolaescu V., Ştefăniţă B. Introducere în probaţiune [Introduction to Probation]. Bucharest, Romania: Editura Naţional, 2001.

Adam A., et al. Ghidul rudelor persoanelor condamnate [The Guide for the Relatives of Convicted Persons]. Chişinău, Republic of Moldova: Institutul de Reforme Penale, 2006.

Ardeleanu, D. (ed.), et al. Raport de monitorizare și evaluare a activității de reintegrare socială a persoanelor liberate din locurile de detenție [Monitoring and Evaluation Report on the Social Reintegration Activity of Persons Released from Places of Detention]. Republic of Moldova; Chișinău: „Cu drag" SRL, 2009.

Balahur D. Fundamente socio-juridice ale probațiunii [Socio-Legal Foundations of Probation]. Iași, Romania: Editura Bit, 2001.

Balahur D. Probaţiune şi reintegrare comunitară. Impactul măsurilor şi sancţiunilor alternative asupra tratamentului copiilor şi tinerilor delicvenţi în sistemul justiţiei penale [Probation and Community Reintegration. The Impact of Alternative Measures and Sanctions on the Treatment of Delinquent Children and Youth in the Criminal Justice System]. Bucharest, Romania: Editura Didactică şi Pedagogică, 2004.

Banciu D. Sociologie Juridică (ipostaze și funcții sociale ale dreptului) [Legal Sociology (Aspects and Social Functions of Law)]. Bucharest, Romania: Editura Hiperion, XXI, 1995.

Bulgaru M. Asistenţa socială: fundamente teoretice şi practice [Social Work: Theoretical and Practical Foundations]. Universitatea de Stat din Moldova, Facultatea de Sociologie şi Asistenţă Socială, CEP USM, Chişinău, 2009.

Caciamac L., et al. Raportul misiunii de evaluare a necesităţilor în domeniul pregătirii pentru liberare a deţinuţilor [The Report of the Needs Assessment Mission in the Field of Preparing Detainees for Release]. Chişinău, Republic of Moldova: Helmax-Exim, 2007.

Ciobanu D., et al. Reintegrarea socială a persoanelor liberate din locurile de detenţie [The Social Reintegration of Persons Released from Places of Detention]. Chişinău, Republic of Moldova: Institutul de Reforme Penale, Chişinău, 2009.

Ciobanu V., et al. Justiţia Juvenilă; Instituţia probaţiunii în sistemul de drept al Republicii Moldova; Medierea penală [Juvenile Justice; The Institution of Probation in the Legal System of the Republic of Moldova; Criminal Mediation]. PNUD Moldova, Institutul Naţional al Justiţiei. Chişinău, Republic of Moldova: Elan Poligraf S.R.L., 2009.

Cojocaru S. Metode apreciative în Asistența Socială. Ancheta, Supervizarea și Managementul de Caz [Appreciative Methods in Social Work. Assessment, Supervision and Case Management]. Iaşi, Romania: Editura Polirom, 2005.

Cojocaru V., et al. Pregătirea pentru liberare a deţinuţilor [Preparing Detainees for Release]. Chişinău, Republic of Moldova: „Cu drag" SRL, 2009.

Corbin J., Strauss A. Basics of qualitative research: techniques and procedures for developing Grounded Theory, third edition. London, UK: Sage Publications Inc, 2008.

Creţu G. Democrație virtuală [Virtual Democracy]. Iaşi, Romania: Editura Lumen, 2009.

Creţu G. Discursul lui Foucault [Foucault's Discourse]. Iași, Romania: Editura Cronica, 2005.

Danileț C. (2016). Educație Juridică pentru Liceeni. Ghid Practic despre Drepturi și Justiție [Legal Education for High School Students. A Practical Guide on Rights and Justice]. Timișoara: Editura Agro.

Dolea I., et al. Capacităţi şi abilităţi de reintegrare socială a deţinuţilor. Cercetare sociologică [Capacities and Skills for the Social Reintegration of Detainees. A Sociological Study]. Chişinău, Republic of Moldova: „Bons Offices" SRL, 2009.

Dolea I. et al. Probaţiunea în Republica Moldova. Raport de monitorizare [Probation in the Republic of Moldova. Monitoring Report]. Chişinău, Republic of Moldova: „Bons Offices" S.R.L., 2011.

Durnescu I. Asistența socială în penitenciar [Social Work in Prison]. Iaşi, Romania: Editura Polirom, 2009.

Durnescu I. (ed.), Probaţiunea. Teorii, legislaţie şi practică [Probation. Theories, Legislation and Practice]. Iaşi, Romania: Editura Polirom, 2011.

Florian Gh., et al. Probaţiunea presentenţială în privinţa minorilor. Teorie şi practică [Pre-Sentence Probation for Minors. Theory and Practice]. Chişinău, Republic of Moldova: Institutul de Reforme Penale, 2005.

Foucault M. A supraveghea şi a pedepsi. Naşterea închisorii [Discipline and Punish. The Birth of the Prison], 2nd edition. Bucharest, Romania: Editura Paralela 45, 2005.

Frunză, A. Către o nouă expertiză etică. Deconstruind valorile etice [Towards a New Ethical Expertise. Deconstructing Ethical Values]. Iaşi, Romania: Editura LUMEN, 2016.

Frunză A. Supervizarea şi dezvoltarea profesională a asistenţilor sociali [Supervision and the Professional Development of Social Workers]. Iaşi, Romania: Editura Lumen, 2017.

Gavriluţă N. Fractalii şi timpul social [Fractals and Social Time]. Cluj: Editura Dacia, 2003, 240p.

Gilligan C. In a Different Voice. Cambridge: Harvard University Press, 1993.

Gilligan C. In a different voice: Psychological theory and women's development. Cambridge, MA: Harvard University Press, 1982.

Goffman E. Aziluri. Eseuri despre situaţia socială a pacienţilor psihiatrici şi a altor categorii de persoane instituţionalizate [Asylums. Essays on the Social Situation of Psychiatric Patients and Other Categories of Institutionalized Persons]. Iaşi, Romania: Editura Polirom, 2004.

Graham W. G. Administrarea justiţiei în comunitate. Standarde și reglementări internaţionale [The Administration of Justice in the Community. International Standards and Regulations]. Bucharest, Romania: Universal Pan, 2001.

Groza D. Drepturile victimei. Recuperarea din uitare [The Rights of the Victim. Recovery from Oblivion]. Iaşi, Romania: Editura Lumen, 2006.

Habermas J. Conștiință morală și acțiune comunicativă [Moral Consciousness and Communicative Action]. Translated by Gilbert Lepădatu, Bucharest, Romania: Editura ALL, 2000.

Hurdubaie I. Spaţiul penal paneuropean din perspectiva Consiliului Europei [The Pan-European Penal Area from the Perspective of the Council of Europe]. Bucharest, Romania: Universal Pan, 1999.

Ignătescu C. Abuzul de drept [Abuse of Rights]. Iași, Romania: Editura Lumen, 2013.

Levinas E. Astfel decât a fi sau dincolo de esență [Otherwise than Being or Beyond Essence]. Bucharest, Romania: Editura Humanitas, 2006.

Levinas E. Totalitate și infinit. Eseu despre exterioritate [Totality and Infinity. An Essay on Exteriority]. Iași, Romania: Editura Polirom, 1999.

Lipovetsky G. Amurgul datoriei: Etica nedureroasă a noilor timpuri democratice [The Twilight of Duty: The Painless Ethics of the New Democratic Times]. Translation and preface by Victor-Dinu Vlădulescu. Bucharest: Editura Babel, 1996.

Lupașcu D. Noul Cod Penal: legislație consolidată, din 10 februarie 2014 [The New Criminal Code: Consolidated Legislation, of 10 February 2014]. Bucharest, Romania: Editura Universul Juridic, 2014.

Lupașcu D. Noul Cod de Procedură Penală: legislație consolidată, din 10 februarie 2014 [The New Code of Criminal Procedure: Consolidated Legislation, of 10 February 2014]. Bucharest, Romania: Editura Universul Juridic, 2014.

Miftode V. et al. Populații vulnerabile și fenomene de automarginalizare. Strategii de intervenție și efecte perverse [Vulnerable Populations and Phenomena of Self-Marginalization. Intervention Strategies and Perverse Effects]. Iași, Romania: Editura Lumen, 2002.

Miftode V. Tratat de metodologie sociologică [Treatise on Sociological Methodology]. Iași, Romania: Editura Lumen, 2011.

Mitrache C. Drept penal român: partea generală [Romanian Criminal Law: The General Part]. Bucharest, Romania: Casa de Editură și Presă, 1994.

Neamțu, G. Tratat de asistență socială [Treatise on Social Work]. Iași, Romania: Editura Polirom, 2015, 1024 p.

Nodding N. Caring. A feminine approach to ethics & moral education. Berkkeley: University of California Press, 1984.

Nodding N. Educating for intelligent belief or unbelief. The John Dewey lecture. New York: Teachers College Press, 1993.

Nodding N. Women and evil. Berkkeley: University of California Press, 1989.

Popa V., Învaţă să trăieşti în comunitate. Ghidul persoanelor liberate din locurile de detenţie [Learn to Live in the Community. The Guide for Persons Released from Places of Detention]. Chişinău, Republic of Moldova: Institutul de Reforme Penale, 2006.

Popa, Vl. Metodologia întocmirii documentelor în procesul de probaţiune şi gestionarea dosarelor [The Methodology of Drafting Documents in the Probation Process and Case File Management]. Chişinău, Republic of Moldova: Institutul Naţional al Justiţiei, 2013

Priţcan V., et al. Reintegrarea socială a persoanelor liberate din locurile de detenţie. Ghid practic [The Social Reintegration of Persons Released from Places of Detention. A Practical Guide]. Chişinău, Republic of Moldova: Institutul de Reforme Penale, 2007.

Sandu A., Unguru E. Medierea și probațiunea. Practici sociale restaurative [Mediation and Probation. Restorative Social Practices], 2nd edition. Iași, Romania: Editura Lumen, 2016. ISBN: 978-973-166-428-6. 250 p.

Sandu A. Asistenţa socială aplicată. Tehnici de cercetare şi modele de intervenţie [Applied Social Work. Research Techniques and Intervention Models]. Iași, Romania: Editura Lumen, 2013. 234 p.

Sandu A. Elemente de sociologie. Sociologie generală, sociologie juridică, metodologia cercetării sociale [Elements of Sociology. General Sociology, Legal Sociology, Social Research Methodology]. Editura Tritonic, Bucharest, Romania, 2014.

Sandu A. Etică profesională și transparență în administrația publică [Professional Ethics and Transparency in Public Administration]. Bucharest, Romania: Editura Didactică şi Pedagogică, 2015.

Sandu A. Etică şi deontologie profesională [Ethics and Professional Deontology]. Iaşi, Romania: Editura Lumen, 2012.

Sandu A. Filosofia social constructionistă. Direcții epistemice, etice și pragmatice [Social Constructionist Philosophy. Epistemic, Ethical and Pragmatic Directions]. Cluj-Napoca, Romania: Editura Presa Universitară Clujeană, 2012.

Sandu A. Perspective semiologice asupra transmodernităţii [Semiological Perspectives on Transmodernity], 2nd edition. Iaşi, Romania: Editura Lumen, 2011. 280 p.

Sandu A. Relaţii Publice şi Comunicare pentru Administraţia Publică [Public Relations and Communication for Public Administration]. Bucharest, Romania: Editura Tritonic, 2016. 195 p.

Spoială A. Probaţiunea şi reintegrarea socială a infractorului [Probation and the Social Reintegration of the Offender], 2nd ed. Chişinău: Centrul Editorial al UASM, 2009.

Ulianovschi X., et al. Ghidul consilierului de probaţiune [The Probation Counsellor's Guide]. Chişinău, Republic of Moldova: Institutul de Reforme Penale, 2004.

Ulianovschi X., et al. Ghid privind munca neremunerată în folosul comunităţii aplicată faţă de minori [Guide on Community Service Applied to Minors]. Chişinău, Republic of Moldova: Institutul de Reforme Penale, 2006.

Vulpescu A., N. Canţer, D. Postu I. A., Pregătirea pentru liberare a deţinuţilor [Preparing Detainees for Release]. Chişinău, Republic of Moldova: Institutul de Reforme Penale, 2007.

Zaharia V. et al. Ghidul consilierului de probaţiune [The Probation Counsellor's Guide]. Chişinău, Republic of Moldova: „Bons Offices" S.R.L., 2009.

Zaharia V., Harconiţă N., Popa V., Ghid de implicare comunitară în activitatea de probaţiune în privinţa minorilor [Guide to Community Involvement in Probation Activity for Minors]. Chişinău, Republic of Moldova: „Bons Offices" S.R.L., 2010.

Zaharia V., Pistrinciuc V., Racu A., Raport de monitorizare şi evaluare a activităţii de reintegrare socială a persoanelor liberate din locurile de detenţie [Monitoring and Evaluation Report on the Social Reintegration Activity of Persons Released from Places of Detention]. Chişinău, Republic of Moldova: „Cu drag" SRL, 2009.

Zaharia V., et al. Alternative la detenţie. Raport de evaluare [Alternatives to Detention. Evaluation Report]. Chişinău, Republic of Moldova: Helmax-Exim, 2009.

Zaharia V., et al. Ghidul consilierului de probaţiune [The Probation Counsellor's Guide]. Chişinău, Republic of Moldova: „Bons Offices" S.R.L., 2009.

In English

Abadinsky H. Probation and Parole: Theory and Practice, tenth edition. Published by Prentice Hall, Pearson Education, Inc., 2009.

Braithwaite J. Crime, shame, and reintegration. Cambridge: Cambridge University Press, 1989.

Braithwaite J. Restorative justice and responsive regulation. New York: Oxford University Press, 2002.

Campbell D., Kinsella K., Coldicott T. Systemic Work with Organizations. A New Model for Managers and Change Agents. London, United Kingdom: Karnak Books, 1994.

Cooperrider D., Whitney D. Appreciative Inquiry Handbook. The First in a Series of AI Workbooks for Leaders of Change. Ohio: Crown Custom Publishing Inc., 2005.

Creswell, J. W. Qualitative Inquiry and Research Design: Choosing Among Five Traditions (second edition). CA: Sage Publication, Inc., 2007.

Derks L. Social Panoramas: Changing the Unconscious Landscape with NLP and Psychotherapy. UK: Crown House Publishing, 2005. 404 p.

Dignan J. Understanding victims and restorative justice. UK: Open University Press, 2005.

Duff A. Punishment, communication, and community. Oxford: Oxford University Press, 2001.

Garhart Mooney C. Theories of Attachment: An Introduction to Bowlby, Ainsworth, Gerber, Brazelton, Kennell, and Klaus. 1st Edition. SUA: Redleaf Press, 2009. 120 p.

Gavrielides T., Artinopoulou V. (eds.), Reconsidering Restorative Justice Philosophy. Surrey, England: Publisher Ashgate Publishing Ltd, 2013.

Gergen K. J. Social Construction in Context. Sage Publishing Inc, 2005.

Gilligan C. In a Different Voice: Psychological Theory and Women's Development. Cambridge: Harvard University, 1982.

Goulding C. Grounded Theory: some reflections on paradigm, procedures and misconceptions. Working Paper Series. Wolverhampton Business School, Management Research Centre, 1999.

Habermas J. Reason and the Rationalization of Society. Volume 1 of The Theory of Communicative Action. English translation by Thomas McCarthy. Boston: Beacon Press (originally published in German in 1981), 1984.

Hudson B. Understanding Justice: An Introduction to Ideas, Perspectives and Controversies in Modern Penal Theory. Buckingam: Open University Press, 1996.

Johnstone G. Restorative Justice: Ideas, Values, Debates. New York, SUA: Routledge, 2011.

Johnstone G., Van Ness D. (Eds.), The Meaning of Restorative Justice. The Handbook on Restorative Justice. Cullompton: Willan Publishing, 2006.

Levinas E. Ethics and Infinity: Conversations with Philippe Nemo. Cohen, R. A. (trans.). Pittsburgh, SUA: Duquesne University Press, 1985.

Nye J. Bound to Lead: The Changing Nature of American Power. New York, SUA: Basic Books, 1990.

Nye J. Soft Power: The Means to Success in World Politics. New York, SUA: Public Affairs, 2004.

Nye J. The Future of Power. New York, SUA: Public Affairs, 2011.

Rawls J. A Theory of Justice. SUA: Belknap Press, 1999.

Rubin H. J., Rubin I. S. Qualitative interviewing: The art of hearing data (3rd ed.). Thousand Oaks: Sage, 2012.

Sandu A. Social Construction of Reality as communicative Action. UK: Cambridge Scholars Publishing, 2016.

Tomiţă M. Probation as a field of study. Institution and profession. Bucharest: Universul Juridic Publishin House, 2012.

Von Hirsh A. Doing Justice: The Choice of Punishment. New-York, SUA: Hill and Wang, 1976.

Ward, T., & Maruna, S. Rehabilitation: Beyond the risk paradigm. New York, NY: Routledge, 2007.

Other Sources

In Romanian

Sondaj „Atitudinea populaţiei faţă de persoanele liberate din detenţie" [Survey "The Population's Attitude Towards Persons Released from Detention"]. Conducted in February 2009 by CJC Chişinău.

Abraham P., Szabo A. Sistemul de probatiune, suport de curs [The Probation System, course material] Universitatea Bucuresti, 2006.

Codul de executare al Republicii Moldova din 24.12.2004 [The Enforcement Code of the Republic of Moldova of 24.12.2004]. In: Monitorul Oficial al Republicii Moldova, 05.11.2010, no. 214-220.

Codul de procedură penală al Republicii Moldova din 14.03.2003 [The Code of Criminal Procedure of the Republic of Moldova of 14.03.2003]. In: Monitorul Oficial al Republicii Moldova, 07.06.2003, no.104-110.

Codul penal al Republicii Moldova din 18.04.2002 [The Criminal Code of the Republic of Moldova of 18.04.2002]. In: Monitorul Oficial al Republicii Moldova, 14.04.2009, no. 72-74.

Durnescu I. Integrarea foştilor deţinuţi [The Integration of Former Detainees]. In Buzducea D. (ed.), Economia socială a grupurilor vulnerabile [The Social Economy of Vulnerable Groups], POLIROM, 2013.

Legea cu privire la probaţiune nr.8-XVI din 14.02.2008 [The Law on Probation no. 8-XVI of 14.02.2008]. In: Monitorul Oficial al Republicii Moldova, 13.06.2008, no.103-105.

Mariț A. et al. Note de curs Drept penal. Parte generală I și II [Criminal Law Course Notes. General Part I and II]. Universitatea de Studii Europene din Republica Moldova, Facultatea de Drept, Chişinău, 2013.

Paicu, O. Managementul situaţiilor de risc în probaţiune - Procedură de lucru [The Management of Risk Situations in Probation – Working Procedure] - Serviciul de Probaţiune Iaşi, 2016.

Recomandarea nr. R (92) 16 a Comitetului de Miniştri al Consiliului Europei către statele membre referitoare la Regulile Europene asupra sancţiunilor aplicate în comunitate [Recommendation No. R (92) 16 of the Committee of Ministers of the Council of Europe to member states concerning the European Rules on Community Sanctions and Measures].

Regulamentul privind organizarea şi funcţionarea organelor de probaţiune [The Regulation on the Organization and Functioning of Probation Bodies], approved by Government Decision no. 827 of 10.09.2010. In: Monitorul Oficial al Republicii Moldova, 14.09.2010, no. 166-168.

Regulile Minime ale Naţiunilor Unite pentru elaborarea unor măsuri neprivative de libertate (Regulile de la Tokyo) [The United Nations Standard Minimum Rules for Non-Custodial Measures (The Tokyo Rules)].

Rezoluţia 40/33 din 29 noiembrie 1985 despre Ansamblul Regulilor Minime ale Naţiunilor Unite cu privire la administrarea justiţiei pentru minori (Regulile de la Beijing) [Resolution 40/33 of 29 November 1985 on the United Nations Standard Minimum Rules for the Administration of Juvenile Justice (The Beijing Rules)].

In English

Kavanagh S. J. An exploration of offenders experiences of being on a Probation Supervision Order, Trinity College, University of Dublin, 2007.

Dissertation Abstracts, Theses

In Romanian

Grecu M. I. Executarea pedepselor în regim neprivativ de libertate [The Execution of Sentences under a Non-Custodial Regime]. PhD thesis, Universitatea "Nicolae Titulescu", Bucharest, Romania, 2009.

In English

Kennington M. Ambiguous Freedom: A Grounded Theoretical Analysis of Life Outside Prison. Dissertation submitted to the faculty of the Virginia Polytechnic Institute and State University in partial fulfillment of the requirements for the degree of Doctor of Philosophy in Human Development. Blacksburg, VA, 2013. 200 p.

Robinson Z. C. Changing Probation Practice: Frontline Perspectives on a New Model for Supervising Offenders. The thesis is submitted in partial fulfilment of the requirements for the award of the degree of Professional Doctorate in Criminal Justice of the University of Portsmouth. Portsmouth, UK: University of Portsmouth, 2014.

Contributions in Journals

In Romanian

Adam, S. Profesia de cadru didactic între reprezentare socială şi vocaţie individuală [The Teaching Profession Between Social Representation and Individual Vocation]. In: Revista de Cercetare în Ştiinţe ale Educaţiei, Sociology of Education, November 2009.

Balica E. Instituţionalizarea probaţiunii în România: Practici şi strategii situaţionale în contextul (Post)Aderării la Uniunea Europeană [The Institutionalization of Probation in Romania: Situational Practices and Strategies in the Context of (Post-)Accession to the European Union]. In: Revista Română de Sociologie, 2009, new series, year XX, no. 3–4, p. 299–317.

Cojocaru Ș. Reabilitarea bazată pe comunitate a persoanelor cu dizabilități [Community-Based Rehabilitation of Persons with Disabilities]. In: Revista de Cercetare și Intervenţie Socială, 2003, Vol.2, 10 p.

Croitor E. Intervenţia socială apreciativă în supravegherea specializată a minorului [Appreciative Social Intervention in the Specialized Supervision of the Minor]. Revista de Cercetare și Intervenţie Socială, 2006, Vol 13, p. 142-161.

Frunză M. Care Ethics as Applied Ethics. Topics for Freedom. Philobiblon, vol. VIII-IX, 2003-2004, p. 143-183.

Fusch P.I., Ness L. R. Are We There Yet? Data Saturation in Qualitative Research. The Qualitative Report, 2015, Vol. 20, Issue 9, p. 1408-1416.

Gregory M. J. Practical Wisdom and the Ethic of Care in Probation Practice. European Journal of Probation, 2011, Vol. 3, No.3, p. 60–77.

Maxim S.-T. Responsabilitatea morală ca virtute și principiu etic fundamental [Moral Responsibility as Virtue and Fundamental Ethical Principle]. In: Analele Universității „Ștefan cel Mare" Suceava. Serie: philosophy, social and human disciplines, 2001, p. 57- 60.

Milicenco S. Dimensiuni ale abordărilor obiective privind fenomenul sărăcie şi excluziune socială în contextul interesului comun naţional [Dimensions of Objective Approaches to the Phenomenon of Poverty and Social Exclusion in the Context of the Common National Interest]. In: Revista ştiinţifică a Universităţii de Stat din Moldova, 2011, no. 3, 43, p. 24-30.

Nichifor E. The Probation Service in Romania: An Overview. Irish Probation Journal, 2013, Vol. 10, p.104-117.

Ólavur C. The Literature Review in Classic Grounded Theory Studies: A methodological note. Grounded Theory Review. An International Journal, 2011, Vol. 10, Issue 3.

Onwuegbuzie A. J., et al. (2012). An exemplar for teaching and learning qualitative research. The Qualitative Report, 17(1), p. 16-77.

Preda A. Probaţiunea în românia, rezultatele unei cercetări empirice evaluative [Probation in Romania, the Results of an Evaluative Empirical Study]. In: Revista română de sociologie, new series, 2015, year XXVI, no. 5–6, p. 459–470.

Sandu A. Cadre normativ-instituţionale ale construcţiei sociale a profesiei de consilier de probaţiune în zona de N-E a României şi în Republica Moldova [Institutional regulatory frameworks of the social construction of the probation counselor profession in N-E Romania and the Republic of Moldova]. In: Sociologie Românească, vol. XIV, no. 1/2016. ISSN 1220 - 5389.

Sandu A., Damian S. Restorative Justice a New (appreciative) paradigm [Justiţa restaurativă. O nouă paradigmă (apreciativa)]. In: Jurnalul de Studii Juridice, 2010, Special no., December, p. 493-505.

Toroipan R., Oancea G. Justiţia restaurativă. Metode de reinserţie pentru tinerii delincvenţi în România [Restorative Justice. Reintegration Methods for Young Offenders in Romania]. In: Jurnalul practicilor pozitive comunitare, 2002, no. 3-4, p. 1-4.

In English

Apel K.-O. How to Ground a Universalistic Ethics of Co-Responsibility for the Effects of Collective Actions and Activities?. In: Philosophica, 1993, 52, 2, p. 9-29.

Apostu, I. Infidelity – the Imorality of the Other. Revista Românească pentru Educaţie Multidimensională, 2016, 8(1), p. 7-10. Doi: http://dx.doi.org/10.18662/rrem/2016.0801.01

Ashwoorth A. Criminal Justice and Deserved Sentences. In: Criminal Law Review, 1989, vol. 36, p. 340-355.

Baciu D. Sociological and Normative Assessment of Juvenile Criminal Justice in Romania. In: Sociologie Românească, No. 4, 2011, p. 18-30.

Barbu S. G. Brief comments regarding the draft of new law on probation. In: Review of the Air Force Academy, 2012, Vol IX, No 2(21), p. 127-132

Bazemore G. Restorative justice and earned redemption: Communities, victims, and offender reintegration. In: American Behavioral Scientist, 1998, 41, p. 768–813.

Bazemore G., Umbreit M. A comparison of four restorative conferencing models. In: Juvenile Justice Bulletin (Vol. February 2001). Washington, DC: U.S. Department of Justice, 2001, p.1-19.

Braithwaite J. Restorative justice: Assessing optimistic and pessimistic accounts. In: Tonry M. (ed.), Crime and justice: A review of research, 1999, Vol. 25, p. 1–127.

Braithwaite V. The value orientations underlying liberalismconservatism. In: Personality and Individual Differences, 1998, 25, p. 575–589.

Brod M., Tesler L. E., Christiansen T. L. Qualitative research and content validity: Developing best practices based on science and experience. Quality of Life Research, 2009, 18(9), p. 1263-1278. doi:10.1007/s11136-009-9540-9

Carroll J. S. et al. Sentencing goals, causal attributions, ideology, and personality. In: Journal of Personality and Social Psychology, 1987, 52, p. 107–118.

Cernica N., et al. Issues in the ethics and aesthetics of new technologies. In: European Journal of Science and Theology, 2013, Vol. 9, nr. 1, p. 77-89.

Chadwick N., Dewolf A., Serin R. Effectively Training Community Supervision Officers A Meta-Analytic Review of the Impact on Offender Outcome. In: Criminal Justice and Behavior, 2015, Vol 42, Issue 10, p. 977-989. DOI: 10.1177/0093854815595661.

Liebling A., Elliot C., Arnold H. Transforming the Prison: Romantic Optimism Or Appreciative Realism. In: Criminology and Criminal Justice, 2001, Vol.I, No.2, p. 161-180.

De Keijser J. W., Van Der Leeden R., Jackson J. L. From moral theory to penal attitudes and back: A theoretically integrated modeling approach. In: Behavioral Sciences & the Law, 2002, 20, 4, p. 317–335.

Dowden C. Andrews D. A. The importance of staff practice in delivering effective correctional treatment: A meta-analytic review of core correctional practice. International Journal of Offender Therapy and Comparative Criminology, 2004, 48, p. 203-214.

Dowden C., Andrews D. A. What works in young offender treatment: A meta-analysis. Forum on Corrections Research, 1999, 11, p. 21-24.

Durnescu I. An Exploration of the Purposes and Outcomes of Probation in European Jurisdictions. In: Probation Journal, 2008, vol. 55, 3.

Fox K. Restoring the social: offender reintegration in a risky world. In: International Journal of Comparative and Applied Criminal Justice, Vol 38, 2014, 235-256.

http://dx.doi.org/10.1080/01924036.2013.848221

Frunză S. Does Communication Construct Reality? A New Perspective on the Crisis of Religion and the Dialectic of the Sacred. In: Revista de Cercetare şi Intervenţie Socială, 2011, vol. 35, p. 180-193.

Gallagher J.R. Nordberg A. A Phenomenological and Grounded Theory Study of Women's Experiences in Drug Court: Informing Practice Through a Gendered Lens. In: Women & Criminal Justice. 2017, Vol. 27, Issue 1, p.1-14.
http://dx.doi.org/10.1080/08974454.2016.1256255 .

Gergen K. J. Construction in Contention: Toward Consequential Resolutions. In: Theory and Psychology, 2001, vol, 11, pp. 419-432.

Hardy M. Practitioner perspectives on risk: Using governmentality to understand contemporary probation practice. In: European Journal of Criminology, 2014, vol. 11, no. 3, p. 303-318.
Doi: 10.1177/1477370813495758.

Killias M., Villetaz P. The effects of custodial vs non-custodial sanctions on reoffending: Lessons from a systematic review. In: Psicothema, 2008, 20, 1, p. 29 – 34.

Louden E. J., et al. Supervising probationers with mental disorder: How do agencies respond to violations? Criminal Justice and Behavior, 2008, Vol. 35, Issue 7, p.832-847. DOI: 10.1177/0093854808319042

Manchak S. M., Kennealy P.J., Skeem J. L. Officer-Offender Relationship Quality Matters: Supervision Process as Evidence-Based Practice. Perspectives. The Journal of the American Probation and Parole Association, 2014, Vol. 38, Issue 2, p. 57-70.

Martin L. Reentry Within the Carceral: Foucault, Race and Prisoner Reentry. In: Critical Criminology, 11/2013, Vol. 21, Issue 4, p. 493-508. DOI 10.1007/s10612-013-9196-1.

Maruna S., LeBel T. Welcome home? Examining the reentry court. Western Criminology Review, 2003, 42, 91–107.

McFatter R. M. Purposes of punishment: Effects of utilities of criminal sanctions on perceived appropriateness. In: Journal of Applied Psychology, 1982, 67, p. 255–267.

McFatter R. M. Sentencing strategies and justice: Effects of punishment philosophy on sentencing decisions. In: Journal of Personality and Social Psychology, 1978, 36, p. 1490–1500.

Miller J., Copeland K., Sullivan M. Keeping Them Off the Corner: How Probation Officers Steer Offenders Away From Crime Opportunities. In: Prison journal, 2015, Vol. 95, Issue: 2, p. 178-198. DOI: 10.1177/0032885515575263.

Nils C. Conflicts as property. In: British Journal of Criminology, 1977, 17, p. 1–15.

Norrie J., Eggleston E., Ringer M. Quality Parameters of Supervision in a Correctional Context. In: New Zealand Journal of Psychology, 2003, Vol. 32, No.2, p. 76-83.

Pascariu L. T. Some Ideas for a Comparative Analysis of the Administrative Contracts. In: European Journal of Law and Public Administration, 2016, 3(1), p. 115-120.

Phillips J. The social construction of probation in England and Wales, and the United States: Implications for the transferability of probation practice. In: British Journal of Community Justice, 2010, Vol. 8, Issue 1, p. 5-18.

Ray, P. H. The Rise of Integral Culture. In: Noetic Sciences Review, 2011, Vol. 10, No.28, p.129-135.

Ricks E., Louden, J. E. The Relationship Between Officer Orientation and Supervision Strategies in Community Corrections. Law and Human Behavior, 2015, Vol. 39 Issue 2, p. 130-141. DOI: 10.1037/lhb0000098.

Sandu A. A levinasian opening on the affirmative ethics of care. In: Journal for the Study of Religions and Ideologies, 2016, 15, 43, p. 28-47.

Sandu A. Freedom as a hermeneutical pretext. In: Revista Romaneasca pentru Educație Multidimensionala, 2010, Vol. 2, issue 3, p. 5-24.

Sandu A. Preliminaries to a Social-Semiotic Model of Communicative Action. In: Postmodern Openings, 2015, Vol. 6, issue 2, p. 59-77. Doi: 10.18662/po/2015.0602.05.

Sandu A. Probation between counselling and supervision. In: Studia Universitatis Moldaviae. Seria Științe Sociale, 2016, 8(98), p. 30-38.

Sandu A. The Development of Human Resources in the Probation Services. A Qualitative Analysis. Under review at the journal Human Service Organizations: Management, Leadership, & Governance, 2016. ISSN: 2330-3131.

Sandu A. The Establishment of Probation Systems in Romania and the Republic of Moldova. In: European Proceedings of Social and Behavioural Sciences, 2016, Vol. 15, p. 865-874. ISSN: 2357-1330. DOI: 10.15405/epsbs.2016.09.108.

Sandu A. The Practice of Probation Centred on Ethical Values. Under review at the journal Social Justice Research, 2016. ISSN: 0885-7466

Sandu A. The social construction of the profession of probation counsellor. An analysis of the instrumental and institutional framework in N.E. Romania and the Republic of Moldova. Under review at the journal Journal of Social Service Research, 2016. ISSN: 0148-8376

Sandu A., Damian S. Applying Appreciative Inquiry Principles in the Restorative Justice Field. In: Postmodern Openings, 2012, Vol. 3, Issue 2, p. 37-52.

Sandu A., Ignătescu C. Retributivity and public perception on the non-custodial sanctions. Forthcoming in Social Research Reports, 2017.

Saulnier A., Sivasubramaniam D. Effects of Victim Presence and Coercion in Restorative Justice: An Experimental Paradigm. In: Law and Human Behavior, 2015, Vol. 39, Issue 4, p. 378-38. DOI: 10.1037/lhb0000130.

Schwalbe C. S. Toward an integrated theory of probation. In: Criminal Justice and Behavior, 2012, Vol. 39, No. 2, p. 185-201. DOI: 10.1177/0093854811430185.

Szabo A. From Restorative Justice to Restorative Practices: Applicability in the Field of Social Work. In: Revista de Asistenţă Socială, 2010, No. 1.

Unguru E., Sandu A. A Socio-Legal Approach of Probation in Light of the New Penal Code. Restorative Justice Versus Retributive Justice. In: European Journal of Law and Public Administration, Issue 1, p. 37-68.

Wenzel M. et al. Retributive and Restorative Justice. In: Law Hum Behav, 2008, 32, p. 375–389. DOI 10.1007/s10979-007-9116-6.

Vlăduțescu Ș. Communication on the difficult route of lie. In: International Letters of Social and Humanistic Sciences, 2014, 16(1), p. 86-95.

Contributions in Scientific Works

In Romanian

Balahur D. Pedeapsă şi control social în modernitatea târzie. Pluralismul socio-juridic şi justiţia alternativă [Punishment and Social Control in Late Modernity. Socio-Legal Pluralism and Alternative Justice]. In: Schiaucu V., Canton R. (eds.). Manual de probaţiune [Probation Manual]. Bucharest, Romania: Editura Eurostandard, 2008, p. 49-68.

Bucur A., Dima M., Oberşterescu E. Elemente de drept [Elements of Law]. In: Schiaucu V., Canton, R. (eds.), Manual de probaţiune [Probation Manual]. Bucharest, Romania: Editura Eurostandard, 2008, p. 69-105.

Bulgaru M. Factori de risc în apariţia comportamentului delincvent [Risk Factors in the Emergence of Delinquent Behaviour]. In: Bulgaru M. (ed.), Asistenţa socială şi justiţia juvenilă: modalităţi de integrare şi cooperare [Social Work and Juvenile Justice: Modalities of Integration and Cooperation]. Collection of articles based on the papers presented at the scientific conference of 22 April 2005. Universitatea de Stat din Moldova. Centrul Republican de Resurse pentru Asistenţă Socială, 2005, p. 7-25.

Cojocaru V. Instituţia probaţiunii în Republica Moldova [The Institution of Probation in the Republic of Moldova]. In: Bulgaru M. (ed.), Asistenţa socială şi justiţia juvenilă: modalităţi de integrare şi cooperare [Social Work and Juvenile Justice: Modalities of Integration and Cooperation]. Collection of articles based on the papers presented at the scientific conference of 22 April 2005.

Universitatea de Stat din Moldova. Centrul Republican de Resurse pentru Asistenţă Socială, 2005, p. 90-98.

Cozma C., Măgureanu L. Valori etice fundamentale, între constanță și metamorfoză [Fundamental Ethical Values, Between Constancy and Metamorphosis]. In: Pivniceru M., Luca M. (eds.), Deontologia profesiei de magistrat. Repere contemporane [The Deontology of the Magistrate Profession. Contemporary Landmarks]. Bucharest, Romania: Editura Hamangiu, 2008.

Dilion M. Efectele mediului penitenciar asupra vieţii persoanelor în conflict cu legea [The Effects of the Prison Environment on the Lives of Persons in Conflict with the Law]. In: Bulgaru M. (ed.), Asistenţa socială şi justiţia juvenilă: modalităţi de integrare şi cooperare [Social Work and Juvenile Justice: Modalities of Integration and Cooperation]. Collection of articles based on the papers presented at the scientific conference of 22 April 2005. Universitatea de Stat din Moldova. Centrul Republican de Resurse pentru Asistenţă Socială, 2005, p. 47-52.

Dongoroz V. Drept penal [Criminal Law]. In: Tanoviceanu I. Tratat de drept şi procedură penală [Treatise on Criminal Law and Procedure], 2nd edition revised and expanded by Dongoroz V. et al. Bucharest, 1924-1927, vol. III.

Dumitraşcu L., Schiaucu V. Supravegherea în comunitate [Community Supervision]. In Schiaucu V., Canton R. (eds.), Manual de Probațiune [Probation Manual]. Bucharest, Romania: Editura Euro Standard, 2008, p. 156-191.

Durnescu I. O istorie a probatiunii în România [A History of Probation in Romania]. In: Schiaucu V., Canton R. (eds.), Manual de Probațiune [Probation Manual]. Bucharest, Romania: Editura Euro Standard, 2008, p. 8-25.

Durnescu I. Recomandări ale Consiliului Europei în Domeniul Probațiunii [Council of Europe Recommendations in the Field of Probation]. In: Durnescu I. (ed.), Probațiunea. Teorii, legislație și practică [Probation. Theories, Legislation and Practice]. Iași, Romania: Editura Polirom, 2011.

Durnescu I. Serviciile de probațiune din România [The Probation Services of Romania]. In Buzducea D. Asistența socială a grupurilor de risc [Social Work with At-Risk Groups]. Iași, Romania: Editura Polirom, 2010.

Haines K. Ce este probaţiunea [What Is Probation]. In: Balahur, D. (ed.), Manualul consilierului de reintegrare socială şi supraveghere [The Manual of the Social Reintegration and Supervision Counsellor]. Craiova: Editura „Themis", 2002.

Maiorescu T. În contra direcţiei de azi în cultura română [Against Today's Direction in Romanian Culture]. In Opere [Works], vol. 1. Bucharest, Romania: Editura Minerva, [1866] 1978.

Maxim S.-T., Dascălu D. I., Hapenciuc V. Relevanţa eticii relaţiilor de afaceri într-o lume în schimbare [The Relevance of Business Relations Ethics in a Changing World]. In: Revista Amfiteatru Economic, 2008, no. 23, p.200-210.

Popa D. Perspective de implementare a justiţiei restaurative în Republica Moldova [Perspectives on Implementing Restorative Justice in the Republic of Moldova]. In: Bulgaru M. (ed.), Asistenţa socială şi justiţia juvenilă: modalităţi de integrare şi cooperare [Social Work and Juvenile Justice: Modalities of Integration and Cooperation]. Collection of articles based on the papers presented at the scientific conference of 22 April 2005. Universitatea de Stat din Moldova. Centrul Republican de Resurse pentru Asistenţă Socială, 2005, p. 81-89.

Popa V. Conceptul de probațiune penitenciară: managementul pedepsei [The Concept of Prison Probation: Sentence Management]. In: Bulgaru M. (ed.), Asistenţa socială şi justiţia juvenilă: modalităţi de integrare şi cooperare [Social Work and Juvenile Justice: Modalities of Integration and Cooperation]. Collection of articles based on the papers presented at the scientific conference of 22 April 2005. Universitatea de Stat din Moldova. Centrul Republican de Resurse pentru Asistenţă Socială, 2005, p. 99-109.

Szabo A. Greșeală, vinovăție și pedeapsă: despre reabilitarea persoanelor care au comis infracțiuni [Fault, Guilt and Punishment: On the Rehabilitation of Persons Who Have Committed Offences]. In Buzducea D. Asistența socială a grupurilor de risc [Social Work with At-Risk Groups]. Iași, Romania: Editura Polirom, 2010.

In English

Apel K.-O. Normative Ethics and Strategical Rationality. The Philosophical Problem of Political Ethics. In: Schurmann, R.(ed.), The Public Realm. Essays on Discursive Types in Political Philosophy. State Univ. of New York Press, 1989.

Apel K.-O. The Ecological Crisis as a Problem for Discourse Ethics. In: Ofsti, A. (ed.), Ecology and Ethics. Trondheim: Nordland Academy of Arts and Sciences, 1992.

Apel K.-O. The Response of Discourse Ethics to the Moral Challenge of the Human Situation as Such and Especially Today. In: Mercier Lectures, Louvain-la-Neuve, March, 1999, p.77-90.

Bandura A. Social Cognitive Theory of Moral Thought and Action. In Kurtines W. M., Gewirtz J. L. (eds.), Handbook of Moral Behavior and Development, Vol. 1. Hillsdale, NJ: Erlbaum, 1991, p. 45-103.

Braithwaite J. Restorative justice. In Tonry, M. (Ed.), The handbook of crime and punishment. Oxford : Oxford University Press, 1998, p. 323–344.

Braithwaite J. Principles of restorative justice. In: Von Hirsch A., Roberts J. V., Bottoms A., Roach K., Schiff M. (eds.), Restorative justice and criminal justice: Competing or reconcilable paradigms? Oxford: Hart, 2003. p.1-20.

Braithwaite J., Strang H. Introduction: Restorative justice and civil society. In: Strang H. , Braithwaite J. (eds.), Restorative justice and civil society. Cambridge: Cambridge University Press, 2001. p.1-13.

Cooperrider D., Srivatsva S. Apreciative Inquiry in Organization Life. In: Cooperrider D., Srivatsva S. (ed.), Research in Organizational Change and Development. Greenwich, CT: JAI Press, 1987.

Daly K. Revisiting the Relationship between Retributive and Restorative Justice. In: Strang H., Braithwaite J. (eds.), Restorative Justice: From Philosophy to Practice. Dartmouth: Aldershot, 2000, p. 33-54.

Foucault M. Governmentality. In Burchell G., Gordon G., Miller P. (eds.), The Foucault Effect: Studies in Governmentality. Chicago, IL: University of Chicago Press, 1991, p. 87–104.

Johnstone G., Van Ness D. V. The Meaning of Restorative Justice. In: Johnstone G., Van Ness D. V. (eds.), Handbook on Restorative Justice. Cullompton: Willan Publishing, 2006.

Levinas E. Ethics as First Philosophy. In Hand S. (ed.), The Levinas Reader. Blackwell Publishing Company, Malden, 2001, p. 75-87.

Levinas E. The Trace of the Other. In Taylor M. C. (ed.), Deconstruction in Context. Chicago, IL: University of Chicago Press, 1986, p. 345-359.

Pavlich G. The force of community. In: Strang H., Braithwaite J. (eds.), Restorative justice and civil society. Cambridge: Cambridge University Press, 2001, p. 56-68.

Sandu A. Probation counsselors' perspectives on their professional practice. Forthcoming in Sandu A., Ciulei T., Frunză A. (eds.), The European Proceedings of Social & Behavioural Sciences. MEPDEV 2nd edition 2016 - 2nd Central & Eastern European LUMEN International Conference - Multidimensional Education & Professional Development. Ethical Values, 2017.

Sandu A. The Functions of Penalty and the Attributions of the Systems of Probation. Comparison between Romania and the Republic of Moldova. In: Sandu, A., Frunza, A., Ciulei, T., Gorghiu, G., Petrovici, A. (eds.), Rethinking Social Action. Core Values. Bologna, Italy: MEDIMOND S R L, 2015, p. 1413-1417.

Sandu A. The Social Construction of the Probation Counsellor Profession. An Ethical Approach. In: Frunză, A., Ciulei, T., Sandu A. (eds.), Transdisciplinarity and Communicative Action. Italy: MEDIMOND-Monduzzi Editore International Proceedings Division, 2015, p. 661-666.

Toader E., Balan G., Bulgaru Iliescu D. Ethical values of the medical education. In: E-Health And Bioengineering Conference (EHB). NEW YORK: IEEE, 345 E 47TH ST. ISBN:978-1-4673-7545-0.

Van Kalmthout A. M., Durnescu I. European Probation Service Systems. A comparative overview. In Van Kalmthout A. M., Durnescu I. (eds.), Probation in Europe, Published by aolf Legal Publishers (WLP) 2008, p. 201.

Contributions in Symposium Proceedings

In English

Sandu A. From Distributive to Procedural Justice. Justice as a Constitutive Value of Public Administration. Presented at World LUMEN Congress, 15th LUMEN Anniversary Edition | 12- 17 April 2016| Iasi, Romania. Available online at: http://conferinta. info/program-wlc2016/

Sandu A. How the Probation Counsellors see the Relationship with the Supervised Persons. Presented at the 2nd Central & Eastern European LUMEN International Conference. Multidimensional Education & Professional Development. Ethical Values, 17-18 November 2016, Târgoviște, Romania. Available online at: http://lumen.international/wp-content/uploads/2016/11/Final-Program_LUMEN_MEPDEV2016_Conference.pdf

Sandu A. Social construction of probation counsellor profession. Presented at the LUMEN 2014 International Scientific Conference – Transdisciplinarity and Communicative Action, 21-22 November 2014, Târgoviște, Romania. Available online at: http://conferinta.info/wp-content/uploads/2014/10/PROGRAM_LUMEN_5th_edition_TCA2014_19.11_13.00.pdf

Sandu A. The Practice of Probation centred on Ethical Values. Presented at the 2nd Central & Eastern European LUMEN International Conference. Multidimensional Education & Professional Development. Ethical Values, 17-18 November 2016, Târgoviște, Romania. Available online at: http://lumen.international/wp-content/uploads/2016/11/Final-Program_LUMEN_MEPDEV2016_Conference.pdf

Sandu A. Three Perspectives on the Ethics of Punishment. Presented in the Plenary Session at the 7th LUMEN International Conference – Multidimensional Education and Professional Development. Ethical Values – MEPDEV 2015, 12th – 14th November 2015, Târgoviște, Romania. Available online at: http://conferinta.info/wp-content/uploads/2015/11/PROGRAM-%E2%80%93-LUMEN-MEPDEV2015.pdf;

Sandu A., Unguru, E. Social Construction of Probation. Professional interferences. Presented at Social Work International Conference (SWIC). Envisioning sustainable social work: Enpowering Communities and Individuals. November 3-4, 2016. Bucharest. Available at: https://swicub.files.wordpress.com/2016/06/2016-11-01-swic-2016_conference-programme_new-version-1.pdf

References to Electronic Documents

In Romanian

Codul de etică al consilierului de probațiune [The Code of Ethics of the Probation Counsellor]. http://cj.md/uploads/Cod%20de%20etica%20final.pdf (accessed 033.02.2017).

Centrul pentru Drepturile Omului din Moldova. Generalizarea şi realizarea studiului privind implementarea legii cu privire la probaţiune în Republica Moldova (Probaţiunea presentinţială şi sentinţială în comunitate), 2012 [The Synthesis and Conduct of the Study on the Implementation of the Law on Probation in the Republic of Moldova (Pre-Sentence and Sentence Probation in the Community), 2012]. http://ombudsman.md/sites/default/files/document/attachments/final_raport_probatiunea_partea2.pdf (accessed 02.02.2017).

Hotărârea 56/3 cu privire la Nota informativă a Procuraturii Generale pe marginea respectării legislaţiei la aplicarea pedepsei sub formă de muncă neremunerată în folosul comunităţii [Decision 56/3 on the Information Note of the Prosecutor General's Office regarding compliance with the legislation on the application of the penalty in the form of community service]. Chişinău, 2013. http://new.csm.md/files/Hotaririle/2013/3/56-3.pdf (accessed 02.02.2017).

Ministerul Justiției al Republicii Moldova, Oficiul Central de Probaţiune. Buletin informativ [Information Bulletin], Issue no. 1/2015. http://probatiune.gov.md/tc_userfiles/file/Buletin%20informativ/Buletin%20Informativ%20nr_%201%20din%2003-2015.pdf (accessed 02.02.2017).

Ministerul Justiției al Republicii Moldova, Oficiul Central de Probaţiune. Ordin cu privire la aprobarea Concepţiei de dezvoltare a instituţiei probaţiunii [Order on the approval of the Concept for the Development of the Probation Institution]. http://www.justice.gov.md/public/files/transparenta_in_procesul_decizional/coordonare/ordin_Conceptia.pdf (accessed 02.02.2017).

Ministerul Justiției, Direcția Națională de Probațiune. Sistemul de Probaţiune. Raport de activitate pentru anul 2015 [The Probation System. Activity Report for the Year 2015]. http://www.just.ro/wp-content/uploads/2015/12/Anexa-1.5.1-Raport-de-activitate-2015-Directia-Nationala-de-Probatiune.pdf (accessed 02.02.2017).

Oficiul Central de Probaţiune. Bilanţul activităţii Oficiului central de probaţiune pentru 9 luni, anul 2015 [The Activity Review of the Central Probation Office for 9 Months, Year 2015]. http://probatiune.gov.md/tc_userfiles/file/Activitatea%20OCP/Bilantul%20-%209%20luni%202015.pdf (accessed 02.02.2017).

Strategia de dezvoltare a sistemului probațiunii pentru anii 2016 – 2020 [The Strategy for the Development of the Probation System for the Years 2016–2020]. http://probatiune.gov.md/tc_userfiles/file/Transparenta/Strategia%20de%20dezvoltare%20a%20sistemului%20de%20proba%C8%9Biune.pdf (accessed 02.02.2017).

In English

Barker K. A. Grounded Theory study of the role of interpersonal processes in community sexual offending group work programmes from a counselling psychology perspective. London Metropolitan University, 2015. http://repository.londonmet.ac.uk/1101/1/Barker Kimberly_GroundedTheoryStudy.pdf (accessed 31.01.2017).

Dale M. Trlin A. Probation practice as social work – viewpoints of practitioners in New Zealand. Social Work Review, 2007, p. 4-11. http://anzasw.nz/wp-content/uploads/SW-Review-19-Winter-07-Article-Dale-and-Trlin.pdf (accessed 02.02.2017).

Epperson M., Lurigio A. Comparative Evaluation of Court-Based Responses to Offenders with Mental Illnesses. https://www.ncjrs.gov/pdffiles1/nij/grants/249894.pdf (accessed 03.02.207).

McNeill F. Probation: Myths, realities and challenges. http://www.coe.int/t/dghl/standardsetting/prisons/Conference_19_files/Word%20Presentation%20McNeill_Helsinki.pdf (accessed 02.02.2017).

Munting L. Offender rehabilitation and reintegration: taking the White Paper on Corrections forward. Cape Town, 2005. https://pdfs.semanticscholar.org/22be/fbbe206bd7178eb748f268dd6e0c7c32ea3b.pdf (accessed 01.02.2017).

Nodding N. Two concepts of caring. Philosophy of Education, 1999, p.36-39. http://ojs.ed.uiuc.edu/index.php/pes/article/view/2024/719 (accessed 03.02.2017).

Case of Atudorei V. Romania, (Application no. 50131/08) Judgment, Strasbourg, 16 September 2014. http://freecases.eu/Doc/CourtAct/4552686 (accessed 03.02.2017).

Legea Nr. 252 din 19 iulie 2013 privind organizarea şi funcţionarea sistemului de probaţiune [Law No. 252 of 19 July 2013 on the organization and functioning of the probation system]. http://anp.gov.ro/documents/10180/57727/Legea+252+din+2013++privind+sistemul+de+probatiune.pdf/a7ed7611-b6ac-43c7-85ac-a31975bbff73 (accessed 03.02.2017).

Legea Nr. 253 din 19 iulie 2013 privind executarea pedepselor, a măsurilor educative şi a altor măsuri neprivative de libertate dispuse de organele judiciare în cursul procesului penal [Law No. 253 of 19 July 2013 on the execution of sentences, educational measures and other non-custodial measures ordered by the judicial bodies during the criminal proceedings]. http://anp.gov.ro/documents/10180/57727/Legea+253+din+2013+-+executarea+pedepselor,a+masurilor+educative+si+a+altor+m%C4%83suri+neprivative+de+libertate.pdf/0d734902-be75-4de2-bcdd-34f5eac9717d (accessed 03.02.2017).

Larkins J. Using Appreciative Inquiry in Parent Teen Mediation, 2004. http://judylarkins.com/news/using-appreciative-inquiry-parentteen-mediation (accessed 07.02.2017).

Appendix 1

Interview Guide for Probation Counsellors

(RO/MD)

I. Thematic axis 1. Experience as a probation counsellor. Description of professional practice / specific features of the practice.

1. How long have you been working as a probation counsellor?
2. How did you come to work as a probation counsellor?
3. What training did you undertake in order to become a probation counsellor?
4. What does your work as a probation counsellor consist of?
5. What are the professional duties incumbent upon you in your capacity as a probation counsellor?
6. Please describe the ordinary activities you carry out during a typical working day.
7. Please describe the activities you undertake in order to bring a case to a successful conclusion.
8. What is the professional context in which your practice is carried out?
9. What do you consider to be the specifically Romanian/Moldovan elements of probation practice?
10. How do you envisage the evolution of probation practice in Romania / the Republic of Moldova?

II. Thematic axis: The meaning that the subject attributes to his or her professional practice

11. What meaning do you attribute to your professional practice? What does it mean to you to be a probation counsellor? To be the manager of a probation service?

12. What meaning do you attribute to the term professionalism?
13. Do you consider that a good probation counsellor should possess solid professional training as a social worker, as a psychologist, or as a jurist? Please justify your choice.
14. What makes you regard yourself as a good professional? What makes you regard someone else (particularly another probation counsellor) as a good professional?
15. What do you consider to have been the greatest achievement of your career as a probation counsellor?
16. What precisely made it possible for this achievement to come about?
17. What was the greatest disappointment you have experienced as a probation counsellor?
18. What precisely made this constitute a disappointment for you?
19. What was the greatest disappointment you have experienced in your capacity as a manager?
20. What, from your point of view, do you consider to be a resolved case?

III. Thematic axis: The relationship with the beneficiaries

21. What is your relationship, in general, with the persons under supervision?
22. What do you do as a professional in order to render communication with supervised persons more effective?
23. How important do you consider trust to be in the relationship between the professional and the beneficiary of the probation system, and what do you do in concrete terms in order to establish a relationship of trust?

IV. Thematic axis: The relationship between the probation counsellor and institutions (the probation service, the courts, penitentiaries)

24. What is your relationship, in your capacity as a probation counsellor, with the court, with the penitentiary, and, more generally, with the other institutions involved in the criminal justice system?

25. What do you think ought to be done in order for the system of probation services to communicate with maximum efficiency with the other systems involved in the field of criminal justice?

V. Thematic axis: The meaning of responsibility and autonomy

26. What is the social role of probation practice?

27. Do you consider yourself rather a professional engaged in the supervision of persons who have committed criminal offences, or a professional engaged in the development and implementation of programmes for their social reintegration?

28. In your opinion, what is the reason for which offenders are punished by society?

29. What is your view of the opinion according to which: the purpose of imposing a punishment is the retribution or sanctioning of a wrong that has been done. Offenders deserve to be punished because they have committed a wrongful or antisocial act.

30. What is your view of the opinion according to which the most important role of punishment is to deter the commission of further offences, both by the offenders in question and by other potential offenders? Punishment must set an example…

31. Should the most important role of punishment be the restoration of equilibrium within society (between the offender, the victim, and the community)?

32. What meaning do you attribute to the term responsibility?

33. Please describe or present reintegration programmes for persons who have committed criminal offences which, in your view, might contribute to fostering their sense of responsibility.

34. Do you believe that it is possible to instil a sense of responsibility in persons who have committed criminal offences?

35. Can you give examples of situations in which persons under the supervision of the probation service, or under your own supervision as a probation counsellor, have demonstrated responsibility?

36. Do you believe that the implementation of offender–victim counselling and mediation programmes would foster a sense of responsibility among offenders? If so, in what manner?

37. How do you define the term autonomy?

38. Do you find a moral or ethical significance in this term?

39. Does the probation service contribute to the construction of the autonomy of the subjects placed under probation?

40. How do you consider that supervision in the community would best be implemented: should the sentence be pronounced and suspended on condition that a probation programme is followed, or should the pronouncement of the sentence be deferred by the judge for an indeterminate period, so that, in the event of the success of the social reintegration programmes, the sentence would not be pronounced at all? Please justify your choice.

Thank you for the time you have devoted to us and for the support you have offered in carrying out this research.

Your answers are exceptionally valuable to us!

Appendix 2

Interview Guide for Beneficiaries

(to be administered to persons who have committed criminal offences and who are under the supervision of the Probation Services)

(RO/MD)

I. Thematic axis 1. Experience as a person under the supervision of the probation service.

1. For how long have you been on the records of the probation service?
2. What are the reasons for which you were placed under the supervision of the Probation Service?
3. What does the supervision carried out in your case by the probation counsellor consist of?
4. Please describe the ordinary activities that you carry out during a meeting held with the probation counsellor.

II. Thematic axis: The meaning that the subject attributes to his or her relationship with the Probation Service

5. What meaning do you attribute to your own social reintegration?
6. Do you consider that a good probation counsellor should possess solid professional training as a social worker, as a psychologist, or as a jurist? Please justify your choice.

III. Thematic axis: The relationship with the probation counsellor

7. What is your relationship, in general, with the probation counsellor?
8. How important do you consider trust to be in your relationship with the Probation counsellor?

IV. Thematic axis: The meaning of responsibility and autonomy

9. What is the social role of probation practice?

10. In your opinion, what is the reason for which offenders are punished by society?

11. What is your view of the opinion according to which: the purpose of imposing a punishment is the retribution or sanctioning of a wrong that has been done. Offenders deserve to be punished because they have committed a wrongful or antisocial act.

12. What is your view of the opinion according to which the most important role of punishment is to deter the commission of further offences, both by the offenders in question and by other potential offenders? Punishment must set an example…

13. Should the most important role of punishment be the restoration of equilibrium within society (between the offender, the victim, and the community)?

14. What meaning do you attribute to the term responsibility?

15. Please describe or present reintegration programmes for persons who have committed criminal offences which, in your view, might contribute to fostering their sense of responsibility.

16. Do you believe that it is possible to instil a sense of responsibility in persons who have committed criminal offences?

17. Do you believe that the implementation of offender–victim counselling and mediation programmes would foster a sense of responsibility among offenders? If so, in what manner?

18. How do you define the term autonomy?

19. Do you find a moral or ethical significance in this term?

20. Does the Probation Service contribute to the construction of the autonomy of the subjects placed under probation?

21. How do you consider that supervision in the community would best be implemented: should the sentence be pronounced and suspended on condition that a probation programme is followed,

or should the pronouncement of the sentence be deferred by the judge for an indeterminate period, so that, in the event of the success of the social reintegration programmes, the sentence would not be pronounced at all? Please justify your choice.

We thank you for the time you have devoted to us and for the support you have offered in carrying out this research.

Your answers are exceptionally valuable to us!

Appendix 3

Interview Guide for Other Professionals

(RO/MD)

1. What is your occupation?
2. In what field do you work?
3. What is your professional experience?
4. For how long have you been interacting with the probation system?
5. What are the specific features of the Probation Service in Romania?
6. In what situation have you interacted with the Probation Service and with the probation counsellor?
7. How useful do you consider the activity of the Probation Service to be for Romanian society? And subsequently I should like you to tell me how you assess it within the context of the Romanian justice system.
8. How do you view the role of the probation counsellor? In what way does he or she benefit Romanian society?
9. There are two positions, according to which: (1) the importance of punishment should be emphasised, and (2) the social reintegration of the offender should be emphasised. Which of the two positions do you subscribe to, and why?
10. How do you view the probation counsellor in relation to other specialists within the justice system and within the system of social services? What would his or her position be?
11. In what manner do you consider that probation fulfils its intended role?
12. Please enumerate, from your point of view, the strengths and the weaknesses of the probation system.
13. What improvements do you believe the probation system in Romania requires?

Appendix 4

Focus Group Guide

(RO/MD)

1. What do you think probation means in general?
2. When did you last interact with a probation counsellor, and what were the activities in which you collaborated?
3. From the perspective of society, and also from your own perspective as professionals, what ought to take precedence? Punishment — and here I am referring to an exemplary punishment of the offender, in the sense of deterring the commission of criminal offences — or, on the contrary, the social reintegration of the offender?
4. Please choose a case, in whatever way you wish, and tell me precisely what you opt for: punishment or reintegration?
5. What do you consider the professional status of the probation counsellor to be?
6. How do you view the development of probation in Romania?
7. Are you now speaking, in a sense, of the specialisation of the activity into distinct niches?
8. If you will allow me, when we refer to status — now from your perspective as a counsellor — you spoke at the outset of that capacity of probation officer.
9. Does the probation officer have a clearly established role?
10. Now, please tell me how you would wish to be known?

Appendix 5

Please select your country of affiliation

*1. * Tick a single box*

☐ Romania ☐ Republic of Moldova

Questionnaire | Research on Public Opinion concerning Non-Custodial Sentences in Romania and the Republic of Moldova

The purpose of this research is to identify the opinion of Probation Counsellors regarding a series of particular aspects relating to non-custodial sentences (that is, sentences which avoid imprisonment) and to the functioning of the Probation Services in Romania. The research is being conducted within the LUMEN Centre for Socio-Human Research, at the Ştefan cel Mare University of Suceava, Faculty of Law and Public Administration, and at the State University of Moldova, as part of the project "The Social Construction of the Profession of Probation Counsellor in Romania and the Republic of Moldova".

What should I expect from my participation in the research | In what follows, you are kindly requested to answer several questions concerning your opinion on non-custodial sentences (that is, sentences which avoid imprisonment) and their social impact. The questionnaire will contain questions relating to the reason for which offenders are punished by society, the usefulness of the custodial sentence for the reintegration of the offender in various contexts, opinions concerning alternative sentences, and the probation services.

Should you have any questions whatsoever concerning the research, please contact:

antonio1907@gmail.com – Antonio Sandu.

None of the questions raises matters of a defamatory character with respect to the persons surveyed or to their working environment, nor does any question involve introspection of a kind that would require reflection liable to produce negative emotions.

If, nevertheless, you identify questions that you would prefer not to answer, you have the possibility of stating this, either by selecting the option DK/NA (do not know / do not answer), or indeed by discontinuing the completion of the questionnaire altogether.

The questionnaire is anonymous, and should identifying data nonetheless be mentioned in your answers, such data will be processed and removed at the stage of transcription. Answering the questions of the questionnaire takes approximately 15–20 minutes.

Your answers are exceptionally important to us, and we thank you most warmly for your availability and for the interest you have shown in completing this questionnaire!

The potential risks and the discomfort created for you if you take part in this study | No harm arising from stress, or of a physical, psychological, social, or economic nature, may be incurred by you as a participant in this study.

Your benefits if you take part in this study | There are no direct benefits for you as a participant.

What you will receive for taking part in this study | Participation in this study is not compensated by any form of financial or material incentive.

What will happen to the information collected in this study | The information collected will be kept confidential, in accordance with the legislation in force.

What rights you have as a participant in this study |

Participation in this research is voluntary. The decision not to participate, or not to form part of this research, will not entail any penalty, fine, or loss of the benefits you already hold. If you have questions concerning your rights as a research subject, or if you wish to report any harm, injury, risk, or risk factor, please contact Dr Roxana Necula – President of the Commission for Research Ethics and Editorial Ethics of the LUMEN Association – necularoxy@gmail.com

Conflict of interests | The researchers have no financial interest in the conduct of this study.

Informed consent | By continuing to provide answers to the following questions, we consider that implicit consent is given to participation in this research, on the basis of your understanding of what has been presented above.

Questionnaire |

Research on Public Opinion concerning Non-Custodial Sentences in Romania and the Republic of Moldova

Please specify your city/county *

Please specify your gender * *Tick a single box*

☐ Female

☐ Male

Please specify your age * *Tick a single box*

☐ under 25 years

☐ 25–34 years

☐ 35–44 years

☐ 44–65 years

☐ over 65 years

Please specify your level of education: * *Tick a single box*

☐ No formal education

☐ Secondary education

☐ University education

☐ Postgraduate education

1. How long have you been working as a probation counsellor?

☐ a) less than one year

☐ b) between one year and 5 years

☐ c) between 5 and 10 years

☐ d) more than 10 years

2. What training did you undertake in order to become a probation counsellor? (multiple choice)

☐ a) Faculty of Social Work

☐ b) Faculty of Law

☐ c) Faculty of Psychology

☐ d) Faculty of Special Psychopedagogy

☐ e) Master's degree in Probation

☐ f) short-term courses in probation

☐ g) other (please specify) ....

....

3. On a scale from 1 to 5, where 1 means of little importance and 5 means very important, how do you assess the importance of knowledge in the following fields for the professional activity of the probation counsellor?

a) social work: 1----2----3----4------5

b) law: 1----2----3----4------5

c) psychology: 1----2----3----4------5

4. In which of the following activities specific to the probation counsellor have you worked, or are you currently working? (multiple choice)

- ☐ a) drafting pre-sentence evaluation reports
- ☐ b) supervising persons sentenced to a suspended sentence
- ☐ c) supervising persons released on parole
- ☐ d) supervising minors serving an educational measure
- ☐ e) social reintegration programmes
- ☐ f) participation in the parole board
- ☐ g) victim–offender mediation
- ☐ h) work with persons held in prison

5. On a scale from 1 to 5, where 1 means of little quality and 5 means very good, please indicate how you assess the relationship between yourself, in your capacity as a probation counsellor, and:

a) persons under supervision	1----2----3----4------5
b) representatives of the courts	1----2----3----4------5
c) representatives of the public authorities	1----2----3----4------5
d) representatives of civil society (NGOs)	1----2----3----4------5
e) representatives of the police	1----2----3----4------5
f) representatives of the penitentiary	1----2----3----4------5

6. Which of the following statements do you consider to apply best to your relations with the other institutions with which you collaborate?

- ☐ a) the most important form of communication is written, formalised, and standardised communication

☐ b) beyond written institutional communication, the interpersonal relationship with the other professionals is important, within the limits of compliance with the law

☐ c) DK/NA

7. Which of the following values do you consider to be the most important for the professional practice of the probation counsellor?

☐ a) respect for and encouragement of the autonomy of beneficiaries (the capacity to take and assume one's own decisions)

☐ b) respect for the dignity of beneficiaries

☐ c) the responsibility of beneficiaries and the fostering of their sense of responsibility

☐ d) effective communication between counsellor and beneficiary

☐ e) trust within the counsellor–beneficiary relationship

☐ f) DK/NA

8. On a scale from 1 to 5, where 1 means I do not agree and 5 means I agree entirely, please indicate how you assess the following statements:

a) offenders deserve to be punished because they have committed a wrongful/antisocial act
1----2----3----4------5

b) offenders are punished in order to set an example for society
1----2----3----4------5

c) offenders are punished so that they may be re-educated
1----2----3----4------5

9. How do you consider your profession would best be designated?

☐ a) probation counsellor

☐ b) supervision officer

☐ c) other (please specify) ....

....

☐ d) DK/NA

10. Which of the following statements best defines the professional success of the probation counsellor?

☐ a) the supervised person has completed the execution of the measures and obligations imposed without any incident

☐ b) the supervised person has not reoffended

☐ c) the supervised person has been reintegrated into the community

☐ d) all the legal provisions have been observed in the work with the beneficiary

☐ e) other (please specify) ....

....

☐ f) DK/NA

About the author

Antonio SANDU is a full professor at "Ştefan cel Mare" University of Suceava, Romania, senior researcher at the LUMEN Center for Socio-Human Research, Iaşi, Romania, professor and doctoral coordinator at the University of Oradea, and also director of LUMEN Publishing House, Iaşi, Romania. His main areas of interest include ethics, bioethics, sociology, social work, and social philosophy, public administration. The original contributions of the author's scientific activities stem from the social construction of reality viewed from a semiological perspective. He analyzes the social construction of reality by developing his own version of this paradigm that operates at the intersection between it and communicative action theory. He has studied the interpretative drift of ethical concepts such as ethical acceptability and ethical values. He has conducted research in autonomy and informed consent in the field of medical ethics and public health ethics. He is also interested in the modifications undergone by the human condition under the influence of the virtualization of social space and humanity's transition toward a trans- and posthuman stage.

He is the author of the volume *Bioethics in Crisis or the Crisis of Bioethics? An Anthropology of the Pandemic in the Medicalized Society*, published by Lumen Publishing House. He has also published the volume *Social Construction of Reality as Communicative Action*, published by Cambridge Scholar Publishing (2016), as well as the volumes *Social Work Practice: Research Techniques and Intervention Models*, *Appreciative Ethics: A Constructionist Version of Ethics*, and *Social-Constructionist Epistemology: A Transmodern Overview*. The last three books were published by Lap Lambert Publishing between 2012-2013. He is coordinator of the books *Ethical Issues in Social Work Practice* and *Ethics in Research Practice and Innovation* published by IGI Global during 2018-2019.

He has published over 150 works in scientific journals, of which 60 are indexed in WoS, the author holding an H-index of 13 in WoS and an H-index of 25 in Google Scholar respectively. He is also the author of over 20 volumes in Romanian and English.

SCAN ME